Deleuze and the History
of Mathematics

Bloomsbury Studies in Continental Philosophy

Bloomsbury Studies in Continental Philosophy is a major monograph series from Bloomsbury. The series features first-class scholarly research monographs across the field of Continental philosophy. Each work makes a major contribution to the field of philosophical research.

Deleuze and the History of Mathematics

In Defense of the "New"

Simon B. Duffy

B L O O M S B U R Y

LONDON • NEW DELHI • NEW YORK • SYDNEY

Bloomsbury Academic
An imprint of Bloomsbury Publishing Plc

50 Bedford Square
London
WC1B 3DP
UK

1385 Broadway
New York
NY 10018
USA

www.bloomsbury.com

Bloomsbury is a registered trade mark of Bloomsbury Publishing Plc

First published 2013
This paperback edition first published 2014

British Library Cataloguing-in-Publication Data
A catalogue record for this book is available from the British Library.

ISBN: HB: 978-1-4411-2950-5
PB: 978-1-4725-9134-0
ePUB: 978-1-4411-7920-3
ePDF: 978-1-4411-1389-4

Library of Congress Cataloging-in-Publication Data
Duffy, Simon B.
Deleuze and the history of mathematics: in defence of the 'new'/Simon B. Duffy.
pages cm. – (Bloomsbury studies in Continental philosophy)
Includes bibliographical references and index.
ISBN 978-1-4411-2950-5 – ISBN 978-1-4411-1389-4 (pdf) – ISBN 978-1-4411-7920-3
(epub) 1. Deleuze, Gilles, 1925–1995. 2. Mathematics–Philosophy. I. Title.
B2430.D454D845 2013
194–dc23
2012049681

Typeset by Deanta Global Publishing Services, Chennai, India
Printed and bound in Great Britain

To Sandra and Samuel

Contents

Acknowledgments

I am grateful to the publishers for granting permission to reprint material from the following articles and chapters:

"Deleuze, Leibniz and projective geometry in *The Fold*." *Angelaki. Journal of the Theoretical Humanities* 15.2 (2010): 129–47. Extracts reproduced with the permission of the publisher, the Routledge, Taylor & Francis Group.

"Leibniz, Mathematics and the Monad." *Deleuze and The Fold. A Critical Reader*. Edited by Niamh McDonnell and Sjoerd van Tuinen, Hampshire: Palgrave Macmillan, 2010. Extracts reproduced with the permission of Palgrave Macmillan.

"The question of Deleuze's Neo-Leibnizianism." *Down by Law: Revisiting Normativity with Deleuze*, edited by RosiBraidotti and Patricia Pisters. London: Bloomsbury, 2012. Extracts reproduced with the permission of Bloomsbury Publishing.

"Schizo-Math. The logic of different/ciation and the philosophy of difference." *Angelaki. Journal of the Theoretical Humanities* 9.3 (2004): 199–215. Extracts reproduced with the permission of the publisher, the Routledge, Taylor & Francis Group.

The logic of expression: quality, quantity, and intensity in Spinoza, Hegel and Deleuze. Aldershot, UK; Burlington, VT: Ashgate, 2006. Extracts from chapters 2, 3, 10, and the conclusion reproduced with the permission of Ashgate Publishers.

"The differential point of view of the infinitesimal calculus in Spinoza, Leibniz and Deleuze." *Journal of the British Society for Phenomenology* 37.3 (2006): 286–307. Extracts reproduced with the permission of the editors.

"The Mathematics of Deleuze's differential logic and metaphysics." *Virtual mathematics: the logic of difference*, edited by Simon Duffy, Manchester: Clinamen Press, 2006. Extracts reproduced with the permission of the editor.

"Deleuze and the Mathematical Philosophy of Albert Lautman." *Deleuze's Philosophical Lineage*, edited by Graham Jones and Jon Roffe. Edinburgh: Edinburgh University Press, 2009. Extracts reproduced with the permission of Edinburgh University Press.

"Badiou's Platonism: The Mathematical Ideas of Post-Cantorian Set Theory." *Badiou and Philosophy*, edited by Sean Bowden and Simon B. Duffy. Edinburgh: Edinburgh University Press, 2012. Reproduced with the permission of Edinburgh University Press.

[with Sean Bowden] "Badiou's Philosophical Heritage." *Badiou and Philosophy*, edited by Sean Bowden and Simon B. Duffy. Edinburgh: Edinburgh University Press, 2012. Extracts reproduced with the permission of Edinburgh University Press.

Among those friends and colleagues who have provided helpful feedback and suggestions, I would like to thank in particular Kieran Aarons, Sabrina Achilles, Philip Armstrong, Jeffrey Bell, HanjoBerressem, Ronald Bogue, John Bova, Sean Bowden, RosiBraidotti, Ray Brassier, Ian Buchannan, Felicity Colman, Mark Colyvan, Sandra

Field, Arne Fredlund, Hélène Frichot, Rocco Gangle, Daniel Garber, Moira Gatens, Melissa Gregg, René Guitart, Graham Harman, Anna Hickey-Moody, Eugene Holland, Joe Hughes, Graham Jones, Christian Kerslake, Stephen Loo, Beth Lord, Craig Lundy, David Macarthur, Robin Mackay, Mary Beth Mader, Talia Morag, Dalia Nassar, Anne Newstead, Paul Patton, ArkadyPlotnitsky, John Protevi, Sebastian Purcell, Paul Redding, Jon Roffe, Anne Sauvagnargues, Daniel W. Smith, HenrySomers-Hall, Julius Telivuo, Paul Thom, Daniela Voss, James Williams, and Jing Wu.

Research for a portion of this book was supported under the Australian Research Council *Discovery Project* funding scheme DP0771436.

List of Abbreviations

Deleuze, Gilles:

B   *Bergsonism* (1991).

CI   *Cinema 1: The Movement-Image* (1986).

CII   *Cinema 2: The Time-Image* (1989).

DR   *Difference and Repetition* (1994).

FLB   *The Fold: Leibniz and the Baroque* (1993).

LS   *The Logic of Sense* (1990).

N   *Negotiations, 1972–1990* (1995).

SEM.   *Seminars*, given between 1971 and 1987 at the Université de Paris VIII Vincennes and Vincennes St-Denis

Deleuze, Gilles and Felix Guattari:

TP   *A Thousand Plateaus: Capitalism and Schizophrenia* (1987).

WP   *What is Philosophy?* (1994).

Bergson, Henri:

CE   *Creative Evolution* (1911).

CM   *The Creative Mind* (1992).

DS   *Duration and Simultaneity* (1999).

IM   *An Introduction to Metaphysics* (1999).

MM   *Matter and Memory* (1911).

TF   *Time and Free Will: An Essay on the Immediate Data of Consciousness* (1910).

Introduction

Deleuze's texts are replete with examples of mathematical problems drawn from different historical periods. These engagements with mathematics rely upon the extraction of mathematical problematics or series of problems from the history of mathematics that have led to the development of alternative lineages in the history of mathematics, in order to use them to reconfigure particular philosophical problems, and to construct new concepts in response to them. Despite the significance of mathematics for the development of Deleuze's philosophy being widely acknowledged, relatively little research has been done in this area. One of the aims of this book is to address this critical deficit by providing a philosophical presentation of Deleuze's relation to mathematics, one that is adequate to his project of constructing a philosophy of difference, and to its application in other domains. This project undertakes an examination of the engagements between the discourse of philosophy and developments in the discipline of mathematics that structure Deleuze's philosophy. It approaches this issue initially by way of a historical study of the developments in the history of mathematics, which Deleuze develops as an alternative lineage in the history of mathematics, and of the relation between these developments in mathematics and the history of philosophy. In doing so, it provides examples of the way that Deleuze extracts mathematical problems from the history of mathematics, and of how these are then redeployed in relation to the history of philosophy. The aim is to provide an account of the mathematical resources that Deleuze draws upon in his project of constructing a philosophy of difference.

Deleuze's engagements with mathematics can be characterized in a general and schematic way as consisting of three different components:

(1) The first component can be characterized as the history of mathematics relevant to each of the programs or mathematical disciplines with which Deleuze engages, and the mathematical problems or problematics that are extracted from them. Deleuze defines a "problematic" as "the ensemble of the problem and its conditions" (DR 177). The alternative lineages in the history of mathematics that are of interest to Deleuze are based on noncanonical research problems and the solutions that have subsequently been offered to these problems. The relation between the canonical history of mathematics and the alternative lineages that Deleuze extracts from it are most clearly exemplified in the difference between what can be described as the axiomatized set theoretical explications of mathematics and those developments or research programs in mathematics that fall outside of the parameters of such an axiomatics, for example, algebraic topology, functional analysis, and differential geometry, to name but a few. Deleuze does not subscribe to what Corfield characterizes as "the logicists idea that mathematics contains nothing beyond an elaboration of the consequences of sets of

axioms" (2003, 23). This difference can be understood to be characteristic of the relation between what Deleuze and Guattari in *A Thousand Plateaus* (1987) refer to as Royal or major science and nomadic or minor science. Royal or major science refers to those practices that fall within the scientific norms and methodological conventions of the time, whereas nomad or minor science refers to those practices that fall outside of such disciplinary habits and resist attempts to be reduced to them. Scientific normativity can therefore be understood to operate as a set of principles according to which respectable research in mathematics is conducted, despite the fact that developments continue to be made that undermine such constraints and, by a process of destabilization and regeneration, lead to the development of alternative systems for structuring such normative frameworks. The aim of this book is to provide an account of the key figures and mathematical problems in the history of mathematics with which Deleuze engages and draws upon to structure the alternative normative framework that is developed in his project of constructing a philosophy of difference. An understanding of each of the mathematical engagements that Deleuze undertakes requires a clear explication of the history of mathematics from which the specific mathematical problematic has been extracted, and of the alternative lineage in the history of mathematics that has developed in relation to it.

(2) The second component of each of Deleuze's engagements with mathematics can be characterized as the explication of the manner by means of which these interventions in the history of mathematics are redeployed by Deleuze in relation to the history of philosophy. The mathematical problematics extracted from the history of mathematics are directly redeployed by Deleuze in order to reconfigure particular philosophical problematics in relation to the history of philosophy. This is achieved by mapping the alternative lineages in the history of mathematics onto corresponding alternative lineages in the history of philosophy, i. e. by isolating those points of convergence between the mathematical and philosophical problematics extracted from their respective histories. This is achieved by using the mathematical problems of these alternative lineages in the history of mathematics as models to reconfigure the philosophical problems and to develop the implications of these reconfigured philosophical problems by constructing an alternative lineage in the history of philosophy. The redeployment of mathematical problematics as models for philosophical problematics is one of the strategies that Deleuze employs in his engagement with and reconfiguration of the history of philosophy.

It is important to note that Deleuze eschews characterizing his redeployment of mathematical problems and problematics as simply analogical or metaphorical. He is careful to distinguish between those mathematical notions that are quantitative and exact in nature, which it is "quite wrong" to use metaphorically "because they belong to exact science" (N 29), and those mathematical problems that are "essentially inexact yet completely rigorous" (N 29) and which have led to important developments not only in mathematics and science in general, but also in other nonscientific areas such as philosophy and the arts. Deleuze argues that this sort of notion is "not unspecific because something's missing but because of its nature and content" (N 29). An example of an inexact and yet rigorous notion, which is presented in Chapter 1, is Henri Poincaré's qualitative theory of differential equations which develops the concept of an essential singularity. The different kinds of essential singularity are observed by virtue of the trajectories of variables across a potential function, rather than because there is a specific mathematical proof of their existence. Another example, which is presented in Chapter 5, is a Riemann Space, which Deleuze describes as occurring "when the connecting of parts is not predetermined but can take place in many ways: it is a space which is disconnected, purely optical, sound or even tactile (in the style of Bresson)" (CII 129). While Deleuze recognizes that citing mathematical notions of the exact kind outside of their particular sphere would rightly expose one to the criticism of "arbitrary metaphor or of forced application" (CII 129), he defends the use he makes of mathematical notions of the inexact kind. He does so on the grounds that by "taking from scientific operators a particular conceptualizable character which itself refers to non-scientific areas" (CII 129), the redeployment of this conceptualizable character in relation to another nonscientific area is justified. What this means is that the other nonscientific area "converges with science without applying it or making it a metaphor" (CII 129). A useful way of characterizing the relation between the conceptualizable character of the inexact mathematical notion and this conceptualizable character as redeployed in other nonscientific areas, insofar as the latter converges with the former, is to refer to it as a modeling relation. That is, the conceptualizable character as redeployed in a nonscientific area is modeled on the conceptualizable character of the inexact mathematical notion. What distinguishes a modeling relation from a relation of analogy or metaphor is that there are "correspondences without resemblance" (DR 184) between them. That is, there is a correspondence between the conceptualizable character in each instance; however, there is no resemblance between the scientific elements of the mathematical problem and the nonscientific elements of the discourse in which this conceptualizable character has been redeployed. It is this conceptualizable character that is characteristic of the two examples above and of all of the mathematical problems that Deleuze deploys in his philosophy as models to reconfigure philosophical problems and to construct alternative lineages in the history of philosophy.

(3) It is the creation of new concepts by bringing together mathematical and philosophical problematics that constitutes the third component of these Deleuzian engagements with mathematics. The reconfigured philosophical problematics that Deleuze extracts and the alternative lineages in the history of philosophy that he develops in relation to them are then redeployed either in relation to mathematical problematics that facilitated this extraction or in relation to one another, or in relation to problematics similarly extracted from other discourses, to create new concepts. One example of the former is the concept of singularity constructed in relation to the problem of the relationship between the universal and the particular in the work of Leibniz and its subsequent development in the history of mathematics.

The way in which these three components are implicated in relation to one another determines the manner by means of which Deleuze's interventions in the history of mathematics serve in his project of constructing a philosophy of difference. The aim of this book is to develop an argument that clearly demonstrates the nature of this implication, more specifically, how the alternative lineages in the history of mathematics are mapped onto or serve as models for the corresponding alternative lineages in the history of philosophy.

The mathematical problematic that will be explored in Chapter 1 is the problem of continuity as encountered by Leibniz's mathematical approach to natural philosophy, which draws upon the law of continuity as reflected in the calculus of infinite series and the infinitesimal calculus. This chapter is seminal in providing the historical background of the main alternative lineage in the history of mathematics that Deleuze draws upon. It will examine the reconstruction of Leibniz's metaphysics that Deleuze undertakes in *The Fold* (1993), which provides a systematic account of the structure of Leibniz's metaphysics in terms of its mathematical foundations, much of the preparatory work for which had already been done in *Logic of Sense* (1990). It is Leibniz's development of the concept of the infinitesimal in his approach to the differential calculus that represents one of the key innovative developments in the history of mathematics that is important for Deleuze. The subsequent development of this concept, and of the mathematical problems to which it is applied, by mathematicians throughout the history of mathematics represents the alternative lineage in the history of mathematics that Deleuze traces in his work.[1]

Chapter 2 examines the role played by Salomon Maimon (b. 1753–1800) in Deleuze's response to Kantian idealism and the development of the his distinctive post-Kantian philosophy, which is a feature of his philosophy of difference. Maimon is critical of the role played by mathematics in Kant's philosophy, and suggests a Leibnizian solution based on the infinitesimal calculus. Deleuze takes up this solution with a number of omissions, notably the concept of the infinite intellect, and a number of modifications that are drawn from the subsequent developments in the history of mathematics that are elaborated in the previous two chapters. Maimon is therefore included in Deleuze's construction of an alternative lineage in the history of philosophy that tracks the development of a series of metaphysical schemes that respond to and attempt to deploy the concept of the infinitesimal.

In addition to the explicit role played by the infinitesimal calculus in Bergson's philosophy, Chapter 3 examines the implicit role of the work of Bernhard Riemann (b. 1826–1866) in the development of Bergson's concept of multiplicity. While Bergson only draws upon one aspect of Riemann's work, specifically the implications of the concept of qualitative multiplicity for the development of his concept of duration, Deleuze rehabilitates and extends Bergson's work by clarifying and drawing upon the full potential of Riemann's mathematical developments, specifically the implications of the concept of qualitative multiplicity for reconfiguring the concept of space in a way that does all of the work required by Bergson's concept of duration.

Chapter 4 examines the implications of the critical program in mathematics undertaken by Albert Lautman (b. 1908–1944) to the development of Deleuze's philosophy. Having provided an account of the mathematical resources that Deleuze draws upon and of how they operate in his work in the previous four chapters, this chapter provides a more thorough account of the broader framework that Deleuze draws upon in order to adequately deploy these resources within his philosophy. This framework is drawn largely from the work of Lautman, with a number of important qualifications, including Deleuze's relation to Lautman's Platonism and his adoption of Cavaillès's reservations as regards the idealist implications in Lautman's work. It is argued that Lautman's concept of the mathematical real, which includes both the sum of all mathematical theories and the structure of the problematic ideas that govern them, provides the blueprint for adequately determining the nature not only of Deleuze's engagement with mathematics, but also of the metaphysics of Deleuze's philosophical logic.

Deleuze is by no means the only contemporary philosopher to have engaged in work of this kind. For this reason, the book is not devoted solely to the explication of this aspect of his work. Chapter 5 is devoted to the critical and comparative investigation of the logic of these Deleuzian engagements with mathematics, and the logic of another related effort to mobilize mathematical ideas in relation to the history of philosophy. The figure that will be used to develop an extended critical comparison with Deleuze's engagement with mathematics will be Alain Badiou (b. 1937–). Badiou is the main contemporary critic of Deleuze's philosophy, and this criticism bears specifically on the way in which the relation between mathematics and philosophy is configured in Deleuze's work. This chapter develops a robust defense of the structure of Deleuze's philosophy, specifically, of its engagement with mathematics, and of the adequacy of the mathematical problems that Deleuze uses to construct his philosophy. As a corollary to these arguments, it provides a defense of the Deleuzian framework for the construction of new concepts. This chapter developed in response to the increasing number of scholars who are quick to appropriate Badiou's criticism of Deleuze without directly engaging with the mathematical aspect of his work and the key role that this plays in his philosophy. One of the aims of the argument developed in this chapter is to dispel any concern that a crisis in legitimacy follows from Badiou's criticism of Deleuze (Badiou 2000; 2005; 2009). The argument developed in this chapter in effect provides a firm footing not only for Deleuze's philosophy and for philosophical engagements with it, but also for other nonphilosophical engagements with and deployments of his work.

Leibniz and the Concept of the Infinitesimal

Gilles Deleuze has gained a lot of respect among historians of philosophy for the rigor and historical integrity of his engagements with figures in the history of philosophy, particularly in those texts that engage with the intricacies of seventeenth century metaphysics and the mathematical developments that contributed to its diversity.[1] One of the aims of these engagements is not only to explicate the detail of the thinker's thought, but also to recast aspects of their philosophy as developments that contribute to his broader project of constructing a philosophy of difference. Each of these engagements therefore provides as much insight into the developments of Deleuze's own thought as it does into the detail of the thought of the figure under examination. In order to test this hypothesis, Deleuze's engagement with Leibniz is singled out for closer scrutiny in this chapter. Much has been made of Deleuze's Neo-Leibnizianism,[2] however, very little detailed work has been done on the specific nature of Deleuze's critique of Leibniz that positions his work within the broader framework of Deleuze's own philosophical project. This chapter undertakes to redress this oversight by providing an account of the reconstruction of Leibniz's metaphysics that Deleuze undertakes in *The Fold* (1993). Deleuze provides a systematic account of the structure of Leibniz's metaphysics in terms of its mathematical foundations. However, in doing so, Deleuze draws upon not only the mathematics developed by Leibniz—including the law of continuity as reflected in the calculus of infinite series and the infinitesimal calculus—but also developments in mathematics made by a number of Leibniz's contemporaries and near contemporaries—including Newton's method of fluxions, the projective geometry that has its roots in the work of Desargues (b. 1591–1661), and the "proto-topology" that appears in the work of Dürer (b. 1471–1528).[3] He also draws upon a number of subsequent developments in mathematics, the rudiments of which can be more or less located in Leibniz's own work—including the theory of functions and singularities, the Weierstrassian theory of analytic continuity, and Poincaré's qualitative theory of differential equations. Deleuze then retrospectively maps these developments back onto the structure of Leibniz's metaphysics. While the Weierstrassian theory of analytic continuity serves to clarify Leibniz's work, Poincaré's qualitative theory of differential equations offers a solution to overcome and extend the limits that Deleuze identifies in Leibniz's metaphysics. Deleuze brings this elaborate conjunction of material together in order to set up a mathematical idealization of the system that he considers to be implicit in Leibniz's work. The result is a thoroughly mathematical explication of the structure of Leibniz's metaphysics. What is provided in this chapter is an exposition of the very mathematical underpinnings of this Deleuzian account of the structure of Leibniz's metaphysics, which subtends the entire text of *The Fold*.

Deleuze's project in *The Fold* is predominantly oriented by Leibniz's insistence on the metaphysical importance of mathematical speculation. What this suggests is that mathematics functions as an important heuristic in the development of Leibniz's metaphysical theories. Deleuze puts this insistence to good use by bringing together the different aspects of Leibniz's metaphysics with the variety of mathematical themes that run throughout his work, principally the infinitesimal calculus. Those aspects of Leibniz's metaphysics that Deleuze's undertakes to clarify in this way, and upon which this chapter will focus, include (1) the definition of a monad; (2) the theory of compossibility; (3) the difference between perception and apperception; (4) the conception of matter and motion; and (5) the range and meaning of the preestablished harmony. However, before providing the details of Deleuze's reconstruction of the structure of Leibniz's metaphysics, it will be necessary to give an introduction to Leibniz's infinitesimal calculus and to some of the other developments in mathematics associated with it.

Leibniz's law of continuity and the infinitesimal calculus

Leibniz was both a philosopher and mathematician. As a mathematician, he made a number of innovative contributions to developments in mathematics. Chief among these was his infinitesimal analysis, which encompassed the investigation of infinite sequences and series, the study of algebraic and transcendental curves[4] and the operations of differentiation and integration upon them, and the solution of differential equations: integration and differentiation being the two fundamental operations of the infinitesimal calculus that he developed.

Leibniz applied the calculus primarily to problems about curves and the calculus of finite sequences, which had been used since antiquity to approximate the curve by a polygon in the Archimedean approach to geometrical problems by means of the method of exhaustion. In his early exploration of mathematics, Leibniz applied the theory of number sequences to the study of curves and showed that the differences and sums in number sequences correspond to tangents and quadratures, respectively, and he developed the conception of the infinitesimal calculus by supposing the differences between the terms of these sequences to be infinitely small (See Bos 1974, 13). One of the keys to the calculus that Leibniz emphasized was to conceive the curve as an infinitangular polygon: [5]

> I feel that this method and others in use up till now can all be deduced from a general principle which I use in measuring curvilinear figures, that a curvilinear figure must be considered to be the same as a polygon with infinitely many sides. (Leibniz 1962, V, 126)

Leibniz based his proofs for the infinitangular polygon on a law of continuity, which he formulated as follows: "In any supposed transition, ending in any terminus, it is permissible to institute a general reasoning, in which the final terminus may also be included" (Leibniz 1920, 147). Leibniz also thought the following to be a requirement for continuity:

> When the difference between two instances in a given series, or in whatever is presupposed, can be diminished until it becomes smaller than any given quantity whatever, the corresponding difference in what is sought, or what results, must of necessity also be diminished or become less than any given quantity whatever. (Leibniz 1969, 351)

Leibniz used the adjective *continuous* for a variable ranging over an infinite sequence of values. In the infinite continuation of the polygon, its sides become infinitely small and its angles infinitely many. The infinitangular polygon is considered to coincide with the curve, the infinitely small sides of which, if prolonged, would form tangents to the curve, where a tangent is a straight line that touches a circle or curve at only one point. Leibniz applied the law of continuity to the tangents of curves as follows: he took the tangent to be continuous with or as the limiting case ("*terminus*") of the secant. To find a tangent is to draw a straight line joining two points of the curve—the secant—which are separated by an infinitely small distance or vanishing difference, which he called "a differential" (See Leibniz 1962, V, 223). The Leibnizian infinitesimal calculus was built upon the concept of the differential. The differential, dx, is the difference in x values between two consecutive values of the variable at P (See Figure 1.1), and the tangent is the line joining such points.

The differential relation, i.e. the quotient between two differentials of the type dy/dx, serves in the determination of the gradient of the tangent to the circle or curve. The gradient of a tangent indicates the slope or rate of change of the curve at that point, i.e. the rate at which the curve changes on the y-axis relative to the x-axis. Leibniz

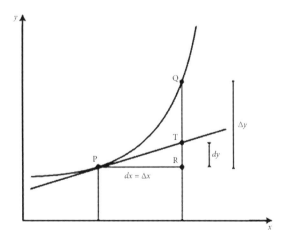

Figure 1.1 The tangent to the curve at P.

thought of the *dy* and *dx* in *dy/dx* as "infinitesimal" quantities. Thus *dx* was an infinitely small nonzero increment in *x* and *dy* was an infinitely small nonzero increment in *y*.

Leibniz brings together the definition of the differential as it operates in the calculus of infinite series, in regard to the infinitangular polygon, and the infinitesimal calculus, in regard to the determination of tangents to curves, as follows:

> Here *dx* means the element, i.e. the (instantaneous) increment or decrement, of the (continually) increasing quantity *x*. It is also called difference, namely the difference between two proximate *x*'s which differ by an element (or by an inassignable), the one originating from the other, as the other increases or decreases (momentaneously). (Leibniz 1962, VII, 223)

The differential can therefore be understood on the one hand, in relation to the calculus of infinite series, as the infinitesimal difference between consecutive values of a continuously diminishing quantity, and on the other, in relation to the infinitesimal calculus, as an infinitesimal quantity. The operation of the differential in the latter actually demonstrates the operation of the differential in the former, because the operation of the differential in the infinitesimal calculus in the determination of tangents to curves demonstrates that the infinitely small sides of the infinitangular polygon are continuous with the curve. Carl Boyer, in *The history of the calculus and its conceptual development*, refers to this early form of the infinitesimal calculus as the infinitesimal calculus from "the differential point of view" (1959, 12).

In one of his early mathematical manuscripts entitled "Justification of the Infinitesimal Calculus by That of Ordinary Algebra," Leibniz offers an account of the infinitesimal calculus in relation to a particular geometrical problem that is solved using ordinary algebra (Leibniz 1969, 545–6). An outline of the demonstration that Leibniz gives is as follows:[6]

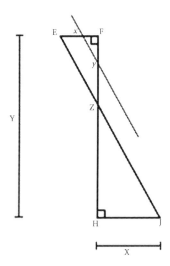

Figure 1.2 Leibniz's example of the infinitesimal calculus using ordinary algebra.

Since the two right triangles, ZFE and ZHJ, that meet at their apex, point Z, are similar, it follows that the ratio y/x is equal to $(Y-y)/X$. As the straight line EJ approaches point F, maintaining the same angle at the variable point Z, the lengths of the straight lines FZ and FE, or y and x, steadily diminish, yet the ratio of y to x remains constant. When the straight line EJ passes through F, the points E and Z coincide with F, and the straight lines, y and x, vanish. Yet y and x will not be absolutely nothing since they preserve the ratio of ZH to HJ, represented by the proportion $(Y-y)/X$, which in this case reduces to Y/X, and obviously does not equal zero. The relation y/x continues to exist even though the terms have vanished since the relation is determinable as equal to Y/X. In this algebraic calculus, the vanished lines x and y are not taken for zeros since they still have an algebraic relation to each other. "And so," Leibniz argues, "they are treated as infinitesimals, exactly as one of the elements which . . . differential calculus recognizes in the ordinates of curves for momentary increments and decrements" (Leibniz 1969, 545). That is, the vanished lines x and y are determinable in relation to each other only insofar as they can be replaced by the infinitesimals dy and dx, by making the supposition that the ratio y/x is equal to the ratio of the infinitesimals, dy/dx. When the relation continues even though the terms of the relation have disappeared, a continuity has been constructed by algebraic means that is instructive of the operations of the infinitesimal calculus.

What Leibniz demonstrates in this example are the conditions according to which any unique triangle can be considered as the extreme case of two similar triangles opposed at the vertex.[7] Deleuze argues that, in the case of a figure in which there is only one triangle, the other triangle is there, but it is only there "virtually" (Sem. 22 Apr 1980). The *virtual* triangle has not simply disappeared, but rather it has become unassignable, all the while remaining completely determined. The hypotenuse of the virtual triangle can be mapped as a side of the infinitangular polygon, which, if prolonged, forms a tangent line to the curve. There is therefore continuity from the polygon to the curve, just as there is continuity from two similar triangles opposed at the vertex to a single triangle. Hence this relation is fundamental for the application of differentials to problems about tangents.

In the first published account of the calculus (Leibniz 1684), Leibniz defines the ratio of infinitesimals as the quotient of first-order differentials, or the associated differential relation. He says that "the differential dx of the abscissa x is an arbitrary quantity, and that the differential dy of the ordinate y is defined as the quantity which is to dx as the ratio of the ordinate to the subtangent" (Boyer 1959, 210). (See Figure 1.1) Leibniz considers differentials to be the fundamental concepts of the infinitesimal calculus, the differential relation being defined in terms of these differentials.

Newton's method of fluxions and infinite series

Newton began thinking of the rate of change, or fluxion, of continuously varying quantities, which he called fluents such as lengths, areas, volumes, distances, and temperatures, in 1665, which predates Leibniz by about ten years. Newton regards his variables as generated by the continuous motion of points, lines, and planes, and offers an account of the fundamental problem of the calculus as follows: "Given a relation between two fluents, find the relation between their fluxions, and conversely" (Newton 1736). Newton thinks of the two variables whose relation is given as changing with time, and, although he does point out that this is useful rather than necessary, it remains a defining feature of his approach and is exemplified in the geometrical reasoning about limits, which Newton was the first to come up with.[8] Put simply, to determine the tangent to a curve at a specified point, a second point on the curve is selected, and the gradient of the line that runs through both of these points is calculated. As the second point approaches the point of tangency, the gradient of the line between the two points approaches the gradient of the tangent. The gradient of the tangent is, therefore, the limit of the gradient of the line between the two points as the points become increasingly close to one another (See Figure 1.3).

He conceptualized the tangent geometrically, as the limit of a sequence of lines between two points, P and Q, on a curve, which is a secant. As the distance between the points approached zero, the secants became progressively smaller, however, they always retained "a real length." The secant therefore approached the tangent without reaching it. When this distance "got arbitrarily small (but remained a real number)" (Lakoff and Núñez 2000, 224), it was considered insignificant for practical purposes, and was ignored. What is different in Leibniz's method is that he "hypothesized infinitely small numbers—infinitesimals—to designate the size of infinitely small intervals" (Lakoff and Núñez 2000, 224). (See Figure 1.1) For Newton, on the contrary, these intervals remained only small, and therefore real. When performing calculations, however, both approaches yielded the same results. But they differed ontologically, because Leibniz had hypothesized a new kind of number, a number Newton did not need, since "his secants always had a real length, while Leibniz's had an infinitesimal length" (Lakoff and Núñez 2000, 224). Leibniz's symbolism also treats quantities independently of their genesis, rather than as the product of an explicit functional relation.

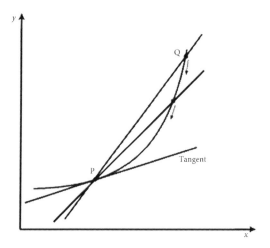

Figure 1.3 Newton's geometrical reasoning about the gradient of a tangent as a limit.

Both Newton and Leibniz are credited with developing the calculus as a new and general method, and with having appreciated that the operations in the new analysis are applicable to infinite series as well as to finite algebraic expressions. However, neither of them clearly understood nor rigorously defined their fundamental concepts. Newton thought his underlying methods were natural extensions of pure geometry, while Leibniz felt that the ultimate justification of his procedures lay in their effectiveness. For the next two hundred years, various attempts were made to find a rigorous arithmetic foundation for the calculus: one that relied neither on the mathematical intuition of geometry, with its tangents and secants, which was perceived as imprecise because its conception of limits was not properly understood, nor on the vagaries of the infinitesimal, which could not be justified either from the point of view of classical algebra or from the point of view of arithmetic, and therefore made many mathematicians wary, so much so that they refused the hypothesis outright despite the fact that Leibniz "could do calculus using arithmetic without geometry—by using infinitesimal numbers" (Lakoff and Núñez 2000, 224–5).

The emergence of the concept of the function

Seventeenth century analysis was a corpus of analytical tools for the study of geometric objects, the most fundamental object of which, thanks to the development of a curvilinear mathematical physics by Christiaan Huygens (b. 1629–1695), was the curve, or curvilinear figures generally, which were understood to embody relations between several variable geometrical quantities defined with respect to a variable point on the curve. The variables of geometric analysis referred to geometric quantities, which were conceived not as real numbers, but rather as having a dimension: for example, "the dimension of a line (e.g. ordinate, arc length, subtangent), of an area (e.g. the area between curve and axis), or of a solid (e.g. the solid of revolution)" (Bos 1974, 6). The relations between these variables were expressed by means of equations. Leibniz actually referred to these variable geometric quantities as the *functiones* of a curve,[9] and thereby introduced the term "function" into mathematics. However, it is important to note the absence of the fully developed concept of function in the Leibnizian context of algebraic relations between variables. Today, a function is understood to be a relation that uniquely associates members of one set with members of another set. For Leibniz, neither the equations nor the variables are functions in this modern sense, rather the relation between x and y was considered to be one entity. The curves were thought of as having a primary existence apart from any analysis of their numeric or algebraic properties. In seventeenth century analysis, equations did not create curves; curves rather gave rise to equations (Dennis and Confrey 1995, 125). Thus the curve was not seen as a graph of a function but rather as "a figure embodying the relation between x and y" (See Bos 1974, 6). In the first half of the eighteenth century, a shift of focus from the curve and the geometric quantities themselves to the formulas which expressed the relations among these quantities occurred, thanks in large part to the symbols introduced by Leibniz. The analytical expressions involving numbers and letters, rather than the geometric objects for which they stood, became the focus of interest. It was this change of focus toward the formula that made the emergence of the concept of function possible. In this process, the differential underwent a corresponding change; it lost its initial geometric connotations and came to be treated as a concept connected with formulas rather than with figures.

With the emergence of the concept of the function, the differential was replaced by the derivative, which is the expression of the differential relation as a function, first developed in the work of Euler (b. 1707–1783). One significant difference, reflecting the transition from a geometric analysis to an analysis of functions and formulas, is that the infinitesimal sequences are no longer induced by an infinitangular polygon standing for a curve, according to the law of continuity as reflected in the infinitesimal calculus, but by a function, defined as a set of ordered pairs of real numbers.

Subsequent developments in mathematics: The problem of rigor

The concept of the function, however, did not immediately resolve the problem of rigor in the calculus. It was not until the late nineteenth century that an adequate solution to this problem was posed. It was Karl Weierstrass (b. 1815–1897) who "developed a pure nongeometric arithmetization for Newtonian calculus" (Lakoff and Núñez 2000, 230), which provided the rigor that had been lacking. The Weierstrassian program determined that the fate of calculus need not be tied to infinitesimals, and could rather be given a rigorous status from the point of view of finite representations. Weierstrass's theory was an updated version of an earlier account by Augustin Cauchy (b.1789–1857), which had also experienced problems conceptualizing limits.

It was Cauchy who first insisted on specific tests for the convergence of series, so that divergent series could henceforth be excluded from being used to try to solve problems of integration because of their propensity to lead to false results (See Boyer 1959, 287).[10] By extending sums to an infinite number of terms, problems began to emerge if the series did not converge, since the sum or limit of an infinite series is only determinable if the series converges. It was considered that reckoning with divergent series, which have no sum, would therefore lead to false results.

Weierstrass considered Cauchy to have actually begged the question of the concept of limit in his proof.[11] In order to overcome this problem of conceptualizing limits, Weierstrass "sought to eliminate all geometry from the study of . . . derivatives and integrals in calculus" (Lakoff and Núñez 2000, 309). In order to characterize calculus purely in terms of arithmetic, it was necessary for the idea of a curve in the Cartesian plane defined in terms of the motion of a point to be completely replaced with the idea of a function. The geometric idea of "approaching a limit" had to be replaced by an arithmetized concept of limit that relied on static logical constraints on numbers alone. This approach is commonly referred to as the epsilon-delta method (See Potter 2004, 85).[12] Deleuze argues that "It is Weierstrass who bypasses all the interpretations of the differential calculus from Leibniz to Lagrange, by saying that it has nothing to do with a process . . . Weierstrass gives an interpretation of the differential and infinitesimal calculus which he himself calls static, where there is no longer fluctuation towards a limit, nor any idea of threshold" (Sem. 22 Feb 1972). The calculus was thereby reformulated without either geometric secants and tangents or infinitesimals; only the real numbers were used.

Because there is no reference to infinitesimals in this Weierstrassian definition of the calculus, the designation "the infinitesimal calculus" was considered to be "inappropriate" (Boyer 1959, 287). Weierstrass's work not only effectively removed any remnants of geometry from what was now referred to as the differential calculus, but also eliminated the use of the Leibnizian-inspired infinitesimals in doing the calculus for over half a century. It was not until the late 1960's, with the development of the controversial axioms of nonstandard analysis by Abraham Robinson (b. 1918–1974), that the infinitesimal was given a rigorous formulation (See Bell 1998),[13] thus allowing the inconsistencies to be removed from the Leibnizian infinitesimal calculus without removing the infinitesimals themselves.[14] Leibniz's ideas about the role of the infinitesimal in the calculus, specifically the hypothesis of the infinitesimal, have therefore been "fully vindicated" (Robinson 1996, 2), as Newton's had been, thanks to Weierstrass.

It is important to note that what is vindicated by Robinson's work is Leibniz's hypothesis of the infinitesimal rather than the specific kind of infinitesimal that Leibniz actually hypothesized. There are a number of differences between their different conceptions of the infinitesimal. Robinson's infinitesimal is a static quantity, whereas Leibniz's infinitesimals are "syncategorematic," i.e. they are as small as is necessary, such that there is always a quantity that is smaller than the smallest given quantity. Their size therefore depends on the size of the smallest variable. The fictional status of infinitesimals is also important for Leibniz's metaphysical speculations.

In response to these protracted historical developments,[15] Deleuze brings renewed scrutiny to the relationship between the developments in the history of mathematics and the metaphysics associated with these developments, which were marginalized as a result of efforts to determine the rigorous foundations of the calculus. This is a part of Deleuze's broader project of constructing an alternative lineage in the history of philosophy that tracks the development of a series of metaphysical schemes that respond to and attempt to deploy the concept, or the conceptualizable character, of the infinitesimal. It is specifically in relation to these developments that Deleuze's appeal to the "barbaric or pre-scientific interpretations of the differential calculus" (DR 171) should be understood. The aim of Deleuze's project is to construct a philosophy of difference as an alternative philosophical logic that subverts a number of the commitments of the Hegelian dialectical logic, which supported the elimination of the infinitesimal in favor of the inverse operation of differentiation as reflected in the operation of negation, the procedure of which postulates the synthesis of a series of contradictions in the determination of concepts.[16]

The theory of singularities

Another development in mathematics, the rudiments of which can be found in the work of Leibniz, is the theory of singularities. A singularity or singular point is a mathematical concept that appears with the development of the theory of functions, which historians of mathematics consider to be one of the first major mathematical concepts upon which the development of modern mathematics depends. Even though the theory of functions doesn't actually take shape until later in the eighteenth century, it is in fact Leibniz who contributes greatly to this development. Indeed, it was Leibniz who developed the first theory of singularities in mathematics, and, Deleuze argues, it is with Leibniz that the concept of singularity becomes a mathematico-philosophical concept (Sem. 29 Apr 1980). However, before explaining what is philosophical in the concept of singularity for Leibniz, it is necessary to offer an account of what he considers singularities to be in mathematics, and of how this concept was subsequently developed in the theory of analytic functions, which is important for Deleuze's account of (in)compossibility in Leibniz, despite it not being developed until long after Leibniz's death.

The great mathematical discovery that Deleuze refers to is that singularity is no longer thought of in relation to the universal, but rather in relation to the ordinary or the regular (Sem. 29 Apr 1980). In classical logic, the singular was thought of with reference to the universal, however, that doesn't necessarily exhaust the concept since in mathematics, the singular is distinct from or exceeds the ordinary or regular. Mathematics refers to the singular and the ordinary in terms of the points of a curve, or more generally concerning complex curves or figures. A curve, a curvilinear surface, or a figure includes singular points and others that are regular or ordinary. Therefore, the relation between singular and ordinary or regular points is a function of curvilinear problems which can be determined by means of the Leibnizian infinitesimal calculus.

The differential relation is used to determine the overall shape of a curve primarily by determining the number and distribution of its singular points or singularities, which are defined as points of articulation where the shape of the curve changes or alters its behavior. For example, when the differential relation is equal to zero, the gradient of the tangent at that point is horizontal, indicating, for example, that the curve peaks or dips, determining therefore a maximum or minimum at that point. These singular points are known as stationary or turning points (See Figure 1.4).

The differential relation characterizes not only the singular points which it determines, but also the nature of the regular points in the immediate neighborhood of these points, i.e. the shape of the branches of the curve on either side of each singular point.[17] Where the differential relation gives the value of the gradient at the singular point, the value of the second order differential relation, i.e. if the differential relation is itself differentiated and which is now referred to as the second derivative, indicates the rate at which the gradient is changing at that point. This allows a more accurate approximation of the shape of the curve in the neighborhood of that point.

Leibniz referred to the stationary points as *maxima* and *minima* depending on whether the curve was concave up or down, respectively. A curve is concave up where the second order differential relation is positive and concave down where the second order differential relation is negative. The points on a curve that mark a transition between a region where the curve is concave up and one where it is concave down are points of inflection. The second order differential relation will be zero at an inflection point. Deleuze distinguishes a point of inflection, as an intrinsic singularity, from the *maxima* and *minima*, as extrinsic singularities, on the grounds that the former "does

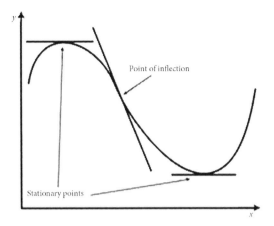

Figure 1.4 The singular points of a curve.

not refer to coordinates" but rather "corresponds" to what Leibniz calls an "ambiguous sign" (FLB 15), i.e. where concavity changes, the sign of the second order differential relation changes from + to −, or vice versa.

The value of the third order differential relation indicates the rate at which the second order differential relation is changing at that point. In fact, the more successive orders of the differential relation that can be evaluated at the singular point, the more accurate the approximation of the shape of the curve in the neighborhood of that point. Leibniz even provided a formula for the nth order differential relation, as n approaches infinity (n→∞). The nth order differential relation at the point of inflection would determine the continuity of the variable curvature in the immediate neighborhood of the inflection with the curve. Because the point of inflection is where the tangent crosses the curve (See Figure 1.4.) and the point where the nth order differential relation as n→∞ is continuous with the curve, Deleuze characterizes the point of inflection as a *point-fold*; which is the trope that unifies a number of the themes and elements of *The Fold*.

The characteristics of a *point-fold* as reflected in the point of inflection

Deleuze considers Baroque mathematics to have been born with Leibniz, and he gives two examples of how infinite variables emerge as the object that defines the discipline of this period, and in both cases Deleuze remarks on the presence of a curved element that he characterizes as a *point-fold*.

(1) The first is the irrational number and the corresponding serial calculus. An irrational number cannot be written as a fraction, and has decimal expansions that neither terminate nor become periodic. Pythagoras believed that all things could be measured by the discrete natural numbers (1, 2, 3, . . .) and their ratios (ordinary fractions, or the rational numbers). This belief was shaken, however, by the discovery

that the hypotenuse of a right isosceles triangle (that is, the diagonal of a unit square) cannot be expressed as a rational number. This discovery was brought about by what is now referred to as Pythagoras's theorem,[18] which established that the square of the hypotenuse of a right isosceles triangle is equal to the sum of the squares of the other two sides, $c^2 = a^2 + b^2$. In a unit square, the diagonal is the hypotenuse of a right isosceles triangle, with sides a = b = 1, hence $c^2 = 2$, and c = √2, or "the square root of 2." Thus there exists a line segment whose length is equal to √2, which is an irrational number. Against the intentions of Pythagoras, it had thereby been shown that rational numbers did not suffice for measuring even simple geometric objects.

Another example of a simple irrational number is π, which is determined by the relation between the circumference, c, of a circle relative to its diameter, d, (where π = c/d). Leibniz was the first to find the infinite series (1 – 1/3 + 1/5 –1/7 + . . .) of which π/4 was the limit. Leibniz only gave the formula of this series, and it was not until the end of the eighteenth century before this formula was demonstrated to be an infinite convergent series by the mathematician Johann Heinrich Lambert (b. 1728–1777).

Irrational numbers can therefore remain in surd form, as for example √2, or they may be represented by an infinite series. Deleuze defines the irrational number as "the common limit of two convergent series, of which one has no maximum and the other no minimum" (FLB 17), thus any irrational number is the limit of the sequence of its rational approximations, which can be represented as follows: increasing series → irrational number ← decreasing series. The diagram that Deleuze provides is of a right isosceles triangle, the sides of which are in the ratio 1:1:√2 (See Figure 1.5).

It functions as a graphical representation of the ratio of the sides of AC:AB (where AC = AX) = 1:√2. The point X is the irrational number, √2, which represents the meeting point of the arc of the circle, of radius AC, inscribed from point C to X, and the straight line AB representing the rational number line. The arc of the circle produces a *point-fold* at X. The "straight line of rational points" is therefore exposed "as a false infinite, a simple indefinite that includes the lacunae" of each irrational number √n, as n→∞. The rational number line should therefore be understood to be interrupted by these curves such as that represented by √2 in the given example. Deleuze considers these to

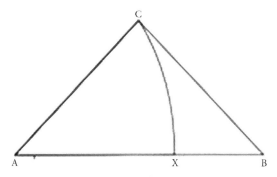

Figure 1.5 The point X, as the irrational number √2, is an event on the line.

be events of the line, and then generalizes this example to include all straight lines as intermingled with curves, *point-folds,* or events of this kind.

(2) The second example is the differential relation and differential calculus. Here Deleuze argues that the diagram from Leibniz's account of the calculus in "Justification of the Infinitesimal Calculus by That of Ordinary Algebra" (See Figure 1.2.) can be correlated with a *point-fold* by mapping the hypotenuse of the virtual triangle onto a side of the infinitangular polygon, which, if prolonged, forms a tangent line to the curve. Once the virtual triangle vanishes or becomes unassigned, the relation dy/dx, and therefore the unassigned virtual triangle, is retained by point F, just as the differential relation designates the gradient of a tangent to the curve at point F, which can therefore be characterized as a *point-fold.*

Deleuze maps these characteristics of a *point-fold* onto the inflection and identifies it as "the pure Event of the line or of the point, the Virtual, ideality par excellence" (FLB 15).

The conceptualizable character of the inflection is deployed throughout *The Fold* as the abstract figure of the event, and any event is considered to be a concrete case of inflection. By means of explanation, Deleuze offers three examples, drawn from the work of Bernard Cache (1995),[19] of the kind of virtual or continuous transformation that the inflection can be understood to be characteristic of.

(1) The first set of transformations is "vectorial, or operate by symmetry, with an orthogonal or tangent plane of reflection" (FLB 15). The example that Deleuze offers is drawn from Baroque architecture, according to which an inflection serves to hide or round out the right angle. This is figured in the Gothic arch which has the geometrical shape of an ogive.

(2) The second set of transformations is characterized as "projective." The example that Deleuze gives is the transformations of René Thom (b. 1923–2002) which refer "to a morphology of living matter." Thom developed catastrophe theory, which is a branch of geometry that attempts to model the effect of the continuous variation of one or more variables of a system that produce abrupt and discontinuous transformations in the system. The results are representable as curves or functions on surfaces that depict "seven elementary events: the fold; the crease; the dovetail; the butterfly; the hyperbolic, elliptical, and parabolic umbilicus" (FLB 16). The role of projective methods in the conceptualization of matter, specifically those of Desargues, is addressed in the paper Duffy 2010a in the section "Projective geometry and point of view."

(3) The third set of transformations "cannot be separated from an infinite variation or an infinitely variable curve" (FLB 17). The example Deleuze gives is the Koch curve, demonstrated by Helge von Koch (b. 1870–1924) in 1904 (FLB 16). The method of constructing the Koch curve is to take an equilateral triangle and trisect each of its sides. On the external side of each middle segment, an equilateral triangle is constructed and the above mentioned middle segment is deleted. This first iteration resembles a Star of David composed of six small triangles. The previous process is repeated on the two outer sides of each small triangle. This basic construction is then iterated indefinitely. With each order of iteration, the length of any side of a triangle is 4/3 times longer than the previous order. As the order of iteration approaches infinity, so too then does the length of the curve. The result is a curve of infinite length surrounding a finite area.

The Koch curve is an example of a nondifferentiable curve, i.e. a continuous curve that does not have a tangent at any of its points. More generalized Koch or fractal curves can be obtained by replacing the equilateral triangle with a regular n-gon, and/ or the "trisection" of each side with other equipartitioning schemes.[20] In this example, the line effectively and continuously defers inflection by means of the method of construction of the folds of its sides. The Koch curve is therefore "obtained by means of rounding angles, according to Baroque requirements" (FLB 16). The problem of the mathematical representation of motion that the Koch curve helps explain is returned to later in the chapter in the section entitled "The Koch curve and the folded tunic: the fractal nature of motion."

Subsequent developments in mathematics: Weierstrass and Poincaré

The important development in mathematics, the rudiments of which Deleuze considers to be in Leibniz's work and that he retrospectively maps back onto Leibniz's account of (in)compossibility, is the Weierstrassian theory of analytic continuity.

Ironically, one of the mathematicians who contributed to the development of the differential point of view is Karl Weierstrass, who considers the differential relation to be logically prior to the function in the process of determination associated with the infinitesimal calculus, i.e. rather than determining the differential relation from a given function, the kinds of mathematical problems in the theory of functions with which Weierstrass dealt involved investigating how to generate a function from a given differential relation. Weierstrass develops a theory of integration as the approximation of functions from differential relations according to a process of summation in the form of series. Despite Weierstrass having been involved separately in the elimination of both geometry and the infinitesimal from the calculus, Deleuze recovers this theory in order to restore the Leibnizian perspective of the differential, as the genetic force of the differential relation, to the differential point of view of the infinitesimal calculus. The kinds of problems in the infinitesimal calculus from the differential point of view that are of interest to Deleuze are those in which a function does not precede the differential relation, but is rather determined by the differential relation itself.

The Leibnizian method of approximation using successive orders of the differential relation is formalized in the calculus according to Weierstrass's theory by a Taylor series or power series expansion. A power series expansion can be written as a polynomial, the coefficients of each of its terms being the successive derivatives evaluated at the singular point. The sum of such a series represents the expanded function provided that any remainder approaches zero as the number of terms becomes infinite (Whittaker and Watson 1990, 95–6); the polynomial then becomes an infinite series which converges with the function in the neighborhood of the singular point.[21] This criterion of convergence repeats Cauchy's earlier exclusion of divergent series from the calculus. A power series operates at each singular point by successively determining the specific qualitative nature of the function at that point, i.e. the shape and behavior of the graph of the function or curve. The power series determines not only the nature of the function at the point in question, but also the nature of all of the regular points in the neighborhood of that singular point, such that the specific qualitative nature of a function in the neighborhood of a singular point insists in that one point. By examining the relation between the differently distributed singular points determined by the differential relation, the regular points that are continuous between the singular points can be determined, which in geometrical terms are the branches of the curve. In general, the power series converges with a function by generating a continuous branch of a curve in the neighborhood of a singular point. To the extent that all of the regular points are continuous across all of the different branches generated by the power series of the singular points, the entire complex curve or the whole analytic function is generated.

The kinds of problems in the infinitesimal calculus that are of interest to Deleuze are those in which the differential relation is generated by differentials and the power series are generated in a process involving the repeated differentiation of the differential relation. In these kinds of problem, it is due to these processes that a function is generated in the first place. The mathematical elements of this interpretation are most clearly developed by Weierstrassian analysis, according to the theorem of the approximation of analytic functions. An analytic function, being secondary to the differential relation, is differentiable, and therefore continuous, at each point of its domain. According to Weierstrass, for any continuous analytic function on a given interval, or domain, there exists a power series expansion which uniformly converges to this function on the given domain. Given that a power series approximates a function in such a restricted domain, the task is then to determine other power series expansions that approximate the same function in other domains. An analytic function is differentiable at each point of its domain, and is essentially defined for Weierstrass from the neighborhood of a singular point by a power series expansion which is convergent with a "circle of convergence" around that point. A power series expansion that is convergent in such a circle represents a function that is analytic at each point in the circle. By taking a point interior to the first circle as a new center, and by determining the values of the coefficients of this new series using the function generated by the first series, a new series and a new center of convergence are obtained, whose circle of convergence overlaps the first. The new series is continuous with the first if the values of the function coincide in the common part of the two circles. This method of "analytic continuity" allows the gradual construction of a whole domain over which the generated function is continuous. At the points of the new circle of convergence that are exterior to, or extend outside, the first, the function represented by the new series is the analytic continuation of the function defined by the first series, what Weierstrass defines as the analytic continuation of a power series expansion outside its circle of convergence. The domain of the function is extended by the successive adjunction of more and more circles of convergence. Each series expansion which determines a circle of convergence is called "an element of the function". In this way, given an element of an analytic function, by analytic continuation one can obtain the entire analytic function over an extended domain. The domain of the successive adjunction of circles of convergence, as determined by analytic continuity, actually has the structure of a surface. The analytic continuation of power series expansions can be continued in this way in all directions up to the points in the immediate neighborhood exterior to the circles of convergence where the series obtained diverge.

Power series expansions diverge at specific "singular points" or "singularities" that may arise in the process of analytic continuity. A singular point or singularity of an analytic function, as with a curve, is any point which is not a regular or ordinary point of the function or curve. They are points which exhibit remarkable properties and thereby have a dominating and exceptional role in the determination of the characteristics of the function, or shape and behavior of the curve. The singular points of a function, which include the stationary points, where $dy/dx = 0$, and points of inflection, where $d^2y/dx^2 = 0$, are "removable singular points," since the power series at these points converge with the function. A removable singular point is uniformly determined by the function and therefore redefinable as a singular point of the function, such that the function is analytic or continuous at that point. The specific singularities of an analytic function where the series obtained diverge are called "poles." Singularities of this kind are those points where the function no longer satisfies the conditions of regularity which assure its local continuity, such that the rule of analytic continuity breaks down. They are therefore points of discontinuity. A singularity is called a pole of a function when the values of the differential relation, i.e. the gradients of the tangents to the points of the function, approach infinity as the function approaches the pole. The function is said to be asymptotic to the pole; it is therefore no longer differentiable at that point, but rather remains undefined, or vanishes. A pole is therefore the limit point of a function, and is referred to as an accumulation point or point of condensation. A pole can also be referred to as a jump discontinuity in relation to a finite discontinuous interval both within the same function, for example periodic functions, and between neighboring analytic functions. Deleuze writes that "a singularity is the point of departure for a series which extends over all the ordinary points of the system, as far as the region of another singularity which itself gives rise to another series which may either converge or diverge from the first" (Deleuze 1994, 278). The singularities whose series converge are removable singular points, and those whose series diverge are poles.

The singularities, or poles, that arise in the process of analytic continuity necessarily lie on the boundaries of the circles of convergence of power series. In the neighborhood of a pole, a circle of convergence extends as far as the pole in order to avoid including it, and the poles of any neighboring functions, within its domain. The effective domain of an analytic function determined by the process of the analytic continuation of power series expansions is therefore limited to that between its poles. With this method the domain is not circumscribed in advance, but results rather from the succession of local operations.

Power series can be used in this way to solve differential relations by determining the analytic function into which they can be expanded. Weierstrass developed his theory alongside the integral conception of Cauchy, which further developed the inverse relation between the differential and the integral calculus as the fundamental theorem of the calculus. The fundamental theorem maintains that differentiation and integration are inverse operations, such that integrals are computed by finding antiderivatives, which are otherwise known as primitive functions. There are a large number of rules, or algorithms, according to which this reversal is effected.

Deleuze presents Weierstrass's theorem of approximation as an effective method for determining the characteristics of a function from the differential point of view of the infinitesimal calculus. The mathematician Albert Lautman (b. 1908–1944) refers to this process as integration from "the local point of view," or simply as "local integration" (Lautman 2011, 99).[22] This form of integration does not involve the determination of the primitive function, which is generated by exercising the inverse operation of integration. The development of a local point of view, rather, requires the analysis of the characteristics of a function at its singular points. The passage from the analytic function defined in the neighborhood of a singular point to the analytic function defined in each ordinary point is made according to the ideas of Weierstrass by analytic continuity. This method was eventually deduced from the Cauchy point of view, such that the Weierstrassian approach was no longer emphasized. The unification of both of these points of view, however, was achieved at the beginning of the twentieth century when the rigor of Cauchy's ideas was improved and fused with those of G. F. Bernhard Riemann (b. 1826–1866), the other major contributor to the development of the theory of functions.[23] Deleuze is therefore able to cite the contribution of Weierstrass's theorem of approximation in the development of the differential point of view of the infinitesimal calculus despite his separate development of the static epsilon-delta method, and thereby establish a historical continuity between Leibniz's differential point of view of the infinitesimal calculus and the differential calculus of contemporary mathematics developed by Cauchy and Riemann.

The development of a differential philosophy

While Deleuze draws inspiration and guidance from Salomon Maimon (b. 1753–1800), who "sought to ground post Kantianism upon a Leibnizian reinterpretation of the calculus" (Deleuze 1994, 170), and "who proposes a fundamental reformation of the *Critique* and an overcoming of the Kantian duality between concept and intuition" (Deleuze 1994, 173),[24] it is in the work of Hoëné Wronski (b. 1778–1853) that Deleuze finds the established expression of the first principle of the differential philosophy. Wronski was "an eager devotee of the differential method of Leibniz and of the transcendental philosophy of Kant" (Boyer 1959, 261). Wronski made a transcendental distinction between the finite and the infinitesimal, determined by the two heterogeneous functions of knowledge, understanding and reason. He argued that "finite quantities bear upon the objects of our knowledge, and infinitesimal quantities on the very generation of this knowledge; such that each of these two classes of knowledge must have laws proper [to themselves], and it is in the distinction between these laws that the major thesis of the metaphysics of infinitesimal quantities is to be found" (Wronski 1814, 35; Blay 1998, 158). It is imperative not to confuse "the objective laws of finite quantities with the purely subjective laws of infinitesimal quantities" (36; 158). He claims that it is this "confusion that is the source of the inexactitude that is felt to be attached to the infinitesimal calculus . . . This is also [why] geometers, especially those of the present day, consider the infinitesimal calculus, which nonetheless they concede always gives true results, to be only an indirect or artificial procedure"

(36; 159). Wronski is referring here to the work of Joseph-Louis Lagrange (b. 1736–1813) and Lazarre Carnot (b. 1753–1823), two of the major figures in the history of the differential calculus, whose attempts to provide a rigorous foundation for the differential calculus involved the elimination of the infinitesimal from all calculations, or as Wronski argued, involved confusing objective and subjective laws in favor of finite quantities (See Blay 1998, 159). Both of these figures count as precursors to the work of Cauchy and Weierstrass. Wronski argued that the differential calculus constituted "a *primitive algorithm* governing the *generation* of quantities, rather than the laws of quantities *already formed*" (Boyer 1959, 262). According to Wronski, the differential should be interpreted "as having an a priori metaphysical reality associated with the generation of magnitude" (262). The differential is therefore expressed as a pure element of quantitability, insofar as it prepares for the determination of quantity. The work of Wronski represents an extreme example of the differential point of view of the infinitesimal calculus which recurs throughout the nineteenth century.[25]

Another significant figure in this alternative history of mathematics that is constructed by Deleuze is Jean Baptiste Bordas-Demoulin (b. 1798–1859), who also champions the infinitesimal against those who consider that infinitesimals had to be eliminated in favor of finite quantities. Bordas-Demoulin does not absolve the differential calculus of the accusation of error, but rather considers the differential calculus to have this error as its principle. According to Bordas-Demoulin, the minimal error of the infinitesimal "finds itself compensated by reference to an error active in the contrary sense . . . . It is in all necessity that the errors are mutually compensated" (Bordas-Demoulin 1874, 414; my translation). The consequence of this mutual compensation "is that one differential is only exact after having been combined with another" (414).[26] Deleuze repeats these arguments of Wronski and Bordas-Demoulin when he maintains that it is in the differential relation that the differential is realized as a pure element of quantitability. Each term of the relation, i.e. each differential, each pure element of quantitability, therefore "exists absolutely only in its relation to the other" (Deleuze 1994, 172), i.e. only insofar as it is reciprocally determined in relation to another.

The question for Deleuze then becomes "in what form is the differential relation determinable?" (172) He argues that it is determinable primarily in qualitative form, insofar as it is the reciprocal relation between differentials, and then secondarily, insofar as it is the function of a tangent whose values give the gradient of the line tangent to a curve, or the specific qualitative nature of this curve, at a point. As the function of a tangent, the differential relation "expresses a function which differs in kind from the so-called primitive function" (172). Whereas the primitive function, when differentiated, expresses the whole curve directly,[27] the differential relation, when differentiated, expresses rather the further qualification of the nature of the function at, or in the immediate neighborhood of, a specific point. The primitive function is the integral of the function determined by the inverse transformation of differentiation, according to the differential calculus. From the differential point of view of the infinitesimal calculus, the differential relation, as the function of the tangent, determines the existence and distribution of the distinctive points of a function, thus preparing for its further qualification. Unlike the primitive function, the differential relation remains tied to the specific qualitative nature of the function at those distinctive points, and, as the function of the tangent, it "is therefore differentiable in turn" (172). When the differential relation is repeatedly differentiated at a distinctive point generating a power series expansion, what is increasingly specified is the qualitative nature of the function in the immediate neighborhood of that point. Deleuze argues that this convergence of a power series with an analytic function, in its immediate neighborhood, satisfies "the minimal conditions of an integral" (174), and characterizes what is for Deleuze the process of "differentiation" (209).

The differential relation expresses the qualitative relation between not only curves and straight lines, but also linear dimensions and their functions, and plane or surface dimensions and their functions. The domain of the successive adjunction of circles of convergence, as determined by analytic continuity, actually has the structure of a surface. This surface is constituted by the points of the domain and the direction attached to each point in the domain, i.e. the tangents to the curve at each point and the direction of the curve at that point. Such a surface can be described as a field of directions or a vector field. A vector is a quantity having both magnitude and direction. The point of departure of the local genesis of functions is from the point of view of the structure of such a surface as a vector field. It is within this context that the example of a jump discontinuity in relation to a finite discontinuous interval between neighboring analytic or local functions is developed by Deleuze, in order to characterize the generation of another function which extends beyond the points of discontinuity that determine the limits of these local functions. Such a function would characterize the relation between the different domains of different local functions. The genesis of such a function from the local point of view is initially determined by taking any two points on the surface of a vector field, such that each point is a pole of a local function determined independently by the point-wise operations of Weierstrassian analysis. The so determined local functions, which have no common distinctive points or poles in the domain, are discontinuous with each other, each pole being a point of discontinuity, or limit point, for its respective local function. Rather than simply being considered as the unchanging limits of local functions generated by analytic continuity, the limit points of each local function can be considered in relation to one another, within the context of the generation of a new function which encompasses the limit points of each local function and the discontinuity that extends between them. Such a function can initially be understood to be a potential function, which is determined as a line of discontinuity between the poles of the two local functions on the surface of the vector field. The potential function admits these two points as the poles of its domain. However, the domain of the potential function is on a scalar field, which is distinct from the vector field insofar as it is composed of points (scalars) which are nondirectional; scalar points are the points onto which a vector field is mapped. The potential function can be defined by the succession of points (scalars) which stretch between the two poles. The scalar field of the potential function is distinct from the vector field of the local functions insofar as, mathematically speaking, it is "cut" from the surface of the vector field. Deleuze argues that "the limit must be conceived not as the limit of a [local] function but as a genuine cut [*coupure*], a border between the changeable and the unchangeable within the function itself. . . . the limit no longer presupposes the ideas of a continuous variable and infinite approximation. On the contrary, the concept of limit grounds a new, static and purely ideal definition" (Deleuze 1994, 172), that of the potential function. To cut the surface from one of these poles to the next is to generate such a potential function. The poles of the potential function determine the limits of the discontinuous domain, or scalar field, which is cut from the surface of the vector field. The "cut" of the surface in this theory renders the structure of the potential function "apt to a creation" (Lautman 2011, 150). The precise moment of production, or genesis, resides in the act by which the cut renders the variables of certain functional expressions able to "jump" from pole to pole across the cut. When the variable jumps across this cut, the domain of the potential function is no longer uniformly discontinuous. With each "jump," the poles which determine the domain of discontinuity, represented by the potential function sustained across the cut, seem to have been removed. The less the cut separates the potential function on the scalar field from the surface of the vector field, the more the poles seem to have been removed, and the more the potential function seems to be continuous with the local functions across the whole surface of the vector field. It is only insofar as this interpretation is conferred on the structure of the potential function that a new function can be understood to have been generated on the surface. A potential function is only generated when there is potential for the creation of a new function between the poles of two local functions. The potential function is therefore always apt to the creation of a new function. This new function, which encompasses the limit points of each local function and the discontinuity that extends between them, is continuous across the structure of the potential function; it completes the structure of the potential function, as what can be referred to as a "composite function." The connection between the structural completion of the potential function and the generation of the corresponding composite function is the act by which the variable jumps from pole to pole. When the variable jumps across the cut, the value of the composite function sustains a fixed increase. Although the increase seems to be sustained by the potential function, it is this increase which actually registers the generation or complete determination of the composite function.

The complete determination of a composite function by the structural completion of the potential function is not determined by Weierstrass's theory of analytic continuity. A function is able to be determined as continuous by analytic continuity across singular points which are removable, but not across singular points which are nonremovable. The poles of the two discontinuous analytic functions are nonremovable, thus analytic continuity between the two functions is not able to be established.

This is the extent of the Weierstrassian theory of analytic continuity that Deleuze retrospectively maps onto Leibniz's theory of singularities and deploys in his account of Leibnizian (in)compossibility, which is explicated in the following section. A singularity is a distinctive point on a curve in the neighborhood of which the second order differential relation changes its sign. This characteristic of the singular point is extended into or continuous with the series of ordinary points that depend on it, all the way to the neighborhood of subsequent singularities. It is for this reason that Deleuze maintains that the theory of singularities is inseparable from a theory or an activity of continuity, where continuity, or the continuous, is the extension of a singular point into the ordinary points up to the neighborhood of the subsequent singularity. And it is for this reason that Deleuze considers the rudiments of the Weierstrassian theory to be in the work of Leibniz, and that it is therefore able to be retrospectively mapped back onto the work of Leibniz.

Weierstrass did recognize a means of solving the problem of the discontinuity between the poles of analytic functions by postulating a potential function, the parameters of the domain of which is determined by the poles of the two discontinuous analytic functions, and by extending his analysis to meromorphic functions.[28] A function is said to be meromorphic in a domain if it is analytic in the domain determined by the poles of two analytic functions. A meromorphic function is determined by the quotient of two arbitrary analytic functions, which have been determined independently on the same surface by the point-wise operations of Weierstrassian analysis. Such a function is defined by the differential relation:

$$\frac{dy}{dx} = \frac{Y}{X}$$

where X and Y are the polynomials, or equations of the power series of the two analytic functions. The meromorphic function, as the function of a differential relation, is just the kind of function which can be understood to have been generated by the structural completion of the potential function. The meromorphic function is therefore the differential relation of the composite function. The expansion of the power series determined by the repeated differentiation of the meromorphic function should generate a function which converges with a composite function. The graph of a composite function, however, consists of curves with infinite branches, because the series generated by the expansion of the meromorphic function is divergent. The representation of such curves posed a problem for Weierstrass, which he was unable to resolve, because divergent series were considered then to fall outside the parameters of the differential calculus, since they defied the criterion of convergence.

The qualitative theory of differential equations

Henri Poincaré (b. 1854–1912) took up this problem of the representation of composite functions, by extending the Weierstrass theory of meromorphic functions into what is called "the qualitative theory of differential equations" (Kline 1972, 732). In place of studying the properties of complex functions in the neighborhood of their singularities, Poincaré was primarily occupied with determining the properties of complex functions in the whole plane, i.e. the properties of the entire curve rather than just the singularity itself. This qualitative method involved the initial investigation of the geometrical form of the curves of functions with infinite branches, only then was numerical determination of the values of the function able to be made. While such divergent series do not converge, in the Weierstrassian sense, to a function, they may indeed furnish a useful approximation to a function if they can be said to represent the function asymptotically. When such a series is asymptotic to the function, it can represent an analytic or composite function even though the series is divergent.

When this geometrical interpretation was applied to composite functions, Poincaré found the values of the composite function around the singularity produced by the function to be undetermined and irregular. The singularity of a composite function would be the point at which both the numerator and denominator of the quotient of the meromorphic function determinative of the composite function vanish (or equal zero). The peculiarity of the meromorphic function is that the numerator and denominator do not vanish at the same point on the surface of the domain. The points at which the two local functions of the quotient vanish are at their respective poles. The determination of a composite function therefore requires the determination of a new singularity in relation to the poles of the local functions of which it is composed. Poincaré called this new kind of singularity an essential singularity. Observing that the values of a composite function very close to an essential singularity fluctuate through a range of different possibilities without stabilizing, Poincaré distinguished four types of essential singularity, which he classified according to the behavior of the function and the geometrical appearance of the solution curves in the neighborhood of these points (See Figure 1.6). The first type of singularity is the node, which is a point through which an infinite number of curves pass. The second kind of singularity is the saddle point or dip, through which only two solution curves pass, acting as asymptotes for neighboring curves. A saddle point is neither a maximum nor minimum, since the value of the function either increases or decreases depending on the direction of movement away from it. The third type of singularity is the point of focus, around which the solution curves turn and toward which they approach in the same way as logarithmic spirals. And the fourth, called a center, is a point around which the curves are closed, concentric with one another and the center.

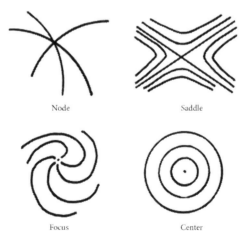

Node   Saddle

Focus   Center

Figure 1.6 The trajectories of the variables of essential singularities.

The type of essential singularity is determined by the form of the constitutive curves of the meromorphic function. While the potential function remains discontinuous with the other functions on the surface from which it is cut, thereby representing a discontinuous group of functions, the composite function, on the contrary, overcomes this discontinuity insofar as it is continuous in the domain that extends across the whole surface of the discontinuous group of functions. The existence of such a continuous function, however, does not express any less the properties of the domain of discontinuity which serves to define it. The discontinuous group of local functions and the continuous composite function attached to this group exist alongside each other, the transformation from one to the other being determined by the process of the generation and expansion of the meromorphic function. The potential function is actualized in the composite function when the variable jumps from one pole to the other. Its trajectory, in the form of a solution curve, is determined by the type of essential singularity created by the meromorphic function. The essential singularity determines the behavior of the composite function, or the appearance of the solution curve, in its immediate neighborhood by acting as an "*attractor*" for the trajectory of the variable across its domain (De Landa 2002, 14). It is the value of this function which sustains a determined increase with each jump of the variable. Insofar as the trajectory of each variable is attracted to the same final state represented by each of the different essential singularities, these essential singularities can be understood to provide a model for what Manuel De Landa describes as the "inherent or intrinsic *long-term tendencies* of a system, the states which the system will spontaneously tend to adopt in the long run as long as it is not constrained by other forces" (2002, 15).[29]

Deleuze distinguishes this differential point of view of the infinitesimal calculus from the Weierstrassian theory of approximation when he writes that:

> No doubt the specification of the singular points (for example, dips, nodes, focal points, centers) is undertaken by means of the form of integral curves, which refer back to the solutions for the differential equations. There is nevertheless a complete determination with regard to the existence and distribution of these points which depends upon a completely different instance - namely, the field of vectors defined by the equation itself. The complementarity of these two aspects does not obscure their difference in kind - on the contrary. (Deleuze 1994, 177)

The equation to which Deleuze refers is the meromorphic function, which is a differential equation or function of a differential relation determined according to the Weierstrassian approach, from which the essential singularity and therefore the composite function are determined according to Poincaré's qualitative approach. This form of integration is again characterized from the local point of view, by what Deleuze describes as "an original process of differenciation" (209). Differenciation is the complete determination of the composite function from the reciprocally determined local functions or the structural completion of the potential function. It is the process whereby a potential function is actualized as a composite function.

Deleuze states that "actualization or differenciation is always a genuine creation," and that to be actualized is "to create divergent lines" (212). The expanded power series of a meromorphic function is actualized in the composite function insofar as it converges with, or creates, the divergent lines of the composite function. Differenciation, therefore, creates an essential singularity, whose divergent lines actualize the specific qualitative nature of the poles of the group of discontinuous local functions, represented by a potential function, in the form of a composite function. According to Poincaré's qualitative theory of differential equations, geometric considerations took precedence over the analysis of series. Jeremy Gray argues that, "as with his theory of automorphic functions, what Poincaré was able to do was to make a geometric insight sufficiently precise to suggest what range of behavior was possible and to couple it to the rigorous methods of analysis" (Gray 2002, 517). Poincaré's pioneering work in this area eventually lead to the definitive founding of the geometric theory of analytic functions, the study of which "has not yet been completely carried out" (Valiron 1971, 173), but continues to be developed with the assistance of computers. Benoit Mandelbrot (b. 1924–2010) considers Poincaré, with his concept of essential singularities, to be "the first student of fractal ("strange") attractors," i.e. of the kinds of attractors operative in fractals which occur in mathematics, and cites certain theories of Poincaré as having "led" him "to new lines of research" (1982, 414).[30]

Deleuze does not consider this process of differenciation to be arrested with the generation of a composite function, but rather presents it as a continuing process, generating those functions which actualize the relations between different composite functions, and those functions which actualize the relations between these functions, and so on. The conception of differenciation is extended in this way when Deleuze states that "there is a differenciation of differenciation which integrates and welds together the differenciated" (Deleuze 1994, 217); each differenciation is simultaneously "a local integration," which then connects with others, according to the same logic, in what is characterized as a "global integration" (211).

The logic of the differential, as determined according to both differentiation and differenciation, designates a process of production, or genesis, which has, for Deleuze, the value of introducing a general theory of relations which unites the Weierstrassian structural considerations of the differential calculus with the concept of "the generation of quantities" (175). "In order to designate the integrity or the integrality of the object," when considered as a composite function from the differential point of view of the infinitesimal calculus, Deleuze argues that, "we require the complex concept of differen*t*/*c*iation. The *t* and the *c* here are the distinctive feature or the phonological relation of difference in person" (209). Deleuze argues that differenciation is "the second part of difference" (209), the first being expressed by the logic of the differential in differentiation. Where the logic of differentiation characterizes a differential philosophy, the complex concept of the logic of differen*t*/*c*iation characterizes Deleuze's philosophy of difference.

The subsequent developments that the Weierstrassian theory of analytic continuity undergoes, up to and including Poincaré's qualitative theory of differential equations, is the material that Deleuze draws upon to offer a solution to overcome and extend the limits of Leibniz's metaphysics. The details of this critical move on Deleuze's part are examined in the final sections of the chapter.

Deleuze's "Leibnizian" interpretation of the theory of compossibility

What then does Deleuze mean by claiming that Leibniz determines the singularity in the domain of mathematics as a philosophical concept? A crucial test for Deleuze's mathematical reconstruction of Leibniz's metaphysics is how to deal with his subject-predicate logic. Deleuze maintains that Leibniz's mathematical account of continuity is reconcilable with the relation between the concept of a subject and its predicates. The solution that Deleuze proposes involves demonstrating that the continuity characteristic of the infinitesimal calculus is isomorphic to, or functions as a model for, the series of predicates contained in the concept of a subject. An explanation of this isomorphism, or modeling relation, requires an explication of Deleuze's understanding of Leibniz's account of predication as determined by the principle of sufficient reason.

For Leibniz, every proposition can be expressed in subject-predicate form. The subject of any proposition is a complete individual substance, i.e. a simple, indivisible, dimensionless metaphysical point or monad.[31] Of this subject it can be said that "every analytic proposition is true," where an analytic proposition is one in which the meaning of the predicate is contained in that of the subject. If this definition is reversed, such that it reads "every true proposition is necessarily analytic," then this amounts to a formulation of Leibniz's principle of sufficient reason. According to which each time a true proposition is formulated, it must be understood to be analytic, i.e. every true proposition is a statement of analyticity whose predicate is wholly contained in its subject. It follows that if a proposition is true, then the predicate must be contained in the concept of the subject. That is, everything that happens to, everything that can be attributed to, everything that is predicated of a subject—past, present and future— must be contained in the concept of the subject. So for Leibniz, all predicates, i.e. the predicates that express all of the states of the world, are contained in the concept of each and every particular or singular subject.

There are, however, grounds to distinguish truths of reason or essence, from truths of fact or existence. An example of a truth of essence would be the proposition $2 + 2 = 4$, which is *analytic*, however, it is analytic in a stronger sense than a truth of fact or existence. In this instance, there is an *identity* of the predicate, $2 + 2$, with the subject, 4.[32] This can be proved by analysis, i.e. in a finite or limited number of quite determinate operations it can be demonstrated that 4, by virtue of its definition, and $2 + 2$, by virtue of their definition, are identical. So, the identity of the predicate with the subject in an analytic proposition can be demonstrated in a finite series of determinate operations. While $2 + 2 = 4$ occurs in all time and in all places, and is therefore a necessary truth, the proposition that "Adam sinned" is specifically dated, i.e. Adam will sin in a particular place at a particular time. It is therefore a truth of existence, and, as will be demonstrated, a contingent truth. According to the principle of sufficient reason, the proposition "Adam sinned" must be analytic. If we pass from one predicate to another to retrace all the causes and follow up all the effects, this would involve the entire series of predicates contained in the subject Adam, i.e. the analysis would extend to infinity. So, in order to demonstrate the inclusion of "sinner" in the concept of "Adam," an infinite series of operations is required. However, we are incapable of completing such an analysis to infinity.

While Leibniz is committed to the idea of potential ("syncategorematic") infinity, i.e. to infinite pluralities such as the terms of an infinite series which are indefinite or unlimited, Leibniz ultimately accepted that in the realm of quantity infinity could in no way be construed as a unified whole by us. As Bassler clearly explains, "So if we ask how many terms there are in an infinite series, the answer is not: an infinite number (if we take this either to mean a magnitude which is infinitely larger than a finite magnitude or a largest magnitude) but rather: more than any given finite magnitude" (Bassler 1998, 65). The performance of such an analysis is indefinite both for us, as finite human beings, because our understanding is limited, and for God, since there is no end of the analysis, i.e. it is unlimited. However, all the elements of the analysis are given to God in an actual infinity. We can't grasp the actual infinite, nor reach it via an indefinite intuitive process. It is only accessible for us via finite systems of symbols that approximate it. The infinitesimal calculus provides us with an "artifice" to operate a well-founded approximation of what happens in God's understanding. We can approach God's understanding thanks to the operation of infinitesimal calculus, without ever actually reaching it. While Leibniz always distinguished philosophical truths and mathematical truths, Deleuze maintains that the idea of infinite analysis in metaphysics has "certain echoes" in the calculus of infinitesimal analysis in mathematics. The infinite analysis that we perform as human beings in which sinner is contained in the concept of Adam is an indefinite analysis, just as if the terms of the series that includes sinner were isometric with $1/2 + 1/4 + 1/8 \ldots$ to infinity. In truths of essence, the analysis is finite, whereas in truths of existence, the analysis is infinite under the above mentioned conditions of a well-founded approximation.

So what distinguishes truths of essence from truths of existence is that a truth of essence is such that its contrary is contradictory and therefore impossible, i.e. it is impossible for 2 and 2 not to equal 4. Just as the identity of 4 and $2 + 2$ can be proved in a series of finite procedures, so too can the contrary, $2 + 2$ not equaling 4, be proved to be contradictory and therefore impossible. While it is impossible to think what $2 + 2$ not equaling 4 or what a squared circle may be, it is possible to think of an Adam who might not have sinned. Truths of existence are therefore contingent truths. A world in which Adam might not have sinned is a logically possible world, i.e. the contrary is not necessarily contradictory. While the relation between Adam sinner and Adam nonsinner is a relation of contradiction since it is impossible that Adam is both sinner and nonsinner, the world in which Adam is a nonsinner is not contradictory with the world in which Adam sinned, it is rather incompossible with such a world. Deleuze argues that to be incompossible is therefore not the same as to be contradictory, it is another kind of relation that exceeds the contradiction, and which Deleuze refers to as "vice-diction" (FLB 59). Deleuze characterizes the relation of incompossibility as "a difference and not a negation" (FLB 150). Incompossibility conserves a very classical principle of disjunction: it is either this world or some other one. So, when analysis extends to infinity, the type or mode of inclusion of the predicate in the subject is compossiblity. What interests Leibniz at the level of truths of existence is not the identity of the predicate and the subject, but rather the process of passing from one predicate to another from the point of view of an infinite analysis, and it is this process that is characterized by Leibniz as having the maximum of continuity. While truths of essence are governed by the principle of identity, truths of existence are governed by the law of continuity.

Rather than discovering the identical at the end or limit of a finite series, infinite analysis substitutes the point of view of continuity for that of identity. There is continuity when the extrinsic case, for example, the circle, the unique triangle or the predicate, can be considered as included in the concept of the intrinsic case, i.e. the infinitangular polygon, the virtual triangle, or the concept of the subject. The domain of (in)compossibility is therefore a different domain to that of identity/contradiction. There is no logical identity between sinner and Adam, but there is a continuity. Two elements are in continuity when an infinitely small or vanishing difference is able to be assigned between these two elements. Here Deleuze shows in what way truths of existence are able to be modeled upon mathematical truths.

Deleuze offers a "Leibnizian" interpretation of the difference between compossibility and incompossibility "based only on divergence or convergence of series" (FLB 150). He proposes the hypothesis that there is compossibility between two singularities "when series of ordinaries converge," that is, when the values of the series of regular points that derive from two singularities coincide, "otherwise there is discontinuity. In one case, you have the definition of compossibility, in the other case, the definition of incompossibility" (Sem. 29 Apr 1980). If the series of ordinary or regular points that derive from singularities diverge, then you have a discontinuity. When the series diverge, when you can no longer compose the continuity of this world with the continuity of this other world, then it can no longer belong to the same world. There are therefore as many worlds as divergences. All worlds are possible, but they are incompossibles with each other.[33] God conceives an infinity of possible worlds that are not compossible with each other, from which He chooses the best of possible worlds, which happens to be the world in which Adam sinned. A world is therefore defined by its continuity. What separates two incompossible worlds is the fact that there is discontinuity between the two worlds. It is in this way that Deleuze maintains that compossibility and incompossibility are the direct consequences of the theory of singularities.

Point of view and the theory of the differential unconscious

While each concept of the subject contains the infinite series of predicates that express the infinite series of states of the world, each particular subject in fact only expresses clearly a small finite portion of it from a certain point of view. In any proposition, the predicate is contained in the subject; however, Deleuze contends that it is contained either actually or virtually. Indeed, any term of analysis remains virtual prior to the analytic procedure of its actualization. What distinguishes subjects is that although they all contain the same virtual world, they don't express the same clear and distinct or actualized portion of it. No two individual substances have the same point of view or exactly the same clear and distinct zone of expression. The point of view of an individual subject at any particular time corresponds to the proportion of the world that is expressed clearly and distinctly by that individual, in relation to the rest of the world that is expressed obscurely and confusedly. The explanation as to why each monad only expresses clearly a limited subdomain of the world that it contains pertains to Leibniz's distinction between "perception, which is the inner state of the monad representing external things, and apperception, which is consciousness or the reflective knowledge of this inner state itself."[34] The infinite series of predicates or states of the world is in each monad in the form of minute perceptions. These are infinitely tiny perceptions that Deleuze characterizes as "unconscious perceptions" (FLB 89), or as the "differentials of consciousness" (FLB 93). Each monad expresses every one of them, but only obscurely or confusedly, like a clamor. Leibniz therefore distinguishes conscious perception as apperception from minute perception, which is not given in consciousness.

When Leibniz mentions that conscious perceptions "arise by degrees from" minute perceptions,[35] Deleuze claims that what Leibniz indeed means is that conscious perception "derives from" minute perceptions. It is in this way that Deleuze links unconscious perception to infinitesimal analysis, the former modeled on the latter. Just as there are differentials for a curve, there are differentials for consciousness.

When the series of minute perceptions is extended into the neighborhood of a singular point, or point of inflection, that perception becomes conscious. Conscious perception, just like the mathematical curve, is therefore subject to a law of continuity, i.e. an indefinite continuity of the differentials of consciousness. We pass from minute perception to conscious perception when the series of ordinaries reaches the neighborhood of a singularity. In this way, the infinitesimal calculus operates as the model for the unconscious psychic mechanism of perception. Deleuze understands the subdomain that each monad expresses clearly in terms of the constraints that the principle of continuity places on a theory of consciousness. "At the limit, then, all monads possess an infinity of compossible minute perceptions, but have differential relations that will select certain ones in order to yield clear perceptions proper to each" (FLB 90). Before addressing Leibniz's understanding of the phenomenal nature of a monad's body, his account of matter, and Deleuze's characterization of it, requires explication.

The mathematical representation of matter, motion, and the continuum

Leibniz considered nature to be infinitely divisible such that "the smallest particle should be considered as a world full of an infinity of creatures."[36] However, his interpretation of infinitesimals as useful fictions, which he arrived at as early as 1676, means that they are without status as actual parts of the continuum. This syncategorematic interpretation of the continuum, which means not only (1) that there is no actually infinitely small but rather for any assignable finite quantity there is always another that is smaller, but also (2) that there is no number of all numbers, or actually infinite number, but only numbers greater than others without bound. The fictional status of the infinite and the infinitely small has significant implications for Leibniz's mathematical approach to natural philosophy and its metaphysical foundations, particularly his understanding of what is perceived in perceptual experience as continuous motion.

It is in the *Pacidius Philalethi*, 1676 (Leibniz 2001), that Leibniz first makes a detailed attempt to work out a theory of motion that is in harmony with his syncategorematic interpretation of the continuum. Indeed, in the *Pacidius,* Leibniz develops an analysis of matter and continuity that prefigures his later metaphysical views.[37] Implicit in Leibniz's reasoning is the assumption of a direct correspondence between a curve as a mathematical object and a curve understood as the trajectory of a physical body. The trajectory of a body that traces or maps directly onto a continuous curve would be both continuous and uniform, i.e. it would be both uninterrupted and moving with constant acceleration respectively. Uniformly accelerated motion is represented mathematically by the curve of a function that pairs a body's change in position with respect to time. The velocity of a body in uniformly accelerated motion at any instant, t, is determined by finding the slope of the tangent to the function's corresponding curve at that point, which is calculated by taking the first derivative of the function with respect to time, t; the acceleration of the body at that moment is calculated by taking the second derivative of the function at that time.

The problem with this picture is that Leibniz actually denies the uniformity of motion, and instead considers the contrary hypothesis of nonuniform motion, which he maintains "is also consistent with reason, for there is no body which is not acted upon by those around it at every single moment" (Leibniz 2001, 208) (See Levey 2003, 384). Leibniz, following Huygens,[38] subscribed to an impulse account of the acceleration of a body, according to which the motion of a body was "due to a series of instantaneous finite impulses punctuating tiny subintervals of uniform motion so that in each successive subinterval the moving body has a fixed higher (or lower) velocity than it had in the preceding one" (Levey 2003, 385). Such accelerated motion is more accurately represented by a polygonal curve that only approximates the "smooth" character of a curve. Leibniz's work on the infinitangular polygon, which actually approaches the smooth character of the curve, comes to the fore here, as it was only by representing motion as a smooth curve that the seventeenth century resources of algebra and geometry were able to be deployed to calculate the velocity and acceleration of a body at any time, t. From the point of view of the syncategorematic definition of the infinitesimal, the representation of a curve as an infinitangular polygon with infinitely many infinitely small sides should be understood as follows: however, many sides are given, and however small those sides are, there are always more that are smaller. The infinitangular polygon functions therefore as a fictional limit of an arbitrarily many-sided, many-angled polygon, just as the infinitesimal functions as a fictional limit of ever decreasing finite quantities.

However, the Leibnizian model of the structure of matter satisfies the premises of the syncategorematic idea of infinite division, such that any finite portion of matter is able to be infinitely divided into progressively smaller finite parts, each of which is also infinitely divisible. The infinity of infinitely divisible parts of matter forms a plenum. The continuously curved trajectory of a body is the mathematical representation of a fictitious limit of the trajectory followed by the body which is constantly subject to the impact of other bodies from all directions in the plenum. So when Leibniz denies the uniformity of motion, he is denying not only the uniformity of acceleration, but also the kind of directionality represented by a polygonal curve. So not only is the mathematical representation of motion that has nonuniform acceleration not a smooth curve, but nor does a polygonal curve, including an infinitangular polygon, adequately represent such nonuniform motion. Leibniz does offer an alternative solution to the representation of such nonuniform motion in the *Pacidius;* however, before explicating this solution, it is necessary to further analyze the account of motion that is offered in that text.

Moving bodies are indeed acted upon by instantaneous impulses that occur at every single instant or moment and from different directions. Since every finite interval of motion is infinitely divisible into increasingly small finite and distinct moments, the moving body suffers the impacts of infinitely many distinct forces during each and every interval of motion, however small. The resulting motion is not accelerated continuously by a force that acts throughout the interval, as accelerative force is now understood to act, but rather each impact adds a distinct and instantaneous change to the motion of the body (See Levey 2003, 386). According to this impulse account of acceleration, the nonuniformity of motion is maintained throughout every subinterval however small, by distinct and instantaneous forces or impulses that add a distinct and instantaneous change in velocity to the moving body in a different direction at each moment. The motion of a moving body is infinitely divided into ever smaller subintervals of motion, each different from the other. It therefore does not persist the same and uniform for any interval. The consequence of this is that there is in fact no motion that remains uniform and continuous throughout any space or time however small.

In the *Pacidius*, Leibniz advances an analysis of the structure of the interval of motion, according to which, each endpoint of an interval of motion assigns "the actual moments in the continuum of time and the actual points in the continuum of space" (Levey 2003, 390).[39] At any moment, the moving body is at a new point, and the transition of the moving body from the end of one interval to the beginning of the next occurs by a single step, which Leibniz characterizes as a "leap" (Leibniz 2001, 79), from an assigned endpoint to what Leibniz describes as the "*locus proximus*" (Leibniz 2001, 168–69), the indistant but distinct beginning point of the next interval.

The conclusion that Leibniz comes to in the *Pacidius* is "that motion is not continuous, but happens by a leap; that is to say, that a body, staying for a while in one place, may immediately afterward be transplanted to another; i.e. that matter is extinguished here, and reproduced elsewhere" (Leibniz 2001, 79). In *Numeri infiniti*, Leibniz further characterizes motion "*per saltus,*" or through a leap, as "transcreation" (Leibniz 2001, 92–3), where the body is "annihilated in the earlier state, and resuscitated in the later one" (Leibniz 2001, 194–95). If motion consists in a body's existing at one moment in one place and in the following moment in an immediately neighboring although indistant place, and the body does not exist at the unassignable times between, then motion itself cannot be continuous across any interval. The motion of a moving body does not persist the same and uniform for any prolonged interval, because it is infinitely divisible into other subintervals of the motion, each different both in direction and velocity from the other. The endpoints of each subinterval of motion remain nothing but bounds, the ends or beginnings of the subintervals of motion into which a whole subinterval is divided by the actions of impulse forces on the apparently moving body.

The impulses at the root of motion, i.e. the leaps between indistant points, are neither intervals nor endpoints of motion. They remain unextended and are rather effected by divine intervention. The body is transcreated according to the dictates of God from one moment to the next. The changes in motion, i.e. the actions of accelerative forces, which Leibniz characterizes as "primary active force," are not the effects of moving bodies upon one another, which he characterizes as "derivative forces," they are rather ascribed to God (See Leibniz 1965, IV, 468–70; 1969, 432–3). For Leibniz, motion is not a real property in bodies, but "merely a positional phenomenon that results from God's creative activity" (Levey 2003, 406). In Leibniz's later metaphysics, he explains that whatever new states a body will possess have been predetermined by virtue of God's selection of the best of possible worlds and the preestablished harmony that it entails. However, before explicating Leibniz's later shift to a metaphysics of monads, a further striking example from this early material will be presented that will allow the structure of the interval of motion to be represented mathematically, although this relies on subsequent developments in mathematics that postdate Leibniz's example.

The Koch curve and the folded tunic: The fractal nature of motion

The example that Leibniz uses in the *Pacidius* to characterize the continuum, of which the interval of motion that has nonuniform acceleration is an instance, is the folded tunic.

> Accordingly the division of the continuum must not be considered to be like the division of sand into grains, but like that of a sheet of paper or tunic into folds. . . . It is just as if we suppose a tunic to be scored with folds multiplied to infinity in such a way that there is no fold so small that it is not subdivided by a new fold. (Leibniz 2001, 185)

The image of the tunic "scored with folds multiplied to infinity" is a heuristic for the structure of the continuum (Levey 2003, 392), and insofar as each moment in the continuum is an endpoint of motion, it is also a heuristic for the structure of the interval of motion. Just as the interval of motion is divided by different subintervals of motion in such a way that it contains subintervals within subintervals *ad infinitum*, so too is the folded tunic "scored with folds" in such a way that it contains folds within folds *ad infinitum*. The interval of motion and the folded tunic therefore display similar structure, and this structure, as Leibniz describes it, displays the very properties that fractal mathematics was later developed to study (See Levey 2003, 393). The fractal curve that best represents the structure of "folds within folds" that is suggested in the image of the folded tunic in the *Pacidius* is the Koch curve.[40] Fractal curves typically are not differentiable, i.e. there are no points on the curve at which tangents can be drawn, no matter what the scale of magnification. Instead, the intervals display only "corners" which are singularities, where the nature of the curve changes. Leibniz's impulse account of accelerated motion, as depicted in the image of the folded tunic, displays fractal structure. The action of impulses at every single moment ensures that the interval of motion of the moving body includes infinitely many singularities in every subinterval of the motion. The fractal curve of the motion, like the Koch curve, is therefore not differentiable.

According to Leibniz, each fold or vertex of the fractal curve, which is a singularity, is a boundary of not one but two intervals of motion, each of which is actually subdivided into smaller subintervals. Each vertex or singularity is in fact an aggregate pair of "indistant points": the end point of one subinterval and the beginning point of the next. A body in motion makes a "leap" from the end of one subinterval to the beginning of the next, and every leap, which occurs at the boundary between the distinct subintervals of motions, marks a change in the motion of the moving body, both of its direction and velocity. Because these subintervals are infinitely divisible, the divisions of a subinterval of motion are distributed across an indefinitely descending hierarchy of distinct scales, of which, according to Leibniz's sycategorematic account of the infinitely small, there is always a subinterval at a scale smaller than the smallest given scale. Any motion across an interval therefore contains a multiplicity of singularities, vertices or boundaries of intervals of motion, i.e. a multiplicity of unextended leaps between the indistant ends and beginnings of its various subintervals of motion, with increasing scales of resolution.

According to Leibniz's theory of motion, the properties of motion are divided into (1) those that apply to the *phenomenon* of motion across an interval of space, i.e. motion as it appears in perceptual experience and is determined by derivative forces, and (2) the conception of motion as a multiplicity of unextended leaps between indistant *loci proximi*, which is reserved for the metaphysical reality that subtends that phenomenon, and which is determined by primary active force. In perceptual experience, motion appears to consist in extended intervals that can be resolved into subintervals, *ad infinitum*. However, metaphysically, motion consists in a multiplicity of unextended leaps. Those leaps that are manifest in experience are the "singularities" at which motion is perceived to be accelerated, but not all leaps nor subintervals of motion are perceived consciously. In the sense perception of finite minds the corporeal world always appears immediately as only finitely complex and piecewise continuous, though upon closer scrutiny it is determined as indefinitely complex and fractal in its structure.

Motion across an interval appears to us to be continuous; however, it actually consists in a multiplicity of leaps. It is presented in experience as continuous, thus giving it the appearance of uniformity, only insofar as most of the subintervals into which it can be divided, and most of the changes in motion, or leaps at the boundaries of the subintervals, remain obscure to perception. While "no particular change in motion is so subtle that it cannot in principle be perceived," there is "no single scale of resolution in the unfolding of reality within experience" (Levey 2003, 404) at which the phenomenon of motion is displaced altogether by a multiplicity of unextended leaps. Motion is metaphysically founded on a multiplicity of unextended leaps between *loci proximi* and cognized constructively such that "sense perception . . . sustains within consciousness an experience of a world of finite complexity and piecewise continuity, though a complexity that can be understood to increase without bound with increasing scales of resolution" (Levey 2003, 404).

The metaphysics of monads, and bodies as "well-founded phenomena"

One of the problems with Leibniz's account of the divisibility of matter in the *Pacidius* that was not resolved until the later development of his metaphysics of monads is the problem of how matter and the objects we perceive in perceptual experience as bodies are grounded. Not only is matter infinitely divided into small finite parts, but each part of matter is itself infinitely divisible into smaller finite parts, *ad infinitum*. The division doesn't terminate in atoms or material indivisibles. Any particular part of matter is infinitely divisible into progressively smaller finite parts without ever reaching or being resolved into a smallest part which could serve as its ground. The problem is that there must be something in virtue of which the bodies, as the objects of our perceptual experience in the corporeal world, are true unities despite their indefinite subdivision into parts. There must be foundations for matter but those foundations cannot be parts of matter. The grounding of bodies that are the objects of our perceptual experience issues from something immaterial in the foundations of matter whose unity is not subject to the same indefinite, and therefore problematic division. The indivisible unities whose reality provides a metaphysical foundation for matter while residing outside of the indefinite regress of parts within parts are immaterial substances that Leibniz calls *monads* (*Monadology*, 1714). It is by means of the monad that the multiplicity of parts of matter that make up a body can be considered as a unity. The monad is prior to the multiplicity that constitutes the body, and the monad exists phenomenally only through the body it constitutes.

The constructivism of the syncategorematic infinite explains the content of our experience of reality; however, it has no place in the account of metaphysical reality. What is real metaphysically, as far as Leibniz is concerned, are simple substances or monads, and aggregates of them. Bodies, as the objects of perceptual experience that are composed of a multiplicity of parts of matter, are the "well-founded phenomenon" that are grounded by monads. In fact, the consensus in Leibniz studies is beginning to swing from an understanding of Leibniz's mature metaphysics as idealist in regard to matter—according to which the bodies perceived in our perceptual experience are mere phenomena, solely the products of our limited understanding—toward an understanding of the actual existence of corporeal substances as constituted by aggregates of monads, or of Leibniz as a realist in regard to matter, although it is not clear that Leibniz himself solved this problem satisfactorily once and for all (Garber 2009, 557). These aggregates of monads are then determined as the bodies perceived in our perceptual experience by the dominant monad that unites them. That is, one dominant monad unites each aggregate of monads which manifests phenomenally as an identifiable body.

In the sense perception of finite minds, the corporeal world always appears immediately as only finitely complex and piecewise continuous, though upon closer scrutiny it is determined as being indefinitely complex and fractal in its structure. Matter "only appears to be continuous" because our imperfect perceptual apparatus obscures the divisions which actually separate the parts of bodies. Leibniz's postulate of the best of possible worlds, chosen by God, can be characterized as an actual infinite, in which all the divisions of matter, and the relations of motion that are exhibited between them in perceptual experience, are actually assigned and the resolution into singularities or leaps, that are more or less perceived in perceptual experience, is complete, independently of the limited capacity of the mind to represent only a temporal section of this in consciousness.

Deleuze's characterization of Leibniz's account of matter

At the most basic level, Leibniz identified *materia prima* or matter with primary passive force, which has the properties of inertia, impenetrability, and extension.[41] Primary active force is associated with velocity and acceleration determined by the impulses of leaps according to the dictates of God's choice of the best of possible worlds and the principle of the preestablished harmony. And derivative forces are modes, accidents or the like of primary forces, and give rise to the mechanist's world of extended bodies in motion. These derivative forces are the immediate cause of the appearance of motion, resistance, impenetrability, and even extension in bodies.[42]

To deal with Leibniz's account of matter, Deleuze extends the trope of the "folded tunic" to characterize matter as "solid pleats" that "resemble the curves of conical forms" in projective geometry, i.e. the actual surface of the projection from apex to a curve of the cone of a conic section "sometimes ending in a circle or an ellipse, sometimes stretching into a hyperbola or a parabola." This accounts for the first type of fold that characterizes the pleats of matter. Deleuze then proposes *origami*, the Japanese art of folding paper, as the model for the sciences of Leibnizian matter (FLB 6), according to which the pleats of matter are then organized according to a second type of fold that Deleuze characterizes mathematically by means of Albrecht Dürer's (b. 1471–1528) projective method for the treatment of solids. Dürer, in his work on the shadow of a cube, devised a "proto-topological method" of developing solids on the plane surface in such a way that "the facets form a coherent "net" which, when cut out of paper and properly folded where the two facets adjoin, will form an actual, three-dimensional model of the solid in question."[43]

What then does this mean for bodies? Bodies are extended insofar as geometry is projected in this prototopological way onto them. In a metaphysical sense, what is really there is force. In his notes on Foucher, Leibniz explains that "Extension or space and the surfaces, lines, and points one can conceive in it are only relations of order or orders of coexistence."[44] The extensionality of bodies is therefore phenomenal in so far as it results from the projection of geometrical concepts onto the "folded tunic" of matter. What to each monad is its everyday spatio-temporal reality is to Leibniz a phenomenal projection, which is only rendered intelligible when it is understood to reflect the mathematical order that determines the structure of Leibniz's metaphysics.[45]

So there is a projection of structure from the mathematico-metaphysical onto the phenomenal, which Deleuze distinguishes according to the distinction canvassed earlier between the functional definition of the Newtonian fluxion and the Leibnizian infinitesimal as a concept. "The physical mechanism of bodies (fluxion) is not identical to the psychic mechanism of perception (differentials), but the latter resembles the former" (FLB 98). So Deleuze maintains that "Leibniz's calculus is adequate to psychic mechanics where Newton's is operative for physical mechanics" (FLB 98), and here again draws from the mathematics of Leibniz's contemporaries to determine a distinction between the mind and body of a monad in Leibniz's metaphysics.

How then does this relate to the body that belongs to each monad? Insofar as each monad clearly expresses a small region of the world, what is expressed clearly is related to the monad's body. Deleuze maintains that "I have a body because I have a clear and distinguished zone of expression" (FLB 98). What is expressed clearly and distinctly is what relates to the biological body of each monad, i.e. each monad has a body that is in constant interaction with other bodies, and these other bodies affect its body. So what determines such a relation is precisely a relationship between the physical elements of other bodies and the monad's biological body, each of which is characterized as a series of microperceptions which are the differentials of consciousness. Deleuze models the relation between these two series on the differential relation. Microperceptions are brought to consciousness by differentiating between the monad's own biological body and the physical affects of its relations with other physical elements or bodies. This results in the apperception of the relation between the body of the monad and the world it inhabits. However, the reality of the body is the realization of the phenomena of the body by means of projection onto the corporeal substance or aggregates of monads that constitutes the body, since the dominant monad draws all perceptive traces from itself. The dominant monad acts as if these bodies were acting upon it and were causing its perceptions. However, among monads there is no direct communication. Instead, each dominant monad or individual subject is harmonized in such a way that what it expresses forms a common compossible world that is continuous and converges with what is expressed by the other monads. So it is necessary that the monads are in harmony with one another, in fact the world is nothing other than the preestablished harmony among monads. The preestablished harmony is, on the one hand, the harmony of relations among monads, and on the other hand, the harmony of souls with their bodies, i.e. the bodies, or aggregates of dominated monads, are realized as phenomenal projections which puts them in harmony with the interiority of souls, or dominant monads.

Overcoming the limits of Leibniz's metaphysics

When Deleuze makes the comment that "The differential relation thus acquires a new meaning, since it expresses the analytical extension of one series into another, and no more the unity of converging series that would not diverge in the least from each other" (FLB 8), this should be understood in relation to what is presented in this chapter as the Weierstrassian development of the meromorphic function as a differential relation. Poincaré's subsequent development of the essential singularity means that in certain circumstances a continuity can be established across divergent series. What this means is that the Leibnizian account of compossibility as the unity of convergent series, which relies on the exclusion of divergence, is no longer required by the mathematics.[46] The mathematical idealization has therefore exceeded the metaphysics, so, in keeping with Leibniz's insistence on the metaphysical importance of mathematical speculation, the metaphysics requires recalibration. Leibniz's metaphysics is limited by the part-whole or one-multiple structure according to which this unity of convergent series is fundamentally determined, whether in terms of the one monad containing the infinite series of predicates which express all of the states of the world—past, present, and future—as determined by the principle of sufficient reason or in terms of one God establishing the harmony of all of the relations—past, present, and future—between a multiplicity of monads, as determined by the choice of the best of possible worlds.

What Poincaré's qualitative theory of differential equations does is offer a way for the part-whole structure of Leibniz's metaphysics to be problematized and overcome. Post Poincaré, the infinite series of states of the world is no longer contained in each monad. There is no preestablished harmony. The continuity of the states of the actual world and the discrimination between what is compossible and what is incompossible with this world is no longer predetermined. The logical possibilities of all incompossible worlds are now real possibilities, all of which have the potential to be actualized by monads as states of the current world, albeit with different potentials. As Deleuze argues "To the degree that the world is now made up of divergent series (the chaosmos), . . . the monad is now unable to contain the entire world as if in a closed circle that can be modified by projection" (FLB 137). So while the Weierstrassian theory of analytic continuity is retrospectively mappable onto the Leibnizian account of the unity of convergent series, the subsequent developments by Poincaré provide a solution that can be understood to overcome the explicit limits of Leibniz's metaphysics.

When it comes to Leibniz's account of motion, Deleuze endorses the hypothesis of a fractal account of our perception of motion. However, the recalibration of Leibniz's metaphysics that Deleuze undertakes in line with the more recent developments in mathematics explicated above has repercussions for Leibniz's impulse account of accelerated motion. According to Leibniz's later metaphysics, the impulses at the root of motion, i.e. the leaps between indistant points that result in changes in motion, are not the effects of moving bodies upon one another, but rather the effects of the actions of accelerative forces, determined by primary active force, that are predetermined by virtue of God's selection of the best of possible worlds and the preestablished harmony of the relations between monads—past, present, and future—that it entails. However, according to Deleuze, one of the repercussions of Poincaré's qualitative theory of differential equations is that there is no longer a preestablished harmony of the relations between monads, and the world is no longer understood to have been the subject of a divine selection as the best of possible worlds. What this means for Leibniz's mature account of accelerated motion is that the impulses at the root of motion can no longer be explained by monads and a preestablished harmony of the relations between them. Instead, a mathematical explanation can be drawn from Poincaré's qualitative theory of differential equations. What displaces the monad on this Deleuzian account and takes on the role of bringing unity to the multiplicity of parts of matter is the essential singularity. The "jump" of the variable across the domain of discontinuity between the poles of two analytic functions, which actualizes the Weierstrassian potential function in the infinite branches of the Poincaréan composite function, corresponds to what Leibniz refers to in his impulse account of accelerated motion as the unextended "leap" made by a body in motion from the end of one subinterval to the *locus proximus*, the indistant but distinct beginning point of the next interval, which marks a change in the direction and velocity of the moving body.[47] However, rather than marking a change in direction and velocity of the moving body, the essential singularity brings unity to the variables of the composite function, which correspond to the compossible predicates contained in the concept of the subject, insofar as it determines the form of a solution curve in its immediate neighborhood by acting as an *attractor* for the trajectory of the variables that "jump" across its domain. Continuing to elaborate the correspondences between Leibniz's later metaphysics and the more recent developments in mathematics that Deleuze calls upon to displace it, each of the singularities (or stationary points) of the discontinuous analytic functions represented in the meromorphic function corresponds to one of the mathematical points, or preindividual singularities, characteristic of point of view, which coincides in what is for Leibniz a metaphysical point, or monad, and what is for Deleuze an essential singularity. The essential singularity fulfills the role of accumulating or condensing the preindividual singularities of the discontinuous analytic functions. It is the number of mathematical points, points of view, or preindividual singularities coincident at any one time in the essential singularity that corresponds to the proportion of the world that is expressed clearly and distinctly as the conscious perception of an individual subject.

According to this Neo-Leibnizian account, in the sense perception of finite minds the corporeal world still appears immediately as only finitely complex and piecewise continuous, and matter "only appears to be continuous" because our imperfect perceptual apparatus, which is differential in nature, obscures the minute perceptions of the divisions which actually separate the parts of bodies. However, the relations of motion that are exhibited between parts of matter which are more or less perceived in perceptual experience are no longer predetermined according to the preestablished harmony, nor are they resolved into leaps in relation to the impulses of monads, determined by primary active force. Instead, motion is actually the result of the impact of bodies upon one another and is explained by mechanics: classical mechanics at the level of perception; quantum mechanics at the subatomic level. And the jumps of variables in relation to essential singularities, which displace the leaps in relation to impulses of monads, no longer determine the forces of motion, but rather determine the transformations of individuals to different levels or degrees of individuation.[48] The essential singularities take on the role of the dominant monads as unities. Any particular degrees of individuation appear immediately as only finitely complex and piecewise continuous, though upon closer scrutiny are determined to be composed of a multiplicity of degrees of individuation and thus to be indefinitely complex and fractal in structure. Rather than motion exhibiting a fractal structure, it is the multiplicity of degrees of individuation that now exhibits fractal structure. The complexity of individuation consists of a mapping of essential singularities that exhibits fractal structure. Of course the resolution of the jumps of variables in relation to essential singularities, or of the compossible propositions in the concept of the individual or monad, because no longer predetermined, is far from complete. It is rather open ended, and the logical possibilities of all incompossible worlds are now real possibilities, all of which have the potential to be actualized by essential singularities, or individuated, as the composite functions characteristic of states of the current world.[49]

The reconstruction of Leibniz's metaphysics that Deleuze provides in the *Fold* draws upon not only the mathematics developed by Leibniz but also developments in mathematics made by a number of Leibniz's contemporaries and a number of subsequent developments in mathematics, the mathematical account of which is offered most explicitly in *Difference and Repetition*.[50] Deleuze then retrospectively maps these developments back onto the structure of Leibniz's metaphysics in order to bring together the different aspects of Leibniz's metaphysics with the variety of mathematical themes that run throughout his work. The result is a thoroughly mathematical explication of Leibniz's metaphysics, and it is this account that subtends the entire text of the *Fold*. It is these aspects of Deleuze's project in *The Fold* that represent the "new Baroque and Neo-Leibnizianism" (FLB 136) that Deleuze has explored elsewhere in his body of work, notably in the ninth and the sixteenth series of the *Logic of Sense*, where Deleuze explicates his Neo-Leibnizian account of the problematic, and his account of the genesis of the individual.

Spinoza and the logic of differen*t*/*c*iation

In *Expressionism in Philosophy, Spinoza* (1992), Deleuze advocates the scientific study of Spinozism, one aspect of which is the relation between Spinoza's ontology and Leibniz's development of the infinitesimal calculus. An appreciation of the role played by the infinitesimal calculus in this context is crucial to understanding how Deleuze's interpretation of Spinoza is implicated in his broader philosophical project. My previous work on Spinoza (Duffy 2006a; 2009b) aimed to develop an understanding of the mechanism of operation of the logic of differen*t*/*c*iation in Deleuze's reading of

Spinoza, and also to position Deleuze's interpretation of Spinoza, and the logic with which it is explicated, within the context of the development of Deleuze's broader philosophical project of constructing a philosophy of difference. By exploiting the implications of the differential point of view of the infinitesimal calculus in his interpretation of the physics of bodies in the second part of the *Ethics*, I argued that Deleuze develops a concept of individuation in relation to Spinoza's theory of relations that is modeled on the logic of differen*t/c*iation.

The logic of the differential, as determined according to both differen*t*iation and differen*c*iation, designates a process of production, or genesis, which has, for Deleuze, the value of introducing a general theory of relations, which unites the structural considerations of the differential calculus to the concept of individuation, insofar as the former serves as a model for the latter. "In order to designate the integrity or the integrality of the object," whether considered as a composite function from the differential point of view of the infinitesimal calculus or as an individual from the point of view of the physics of bodies, Deleuze argues that, "we require the complex concept of differen*t/c*iation. The *t* and the *c* here are the distinctive feature or the phonological relation of difference in person" (DR 209). Deleuze argues that differen*c*iation is "the second part of difference" (DR 209), the first being expressed by the logic of the differential in differen*t*iation.[51] Where the logic of differen*t*iation characterizes a differential philosophy, the complex concept of the logic of differen*t/c*iation characterizes Deleuze's "philosophy of difference."

The alternative lineage in the history of mathematics is implicated in Deleuze's alternative lineage in the history of philosophy by deploying the logic of the differential from the differential point of view of the infinitesimal calculus as a model for the logic of the theory of relations. The manner by means of which a mathematical function— the relation between infinitely small differentials—is implicated in the mathematical logic which determines it serves as a model for the manner by means of which a philosophical concept—the relation between the most simple bodies—is implicated in the philosophical logic which determines it. There are what Deleuze considers to be "correspondences without resemblance" (DR 184) between them, insofar as both are determined according to the logic of differen*t/c*iation; however, there is no resemblance between differentials and the most simple bodies. Differentials are mathematical, not physical. The correspondence is between the conceptualizable character of the differential and the concept of the most simple body. The philosophical implications of this correspondence are developed by Deleuze in *Expressionism in Philosophy* in relation to his reading of Spinoza's theory of relations in the *Ethics*. By exploiting the implications of the differential point of view of the infinitesimal calculus in his interpretation of the physics of bodies in the second part of the *Ethics*, Deleuze is able to read the system of the *Ethics* as a whole as determined according to the logic of differen*t/c*iation. This strategy of reading the *Ethics* as determined according to a logic of differen*t/c*iation marks the originality of Deleuze's interpretation of Spinoza, which traces an alternative lineage in the history of philosophy between Spinoza's ontology and the mathematics of Leibniz. There is therefore a convergence between Leibniz and Spinoza in Deleuze's philosophy in terms of the seventeenth century theory of relations that he traces through their work.

The main problematic that has determined the direction of the investigation so far, and which continues to do so throughout the following chapters, is the question of the nature of the relation between, on the one hand, the mathematical function and the mathematical logic that determines it, and, on the other hand, the philosophical concept and the philosophical logic that determines it. This has taken the form of asking whether or not mathematics can be understood to serve as a model for philosophy, and if so, how? While having demonstrated in Duffy 2006a how the logic of the differential from the differential point of view of the infinitesimal calculus, which is deployed by Deleuze in the form of the logic of differen*t/c*iation, does function as a model for the development of the concept of individuation in Deleuze's reading of Spinoza, the next chapter takes up the question of how this logic is deployed by Deleuze in his overall project of constructing a philosophy of difference, specifically in relation to his reading of Maimon and of Maimon's response to Kant's first *Critique*.

Maimon's Critique of Kant's Approach to Mathematics

Kant on the construction of mathematical concepts in pure intuition

Kant has problems similar to those of Deleuze with the implications of Leibnizian compossibility for the subject-predicate logic. This is brought out in particular in the distinction between mathematical and philosophical knowledge that Kant establishes in the *Critique of Pure Reason* (1998), which is in contrast to Leibniz, for whom philosophical inquiry is modeled on the prototype of mathematical analysis. For Leibniz, any mathematical proposition expresses a demonstrable identity. This is explicable in terms of the Leibnizian understanding of the subject-predicate logic, according to which an infinite series of predicates is contained in the concept of the subject, i.e. that mathematical propositions are analytic and that every step in a mathematical demonstration is in accord with/bound by the law of noncontradiction. While Kant agrees that mathematical propositions are expressed as judgments that relate a subject concept to a predicate concept, the main point of contention for him is the claim that mathematical propositions are analytic, i.e. that such propositions can be understood solely by virtue of conceptual analysis of the subject and predicate concepts.[1] While Kant concedes the claim that mathematical propositions are deduced in accordance with the law of noncontradiction, he denies that this demonstrates their analyticity. The distinction between Leibniz and Kant on this point is most stark when considering the propositions of geometry. For Leibniz, geometrical propositions are derived from general principles, rather than from their corresponding geometric diagrams.

> You must understand that geometers do not derive their proofs from diagrams, although the expository approach makes it seem so. The cogency of the demonstration is independent of the diagram, whose only role is to make it easier to understand what is meant and to fix one's attention. It is universal propositions, i.e. definitions and axioms and theorems which have already been demonstrated, that make up the reasoning, and they would sustain it even if there were no diagram. (Leibniz 1996, 360–1)

In denying the analyticity of mathematical propositions, Kant is contrasting the method of determining mathematical knowledge with that of determining philosophical knowledge. While philosophical knowledge is rational knowledge from concepts and depends solely upon the analysis of concepts, mathematical knowledge for Kant is determined by the construction of concepts, which implicates geometrical diagrams in a very specific way, i.e. as the *a priori* intuitions of mathematical concepts. Kant explains this implication as follows:

> to construct a concept means to exhibit a priori the intuition corresponding to it. For the construction of a concept, therefore, a non-empirical intuition is required, which consequently, as intuition, is an individual object, but which must nevertheless, as the construction of a concept (of a general representation), express in the representation universal validity for all possible intuitions that belong under the same concept. (Kant 1998, A713/B741–A714/B742)

When the constructed mathematical concept is exhibited *a priori* by the imagination, it is exhibited solely in accordance with the conditions of the pure intuitions of space and time, the forms, respectively, of outer and inner intuition, and is therefore referred to by Kant as itself a "pure intuition" (Kant 1998, A721/B749). However, it can also be exhibited as an empirical intuition in the form of a figure drawn on paper.

In the Preface to the *Critique of Pure Reason*, Kant appeals to the figure of a triangle as an example of such a figure (Kant 1998, Bxi), and he repeatedly returns to the example of a triangle as a model for mathematical construction. To construct a triangle is to exhibit "an object corresponding to this concept, either through mere imagination, in pure intuition, or on paper, in empirical intuition" (Kant 1998, A713/B741–A714/B742). When the figure of a triangle is represented as an empirical "intuition, the drawn figure is an empirical sensible object which nevertheless serves to construct its corresponding concept universally" (Shabel 2003, 92), since what Kant refers to as "the pattern for it" (Kant 1998, A713/B741–A714/B742) is not borrowed from experience. That is, as Kant explains, "we have taken account only of the action of constructing the concept, to which many determinations, e.g., those of the magnitude of the sides and the angles, are entirely indifferent, and thus we have abstracted from these differences, which do not alter the concept of the triangle" (Kant 1998, A713/B741–A714/B742). Kant's claim that mathematical knowledge is synthetic a priori and universal follows directly from the view that mathematical concepts are constructed in pure intuition, as opposed to empirical intuitions, which are, by definition, *a posteriori*. When the mathematical concept is constructed in pure intuition, the so constructed object functions as a representative of all possible intuitions falling under the same concept, it thus confers universality on the mathematical concept and on the mathematical judgments that are made in relation to it. What is important for Kant is the rule-governed and therefore repeatable nature of the procedure of constructing the empirical intuition, not the resulting drawn figure itself. The point is that the entire procedure is carried out in pure intuition by abstracting from the particular determinations of the drawn figure, in the case of a triangle for example, from the magnitudes of its sides and angles. The pure intuition that corresponds to, and constructs, the mathematical concept can therefore actually be drawn, and thus rendered empirically, without ceasing to function as a "pure" intuition.

It is, however, sufficient to consider the rule-governed procedure for the construction of the object in pure intuition for the concept to be constructed, and to thus attain synthetic a priori knowledge of the mathematical proposition. Whereas if only the resulting construction as rendered empirically is inspected, this would lead simply to diagrammatic knowledge of the empirical intuition, which would consist of knowledge of the construction solely by means of measurement using a ruler and protractor. It is solely by virtue of information provided by the construction of the object in intuition that properties can be predicated both of it and of any resulting empirical construction of it. Such properties, whether general or particular, are then subsumed under the concept constructed in pure intuition. "Thus we think of a triangle as an object by being conscious of the composition of three straight lines in accordance with a rule according to which such an intuition can always be exhibited" (Kant 1998, A105).

Kant's conception of mathematics commits him to the understanding that we need to be conscious of the rule-governed procedures followed in effecting mathematical constructions, i.e. that the diagrams of Euclidean geometry must actually be drawn in order for us to cognize and thereby gain any understanding of the relationships among the elements of geometry, whether this occurs solely in pure intuition or also in empirical intuition. In order to illustrate the differences between the mathematical construction of concepts and the philosophical analysis of concepts, Kant again turns to the example of the triangle:

> Give a philosopher the concept of a triangle, and let him try to find out in his way how the sum of its angles might be related to a right angle. He has nothing but the concept of a figure enclosed by three straight lines, and in it the concept of equally many angles. Now he may reflect on this concept as long as he wants, yet he will never produce anything new . . . . But now let the geometer take up this question. He begins at once to construct a triangle . . . (Kant 1998, A716/B745).

The particular example of a triangle that Kant turns to in order to explicate this distinction is the classical proof of Proposition I.32 of Euclid's *Elements*: "In any triangle, if one of the sides be produced, the exterior angle is equal to the two interior and opposite angles, and the three interior angles of the triangle are equal to two right angles" (Euclid 1956, 316). The problem for the philosopher is that they are unable to demonstrate proposition I.32 analytically. This is so because the original concept of the interior sum of the angles of a triangle does not contain within it the concept of two right angles. The geometer on the other hand can construct the concept of the triangle by constructing a triangular figure and, by extending the sides using the geometrical relationship between the angles contained by parallel lines and a transversal, can connect the original concept of the interior sum of the angles of a triangle with the concept of two right angles. Kant describes the procedure of the geometer as follows:

> Since he knows that two right angles together are exactly equal to all of the adjacent angles that can be drawn at one point on a straight line, he extends one side of his triangle, and obtains two adjacent angles that together are equal to two right ones. Now he divides the external one of these angles by drawing a line parallel to the opposite side of the triangle, and sees that here there arises an external adjacent angle which is equal to an internal one, etc. (Kant 1998, A716/B744).

The extensions made to the original figure give the geometer more conceptual information than the philosopher can attain by mere analysis. The geometer is therefore able to connect the original concept "to properties which do not lie in this concept but" that, by means of geometrical construction and therefore demonstration, do "still belong to it" (Kant 1998, A718/B746). The judgment that these concepts are able to be connected in this way is therefore not an analytic judgment but rather a synthetic judgment. Kant further qualifies the nature of synthetic judgments depending on the specific intuition in relation to which they are made. He maintains that:

> I can go from the concept to the pure or empirical intuition corresponding to it in order to assess it *in concreto* and cognize *a priori* or *a posteriori* what pertains to its object. The former is rational and mathematical cognition through the construction of the concept, the latter merely empirical (mechanical) cognition, which can never yield necessary and apodictic propositions (Kant 1998, A721/ B749).

Just as there is a distinction between the pure and empirical intuitions that are implicated in the construction of a mathematical concept, so too is there a distinction, indeed the same distinction, between the kinds of mathematical judgments that result, or can be made about them. A mathematical judgment can be either synthetic *a priori*, or synthetic *a posteriori*, depending on the kind of intuition used to demonstrate it. Kant maintains that a mathematical judgment, such as that made upon mathematically demonstrating Euclid's proposition I.32, when focusing solely on the rule-governed nature of the construction of the figure in pure intuition, yields synthetic *a priori* knowledge. A synthetic judgment is formed by attributing a property to a concept that was not previously contained in it. A synthetic *a priori* judgment about a concept, such as the interior sum of the angles of a triangle, goes beyond this concept "to the intuition in which it is given" (Kant 1998, A721/B749), i.e. to the construction in pure intuition that connects it with the construction of the concept of the two right angles. So, regardless of whether or not the geometrical figure is actually constructed *in concreto*, or if its construction is just imagined, mathematical knowledge is derived from the inferences drawn from these constructions. It is synthetic a priori judgments made in relation to constructions, or a priori exhibitions, in pure intuition that effect the construction of mathematical concepts and thereby yield necessary and apodictic propositions characteristic of rational and mathematical cognition. Judgments made in relation to the actually constructed, or exhibited, figures are synthetic a posteriori judgments characteristic of empirical (mechanical) cognition that yield diagrammatic knowledge about the measurable properties that can be predicated of these figures and that are subsumable under the constructed concept.[2]

That mathematical judgments are synthetic and *a priori* therefore follows from Kant's understanding of the role of pure intuitions in mathematical demonstration.[3] The corollary to this is that Kant's philosophy of mathematics plays a central role in the determination of the solution that he provides in the first *Critique* (1998) to the problem of the application of pure concepts of the understanding, or the categories, to empirical intuitions, or appearances, which are heterogeneous by nature. Indeed, Kant maintains that "The understanding can intuit nothing, the senses can think nothing.

Only through their union can knowledge arise. But that is no reason for confounding the contribution of either with that of the other; rather it is a strong reason for carefully separating and distinguishing the one from the other" (Kant 1998, A51/B75). In his correspondence with Reinhold, Kant provides a clear account of the extension of this principle to all synthetic judgments, both a priori and a posteriori. Kant's principle for synthetic judgments, implicit in the first *Critique*, is that

> all synthetic judgments of theoretical cognition are possible only by the relating of a given concept to an intuition. If the synthetic judgment is an experiential judgment, the intuition must be empirical and if the judgment is a priori synthetic, there must be a pure intuition to ground it. (Kant 1967, 141)

The solution that Kant comes up with in the first *Critique* relies on positing a "third thing"

> which must stand in *homogeneity* with the category on the one hand and the appearance on the other, and makes possible the application of the former to the latter. This mediating representation must be pure (without anything empirical) and yet intellectual on the one hand and sensible on the other. Such a representation is the transcendental schema. (Kant 1998, A138/B177)

Kant introduces the Schematism in order to resolve the concept-intuition problem. The ability of the mathematical diagram to function purely as an intuition in the construction of a mathematical concept provides Kant with a model for the function of the transcendental schema. The way a mathematical concept is constructed by a pure intuition, which thereby mediates between the concept and its empirical instantiation, provides the framework for the way transcendental schemata mediate between a pure concept and the empirical intuition that instantiates it. The link is provided, not by the image of the geometrical object, but by the pure intuition which signifies a rule-governed procedure for the construction of the mathematical concept. As Kant explains in his discussion of the schemata of mathematical concepts, which he refers to in this passage as "pure sensible concepts" as opposed to pure concepts, or categories:

> In fact it is not images of objects but schemata which ground our pure sensible concepts. No image of a triangle would ever be adequate to the concept of it. For it would not attain the generality of the concept, which makes this valid for all triangles, right or acute, etc., but would always be limited to one part of this sphere. The schema of the triangle can never exist anywhere except in thought, and signifies a rule of the synthesis of the imagination with regard to pure shapes in space. (Kant 1998, A142/B181)

The schema of a mathematical concept is that aspect of the intuition of a mathematical concept that is pure rather than empirical. It signifies the rule that determines the procedure for constructing that concept. It is only because the mathematical concept of "triangle" is constructed according to a rule that it is linked to its empirical intuition. A mathematical concept is therefore not grounded by the concrete image that results from performing the construction in accordance with a rule but by the schema, or rule itself, for its possible construction in empirical intuition. The empirical construction itself is not necessary for a pure intuition to function as a rule of construction, since the schema provides a general rule that guarantees the possibility of such a construction. The mathematical schema therefore specifies the rule according to which a mathematical object can be intuited purely independent of its empirical instantiation. However, any individual triangle constructed in empirical intuition has the capacity to represent "triangle" universally insofar as it is constructed in accord with the rule of construction specified by the schema for the concept of triangle. As Kant explains:

> . . . mathematical cognition considers the universal in the particular, indeed even in the individual, yet nonetheless a priori and by means of reason, so that just as this individual is determined under certain general conditions of construction, the object of the concept, to which this individual corresponds only as its schema, must likewise be thought as universally determined. (Kant 1998, A714/B742)

The demonstration of Euclid's proposition I.32 presented by Kant, and indeed any mathematical demonstration that employs general or universally determined pure intuition, is therefore an example of a synthetic *a priori* and universal judgment.

The concept of the straight line

Kant also considers geometric principles, or axioms, to be examples of synthetic a priori propositions, in particular, the proposition that the straight line between two points is the shortest distance (Kant 1998, B16).[4] He maintains that because the "concept of the straight contains nothing of quantity, but only a quality," then "the concept of the shortest is therefore entirely additional to it, and cannot be extracted out of the concept of the straight line by any analysis" (Kant 1998, B16). What he means by this is that the concept of the shortest distance between two points is not analytically contained in the concept of the straight line between them, since it refers solely to the shape and not the measure of the distance between the points. The straight line between the points can therefore not be judged by conceptual analysis to be the shortest distance between the points. To make a judgment about the relation of the concept of the straight line and that of the shortest distance between two points, the concept of the straight line must be synthesized with the concept of the shortest distance by constructing, or exhibiting, the latter in intuition, whether solely in pure intuition or also in empirical intuition as a concrete drawing. Kant considers the synthesis between the concepts to be immediately evident because a line that was longer than the shortest distance between the two points would either be curved or bent, and therefore no longer the shortest.

Just as the relation between a mathematical concept and its empirical intuition is linked by the schema or rule of construction, which in this case is signified by the pure intuition, so too is a pure concept linked with its empirical intuition by its schema. However, rather than considering the universal in the particular, as in mathematical cognition, philosophical cognition "considers the particular only in the universal" (Kant 1998, A714/B742).

The pure concepts of the understanding, or categories, whose content for Kant is derived solely from the logical structures of judgment, and is therefore universal, provide the conditions according to which particular empirical sensible intuitions can be cognized. Each category is associated with its own schema in imagination, which provides the rules or procedures for the representation in intuition of the logical form or relation of that category. To do this, each category must be associated with, on the one hand, a temporal schema, since time as the form of inner intuition is the form of every sensible intuition whatsoever, and on the other hand, for those intuitions of spatial properties or relations, a spatial schema, since space is the form of outer intuition. Thus, the categories provide the conditions according to which particular empirical intuitions can be given in space and time. While the schemata of mathematical concepts do provide a model for understanding the schemata of pure concepts, there are important differences between the two. Since mathematical concepts are constructible, their schemata are rules for constructing universalizable images that instantiate them, whereas pure concepts are necessarily linked to existing appearances via rules for representing images in accordance with a particular category. While mathematical concepts can be constructed in the form of images, insofar as the images are geometrical diagrams functioning as pure intuitions, pure concepts cannot be directly connected to an image. As Kant explains:

> the schema of sensible concepts (such as figures in space) *is* a product and as it were a monogram of pure *a priori* imagination, through which and in accordance with which the images first become possible, but which must be connected with the concept, to which they are in themselves never fully congruent, always only by means of the schema which they designate. (Kant 1998, A140/B180–A142/B181)

Instead, the schemata of pure concepts provide rules for cognizing images or empirical intuitions, i.e. rules for picking them out and making them available to be subsumed under certain general concepts. The difference between mathematical and philosophical cognition is therefore determined by the difference between the rules signified by their schemata. While the schemata of mathematical concepts are rules for constructing, or exhibiting a priori, pure intuitions and the empirical instantiations of them, the schemata of pure concepts are rules for the recognizing and subsuming empirical intuitions under general concepts.[5]

The schema of pure concepts differ from those of mathematical concepts insofar as the link provided by the schematism between the pure concept and its empirical intuition is necessary because the pure concept is heterogeneous with its corresponding intuitions, i.e. the appearances which fall under it, while for Kant there is no analogous heterogeneity between mathematical concepts and the intuitions that correspond to them directly via construction. The explanation for this is that the construction of the concept triangle is not exhausted by the exhibition of the concept itself, but requires the exhibition of a triangular figure in the pure intuition of space. The mathematical concept of a triangle is therefore homogeneous with its pure intuition of a triangle by virtue of the necessity of construction, and indeed with all pure and empirical intuitions of triangles. This homogeneity also extends to all triangular objects of experience, since the concept triangle provides the rule for the representation of any three-sided rectilinear object. In this way, geometric concepts provide the framework for constructing sensible intuitions of the spatial magnitudes of objects of outer sense, and it is the schemata of arithmetic concepts, such as the concept of number, that provide the rule or procedure for the construction of sensible intuitions of the magnitudes of objects in general. This includes the quantitative measures of objects of both inner and outer sense, i.e. both spatial and temporal magnitudes. The intuitions that construct these concepts are found in "the fingers, in the beads of an abacus, or in strokes and points that are placed before the eyes" (Kant 1998, A240/B299). Thus, the concept five, for example, can be constructed in intuition by the representation of five discrete strokes: | | | | |. This rule or procedure, which "summarizes the successive addition of one (homogeneous) unit to another," is what Kant refers to as an "*a priori* time-determination in accordance with rules" (Kant 1998, A142/B182), "because the 'rule of counting' or procedure for representing each of a collection of objects by strokes or points determines the same pattern as the representation of successive moments or instants in (a finite period of) time" (Shabel 2003, 111). Thus, Kant writes that "number is nothing other than the unity of the synthesis of the manifold of a homogeneous intuition in general, because I generate time itself in the apprehension of the intuition" (Kant 1998, A142/B182). It is precisely because mathematical concepts are derived from the combination of the categories of quantity with space and time that Kant conceives them to be constructible. For Kant, it is sufficient for intuitions of the constructed figures of elementary mathematics (arithmetic, geometry, and algebra)[6] to be pure, rather than empirical for their respective concepts to be constructed. What this means is that by following a specified rule or procedure, the act of construction in pure intuition is sufficient to bring out those properties of the constructed object that are not evident in its concept alone.

When it comes to the schematism of the understanding with regard to empirical or sensible concepts, Kant maintains that "an object of experience or image of it," an appearance, doesn't relate directly to the empirical concept, as it does with a mathematical concept. Instead, the empirical concept "is always related immediately to the schema of the imagination, as a rule for the determination of our intuition in accordance with a certain general concept" (Kant 1998, A141/B181). The example of a general concept that Kant provides, which subsumes the empirical concept in this cognitive process, is the concept of a dog, which "signifies a rule in accordance with which my imagination can specify the shape of a four-footed animal in general, without being restricted to any single particular shape that experience offers me or any possible image that I can exhibit *in concreto*" (Kant 1998, A141/B181).

Kant describes the schematism of sensible concepts as "a hidden art in the depths of the human soul, whose true operations we can divine from nature and lay unveiled before our eyes only with difficulty" (Kant 1998, A141/B181). It is to the schemata of mathematical concepts that Kant turns in order to explicate the framework for the mode of operation of the schemata of sensible concepts. Kant's account of mathematical cognition therefore provides the framework for cognition in general, and his philosophy of mathematics can therefore be understood to play a fundamental role in the critical project as a whole.

Maimon's critique of Kant

Maimon's *Essay on Transcendental Philosophy* is presented as a refutation of Kant's *Critique of Pure Reason*. Maimon's critique of Kant concerns the central thesis of the first *Critique* that purports to resolve the problem of the relation between concepts of the understanding and empirical intuitions by means of the schematism. In the preface to the *Essay*, Maimon provides a concise summary of his response to Kant and of the subsequent system that he builds:

> In particular I present the following remarks to the thoughtful reader for examination. First, the distinction between mere *a priori* cognition and pure *a priori* cognition, and the difficulty that still remains with respect to the latter. Second, my derivation of the origin of synthetic propositions from the incompleteness of our cognition. Third, doubts with respect to the question *quid facti*, to which Hume's objection appears to be irrefutable. Fourth, the clue I give to the answer to the question *quid juris* and the explanation of the possibility of metaphysics in general, through the reduction of intuitions to their elements, elements that I call ideas of the understanding. (Maimon 2010, 9)

The question *quid juris* for Maimon is a query concerning Kant's solution to the problem of the relation between pure concepts and empirical intuitions. He questions whether the objective use of the concept is legitimate, and if it is, what exactly is the nature of this legitimacy (Maimon 2010, 51)?[7] It was Kant who first posed the question *quid juris* in the first *Critique*. Kant argues that "proofs from experience are not sufficient for the lawfulness of such a use, and yet one must know how these concepts can be related to objects that they do not derive from any experience" (Kant 1998, A85/ B117). The solution that Kant provides is in the chapter on the Schematism (A137/ B176). Maimon does not accept Kant's response to the question. He considers Kant to have presupposed that concepts and intuitions necessarily unite in cognition. It is not the necessity of this relation that Maimon disputes but the presumption, because he does not think that Kant can justify the presumption. Nor does Maimon accept the implications that follow from Kant's characterization of geometry as an inquiry into the properties of the form of sensation, namely that our pure intuition of space is the actual source of our cognition of the first principles of geometry. What Maimon demands in the *Essay* is a response to the question *quid juris* in light of the Kantian solution that he sees as problematic. The alternative solution that Maimon proposes is first presented in chapter two of the *Essay*:

> In the Kantian system, namely where sensibility and understanding are two totally different sources of our cognition, this question is insoluble as I have shown; on the other hand in the Leibnizian-Wolffian system, both flow from one and the same cognitive source (the difference lies only in the degree of completeness of this cognition) and so the question is easily resolved. (Maimon 2010, 64)

Maimon maintains that as long as sensibility is regarded as independent of the understanding, the possibility of applying concepts to sensible intuition cannot be comprehended. The connection between the two can only be explained by demonstrating that they both derive from the same source. While Kant only asked the quid juris question about the relation between the pure concepts and a posteriori intuitions, Maimon extends this to include a priori intuitions as well, and it is in relation to mathematics that Maimon demonstrates the primacy of this question:

> I also take a fact as ground, but not a fact relating to *a posteriori* objects (because I doubt the latter) but a fact relating to *a priori* objects (of pure mathematics) where we connect forms (relations) with intuitions, and because this undoubted fact refers to a priori objects, it is certainly possible, and at the same time actual. But my question is: how is it comprehensible? . . . Kant shows merely the possibility of his fact, which he merely presupposes. By contrast, my fact is certain and also possible. I merely ask: what sort of hypothesis must I adopt for it to be comprehensible? (Maimon 2010, 364)

The purpose of the following section is to provide an account of the hypothesis that Maimon adopts in order to render this connection comprehensible. Maimon's starting point is to distinguish between two types of a priori cognition, that which is pure and a priori, and that which is merely a priori.

> Something is pure when it is the product of the understanding alone (and not of sensibility). Everything that is pure is at the same time a priori, but not the reverse. All mathematical concepts are a priori, but nevertheless not pure. (Maimon 2010, 56)

Cognition that is both a priori and pure does not refer to sensibility in any way, neither to the a posteriori, i.e. to specific sensations, nor to that which constitutes a condition for the sensation of objects, namely, space and time. This type of a priori is completely conceptual. The other type of a priori, which is not pure, also doesn't refer to specific sensations, but does involve space and time and therefore the forms of sensation. The range and philosophical significance of Maimon's two types of a priori cognition differ from that of the types of cognition discussed by Kant. While for both, pure cognition involves the categories,[8] Kant also refers to mathematical concepts as pure sensible concepts. Maimon on the other hand claims that while mathematical concepts are indeed a priori, not all of them are pure. What this means for Maimon is that there is a distinction between mathematical concepts that are pure, and about which we can only think, and those that are not pure and of which we are only conscious because of their representation in a priori intuition. The difference between Kant and Maimon on this issue comes down to the difference in the nature of the representation of mathematical concepts in a priori intuition. If the concepts of the numbers are taken as a preliminary example of this difference, for Kant, the concept of a number, 5 for example, is constructed in pure intuition by means of the representation of discrete strokes, for example | | | | | (Kant 1998, A240/B299). Whereas Maimon considers the concepts of the numbers to be "merely relations" that

> do not presuppose real objects because these relations are the objects themselves. For example, the number 2 expresses a ratio of 2:1 at the same time as it expresses

the object of this relation, and if the latter is necessary for its consciousness, it is certainly not necessary for its reality. All mathematical truths have their reality prior to our consciousness of them. (Maimon 2010, 190)

Maimon considers it to be "an error to believe that things (real objects) must be prior to their relations" (Maimon 2010, 190). The difference between these two accounts is that, for Kant, the a priori intuitions are supplements to and given independently of the concepts of magnitude that are applied to them. Whereas for Maimon, the a priori intuition is merely "an image or distinguishing mark" (Maimon 2010, 69) of the relational concept of the magnitude itself, which results from what Maimon characterizes as our limited knowledge of it, and is therefore not so heterogeneous with it. Maimon maintains that:

> the representation or concept of a thing is not so heterogeneous with the thing itself (or with what belongs to its existence) as is commonly believed. . . . The reality of the former stems merely from the negation or limitation of the latter. For an infinite understanding, the thing and its representation are one and the same. An idea is a method for finding a passage from the representation or concept of a thing to the thing itself; it does not determine any object of intuition but still determines a real object whose schema is the object of intuition. (Maimon 2010, 365)

Before considering the role of the infinite understanding in Maimon's system and how the relation between ideas and concepts of *a priori* cognition relate to those of *a posteriori* cognition, the broader implications of the difference between the representation or concept of a thing and the thing itself, which Maimon characterizes as not so heterogeneous, will be developed in relation to mathematics, where Maimon's difference in understanding of arithmetic is deployed in relation to Kant's account of synthetic *a priori* judgments in the first *Critique*. It is this distinction between their accounts of arithmetic, and the implications for the role of mathematics in their respective philosophical systems that this entails, that will be the focus of this treatment of Maimon.

The distinction between their different approaches to arithmetic allows Maimon's question *quid juris* to be formulated specifically in relation to mathematical cognition. For Maimon, the question regarding the connection between the categories of the understanding and the forms of sensibility is generalized into a demand to understand the connection between mere a priori cognition, which draws on intuition, and pure a priori cognition which doesn't. What this amounts to in relation to mathematical cognition is the question of the connection between an image and that of which it is an image.

Maimon acknowledges the problem of the connection between pure cognition and a priori cognition that Kant attempts to explain by means of the schematism. However, he considers the schematism, which is modeled on the relation between mathematical concepts and what Kant refers to respectively as their pure and empirical intuitions, to simply posit a false resolution, and he considers himself to take the issue further than Kant in demanding how such a relation is comprehensible. The question that Maimon poses is how the possibility of such a connection can be accounted for, i.e.

the possibility of applying a pure relational concept to an intuition that is a priori but not pure? The example that Maimon gives of this connection is the proposition that "the straight line is the shortest between two points" (Maimon 2010, 65), which is also one of Kant's examples of a synthetic a priori judgment in the first *Critique* (Kant 1998, B16). It facilitates the comparison of the difference between Maimon and Kant and enables a close examination of one of Maimon's main moves against Kant in the *Essay*. On Kant's analysis, the judgment that a straight line is the shortest between two points adds a further property, i.e. the intuited property of the line being straight, to the conceptual property of being the shortest distance between two points. Maimon understands this example quite differently. According to him, the intuition in question is not a supplement to the concept, but rather "an image" of that concept, i.e. it represents the concept on which it is founded. What is represented as a straight line, i.e. a line with a single, fixed direction, is in fact an image of the shortest distance between two points. Maimon acknowledges that there is a synthesis between the two components of the proposition. On the one hand, there is the straight line, which, as far as Maimon is concerned, is an a priori cognition which appears in intuition and is therefore impure. On the other hand, there is the property of being the shortest distance between two points, which refers solely to the magnitude of the distance, which is a category and therefore belongs to pure cognition. The two are synthesized in the proposition. It therefore remains a synthetic a priori proposition for Maimon; however, the nature of the synthesis is different.

Maimon agrees with Kant that the Wolffian definition of the straight line as the "identity of direction of its parts" is "useless" (Maimon 2010, 70), as Maimon puts it, since it presupposes that the parts have already arisen and, "because the similarity of the parts to the whole can only be in direction," it also "already presupposes lines" (Maimon 2010, 70). However, he disagrees with Kant, who Maimon argues makes "a concept of reflection," that is, the shortest distance between two points, "into the rule for the production of an object" (Maimon 2010, 68), i.e. of the straight line as a real object of mathematics, by claiming that it is constructed by being represented in intuition. Maimon on the contrary argues that "a concept of reflection should really be thought between already given objects" (Maimon 2010, 68), i.e. between real objects of mathematics which are pure a priori concepts of the understanding. Maimon is thinking here of the phrase "the shortest distance between two points," which he argues that the understanding thinks as a rule in order to produce the straight line as an object. Maimon considers this rule to be a concept of reflection, "a relation of difference with respect to magnitude" (Maimon 2010, 68), i.e. thought between two already given real objects of mathematics or pure a priori concepts of the understanding, i.e. the two points between which a judgment of magnitude is made, both of which can be defined independently of the intuitions. This is achieved according to Euclid's definition 1.1, "A point is that which has no point" (Euclid 1956, 153), and from Maimon's argument presented above about numbers being "merely relations" that "do not presuppose real objects because these relations are the objects themselves" (Maimon 2010, 190). Maimon argues that the two points referred to in this rule of the understanding are "pure magnitudes prior to their application to intuition"

(Maimon 2010, 69), and that this "cannot be supposed otherwise, because it is only by means of such relations that the magnitudes become objects in the first place" (Maimon 2010, 69). So, contrary to Kant, Maimon distinguishes arithmetic from geometry in this respect insofar as in arithmetic "without the thought of a relation there is indeed no object of magnitude" (Maimon 2010, 69), whereas geometry "does provide us with objects prior to their subsumption under the category of magnitude, namely figures that are already determined through their position" (Maimon 2010, 69). In arithmetic, "the inner (the thing in itself) does not precede the outer (the relation to other things) as is the case with other objects, but rather the reverse" (Maimon 2010, 69).

In the next step of his argument, Maimon provides an analytic proof "that one line (between two points) must be shorter than several lines (between the same points)" (Maimon 2010, 65). He does this by initially comparing two lines between the points with one line between the same points. These three lines can be understood to constitute a triangle, and therefore allow the use of Euclidian proposition I.20, which concerns the relations between the sides of a triangle. Proposition 20 states that "In any triangle two sides taken together in any manner are greater than the remaining one" (Euclid 1956, 293). Maimon then claims that this proof can be extended to "several lines that lie . . . between the same points." The reason being that "a rectilinear figure will always arise that can be resolved into triangles" (Maimon 2010, 66).

What this means for Maimon is that, just as an intuited number 2 is necessary for consciousness of the magnitude, but is not necessary for the reality of the object 2 in the understanding, because the relation 2:1 is the object itself, so too can the rule, "the shortest distance between two points," be thought by the understanding independently of the intuition, even though it can only be brought to consciousness as an object by means of the intuition. What is brought to consciousness is "the straight line," which, in keeping with Maimon's solution to the quid juris question, that sensibility and understanding flow from one and the same cognitive source, is "an image [*Bild*] or the distinguishing mark [*Merkmal*] of this relational concept" (Maimon 2010, 69). Maimon acknowledges that we can and do "already have cognition of this proposition by means of intuition alone prior to its proof," (Maimon 2010, 70); however, he maintains that this perception of the "distinguishing mark or image in intuition . . . can only be made clear, not distinct" (Maimon 2010, 70). Maimon characterizes this clarity without distinction as "a presentiment of the truth in advance (a presentiment that I believe must play no insignificant role in the power of invention)" (Maimon 2010, 70). This provides a good example of how to account for Maimon's claim that the sensible is an "image" (Maimon 2010, 69) of the intellectual and that "sensibility and understanding . . . flow from one and the same cognitive source" (Maimon 2010, 64). Rather than there being a sensible intuition belonging to the faculty of the imagination that represents the concept in a different faculty, i.e. in the faculty of the understanding, and which is necessary for its construction, for Maimon, the straight line is an image in intuition; however, intuition, as an image or mark of the concept, is itself conceptual, although only a limited version of the conceptual. The relational concept, "the shortest distance between two points," is thought as a mathematical rule of the understanding in order to produce the straight line as an object of the understanding independently of the intuition. So for Maimon, the synthesis is between different conceptual components of the proposition, rather than between a concept and an intuition. For Kant, the representation in intuition results in the construction of the mathematical concept, whereas for Maimon, it merely brings the concept to consciousness. This understanding is consistent with Maimon's broader logical principles and is the key to his system as a whole.

Maimonic reduction

In keeping with his claim that an intuition is itself conceptual, Maimon argues that the image perceived by intuition is reducible to the concept on which the intuition is founded, the paradigm case being the straight line proposition. To state that the straight line is an image of the shortest distance between two points amounts to claiming that the property granted to the intuition "straight line" is reducible to that expressed in the concept "the shortest distance between two points." Maimon's point is that by reduction, one term is determined as being grounded in the other, i.e. that one term can be understood solely by virtue of the conceptual analysis of the other term, such that there is an analytic relationship between them. For Maimon, the straight line is reducible to the shortest distance between two points if all the conclusions that are derived from the limited concept of the straight line still hold with the concept of the shortest distance between two points. In support of this thesis, and of this specific reduction, he argues that "If we survey all the theorems concerning a straight line, we will find that they follow not from its straightness, but from its being the shortest" (Maimon 2010, 70). So, for Maimon, intuition is in itself conceptual, though of a limited state; it does not merely correspond to the concept, but is actually grounded in it. Maimon's response to the quid juris question reduces the autonomy of a priori intuitions, compared to their treatment by Kant, insofar as he regards a priori intuition as an image of the conceptual. Judgments based on intuition are therefore actually conceptual judgments. It is this move that provides the ground for Maimon's challenge to Kant.

Two important intuitions that are subjected to Maimonic reduction are space and time. Maimon disputes Kant's claim that these are pure intuitions, instead arguing that space and time, as a priori intuitions, are the images of particular concepts. In relation to space, Maimon claims that:

> The difference between Kant's theory and mine is this: for Kant, space is merely a form of intuition, whereas for me it is, as concept, a form of all objects in general and, as intuition, an image of this form. For Kant, it is nothing in the object itself abstracted from our way of representing it; by contrast, for me it is always *something* in relation to any subject at all and certainly a form, but a form grounded in the object. (Maimon 2010, 427)

Maimon draws upon the Leibnizian proposal that space is related to conceptual difference to claim that the concept in which space is grounded, and of which it is the image, is the concept of difference. According to Maimon, space is "the image of the difference between given objects," i.e. "the subjective way of representing this objective difference" (Maimon 2010, 179). Maimon claims to be speaking "here as a Leibnizian, who treats time and space as universal undetermined concepts of reflection that must have an objective ground" (Maimon 2010, 132). When two bodies are perceived in space, they are recognized as different by virtue of the application of the rule of the understanding enshrined in the concept of difference, i.e. that the intuition of two bodies in space is grounded in their conceptual difference from one another. Maimon insists that this is "a necessary condition of thinking things in general" (Maimon 2010, 179). This also extends to Maimon's understanding of time as "an image of the difference between mental states" (Maimon 2010, 179), which is thought through them preceding and succeeding one another. In fact, Maimon argues that simultaneity, as the condition of conceptual difference in space, is "the cancelling out" (Maimon 2010, 26) of this very understanding of time. Maimon therefore agrees with Kant that space and time are a priori intuitions, but in addition, claims that they are a priori intuitions because they are images of difference. He therefore advocates the reduction of the representation of space and time to the representation of conceptual difference. The conceptual difference underlying sensible objects is perceived in intuition as the occurrence of different objects at different points in space and time. Space and time therefore apply to all sensible objects of intuition because the concept of difference applies to all such objects. Any conceptual difference between sensible objects of intuition is perceived as a difference in position in space and time.

> So space and time are these special forms by means of which unity in the manifold of sensible objects is possible, and hence by means of which these objects themselves are possible as objects of our consciousness. (Maimon 2010, 16)

Space and time, as images of conceptual difference, are therefore the conditions for the perception of empirical difference and for the consciousness of sensible objects themselves.

An important corollary to this account is that Maimon's general move can be implemented in other ways, which are not necessarily Leibnizian. Any account of space and time as deriving from conceptual relations, where the a priori intuitions of space and time are images of the conceptual relations, can serve as a substitute for Maimon's account. For this reason, other mathematical concepts can be considered as candidates for the ground of the a priori intuitions of space and time, a number of which emerge in subsequent developments in mathematics. Such an alternative account would serve the same critical function in relation to Kant's work, and, in addition, would provide the opportunity to extend Maimon's work in relation to more recent developments in mathematics: for example, Carl Gauss's *theorema egregium*, according to which the curvature of a surface embedded in three dimensional space may be understood intrinsically to that surface, i.e. independently of the three dimensional space in which it is embedded, and Bernhard Riemann's generalization of Gauss's work on the geometry of surfaces into higher-dimensions.[9]

The laws of sensibility

Maimon's point about the relation between a priori cognition and pure cognition, i.e. the idea that intuition as the image of the concept is always already conceptual though limited, is also applicable to the empirical realm. In fact, this relation functions as a model for the way empirical intuitions are understood to relate to the objects of which they are the images. Just as the a priori intuition of the straight line is an image of the concept of the shortest distance between two points, which serves as the rule of the understanding by means of which it is defined, by the same procedure, an empirical intuition can be understood to be the image or representation of the concept of a sensible object. However, sensible objects are not the same kind of object as the real objects produced by the understanding according to rules that are determined by mathematics. Instead, what is immediately striking about Maimon's account of the concept of the sensible object is the fact that for Maimon there are no objects outside consciousness. Maimon gives new meaning to the Kantian idea of the "thing in itself" by conceiving "the thing itself" and phenomena solely as functions of knowledge.

Maimon's solution to the quid juris question, which involves the claim that intuitions are images of concepts, supplants the role proposed by Kant for the thing in itself as what produces the affections of sensibility, because, unlike Kant, Maimonic intuition has a ground which is not extracognitive.

> If I say that: I am conscious of something, I do not understand by this something that is outside consciousness, which is self-contradictory; but merely the determinate mode of consciousness; i.e. of the act. (Maimon 2010, 30)

While Maimon's solution renders the thing in itself redundant, sensible objects of the intuitions are still represented to the understanding as being extracognitive. Maimon argues that this "illusion" can be described as follows:

> the representations of the objects of intuitions in space and time are like images produced in the mirror (the empirical I) by the transcendental subject of all representations (the pure I, though by means of its pure *a priori* form); but they appear as if they came from something behind the mirror (from objects that are different from ourselves). . . . But we must not let ourselves be misled by the expression "outside us," as if this something were in a spatial relation to us; the reason is that space itself is only a form within us. (Maimon 2010, 203)

Maimon's explanation of this illusion is that sensible objects of intuition are represented to the understanding from "outside of us" as a consequence of being represented from the point of view of our limited understanding, i.e. the cognized sensible object is restricted to the finite point of view of human consciousness.

Unlike Kant, who treats sensibility and understanding as two different faculties, for Maimon "sensibility is incomplete understanding." He argues that this affects us in three ways:

> 1) we are not conscious of the concepts contained within sensibility; 2) with respect to the concepts that we can attain, we must attach them to sensibility in order to

achieve consciousness of them; 3) so, for the most part, we come by both these concepts themselves as well as their relations to one another incompletely and in a temporal sequence according to the laws of sensibility. (Maimon 2010, 182)

Consciousness is therefore limited insofar as it remains oblivious to the cause and the mode of production of what is given in sensibility as an empirical intuition. If it is not extra cognitive objects that we are conscious of, then what is it that we are conscious of in sensibility? What is it that constitutes an empirical intuition? First of all, empirical intuitions are distinct from a priori intuitions. This is made clear by the second criteria mentioned above. An example of a concept the consciousness of which can be attained is the mathematical concept of the straight line as the shortest distance between two points. The rule of the understanding must be attached to the a priori intuition in order to achieve consciousness of a straight line as a mathematical concept rather than just as an empirical intuition of something like an extended stroke. Mathematical concepts in general would belong to this second of the three criteria above; however, even with mathematical concepts, the question of what exactly we are conscious of in an a priori intuition, or what is its content, is yet to be answered. So, before addressing the question of the content of empirical intuitions, another mathematical example will be presented in order to determine the content of a priori intuitions, which will assist in setting up the discussion of the contents of empirical intuitions.

One of the other paradigm examples of a mathematical concept that Maimon discusses is the concept of the circle. To define the circle, "the understanding prescribes for itself this rule or condition: that an infinite number of equal lines are to be drawn from a given point, so that by joining their endpoints together the concept of the circle is produced" (Maimon 2010, 75). Maimon maintains that "the possibility of this rule, and hence of the concept itself, can be shown in intuition" (Maimon 2010, 75) in the image of a circle, which is constructed by "rotating a line around the given point" (Maimon 2010, 75).

This seems to fit with the example of the straight line insofar as the empirical intuition seems to be an image of the concept which brings the concept into consciousness. However, the example of the circle allows a greater degree of scrutiny to be brought to bear upon Maimon's account of the consciousness that we have of mathematical concepts than is initially provided in the example of the straight line. In the example of the circle, what Maimon refers to as the "material completeness of the concept" cannot be given in intuition because "only a finite number of equal lines can be drawn" in intuition, whereas the rule of the understanding calls for an infinite number of lines. What is provided in conscious intuition is described by Maimon as the "unity of the manifold," which he refers to as the "formal completeness of the concept," rather than the "completeness of the manifold" itself, or the "material completeness of the concept." The intuition of a circle as an image is therefore not of the material completeness of the concept of the circle, but of the formal completeness of the concept. Maimon maintains that the material completeness of the concept of the circle is therefore "not a concept of the understanding to which an object corresponds, but only an idea of the understanding" (Maimon 2010, 75), and he argues that such an idea of the understanding is understood as "a limit concept." Rather than the material completeness of the concept being understood as an idea of the understanding, it is instead understood as a limit concept, which can only be approached, like an asymptote. Maimon describes the asymptotes of a curved line as "complete according to their rule, but in their presentation they are always incomplete. We grasp how their construction must be completed without being able to construct them completely" (Maimon 2010, 79).

In contrast to the material completeness of the concept, which is an idea of the understanding and can only be understood as a limit concept, Maimon characterizes the formal completeness of a concept as "an idea of reason" (Maimon 2010, 80). What is brought to consciousness by the a priori intuition, or image, of the circle is therefore the concept of the circle as an idea of reason, i.e. the concept of a circle as formally complete, and not the concept of the circle as materially complete, which is instead an idea of the understanding that is understood as a limit concept.

This distinction between the formal completeness of a concept and its material completeness also holds in the example of the straight line. Maimon maintains that "the principle that a straight line is the shortest between two points is all the more correctly applied to a given line, the more straight parts can be identified in it" (Maimon 2010, 80). The a priori intuition, or image, of the straight line is therefore an idea of reason of the formal completeness of the concept, rather than an idea of the understanding, because identifying the straight parts of a line by distinguishing them from curved parts as an intuitive exercise would remain incomplete on the understanding that a line is divisible into an infinite number of parts. The straight line and the circle are therefore examples of concepts that we can attain and achieve consciousness of as ideas of reason by means of them being attached to their respective a priori intuitions, or images. While these concepts are brought to consciousness as ideas of reason, we do not understand each of them as ideas of the understanding, but only as limit concepts. Maimon maintains that the distinction between ideas of reason and ideas of the understanding is "indispensible for extending the use of the understanding" (Maimon 2010, 78) in his account of cognition. Having introduced this distinction, the third of the three criteria in Maimon's account of the "laws of sensibility" can now be addressed.

When it comes to empirical intuitions and the concepts of the sensible objects of which they are intuitions, Maimon maintains that we only come across these concepts "themselves as well as their relations to one another incompletely and in a temporal sequence according to the laws of sensibility" (Maimon 2010, 182). Maimon's characterization of the incomplete nature of our consciousness of the concepts of sensible objects and of the temporal sequence in which this incomplete consciousness is attained is explicable by means of his account of the laws of sensibility. In his discussion of the role of sensation in intuition, sensation and intuition being the two constituents of sensibility, Maimon argues that

> sensation is a modification of the cognitive faculty that is actualized within that faculty only passively (without spontaneity); but this is only an idea that we can approach by means of ever diminishing consciousness, but can never reach because the complete absence of consciousness = 0 and so cannot be a modification of the cognitive faculty. (Maimon 2010, 168)

When it comes to sensation, we can only ever have an idea of it, and here Maimon means an idea of reason, because we are not talking about an a priori intuition of it, but rather about an empirical intuition of it. However, the way that we understand sensation as an idea of reason involves applying an a priori concept to it in intuition. For Maimon, the idea of sensation is the lowest degree of consciousness that can be accounted for by the ever diminishing series of degrees that distinguishes clearly determined consciousness from the privation of consciousness, which would result if this exercise were carried out to its limit, i.e. to zero. The limit can therefore only be approached, without ever being reached. Maimon argues that what we understand to be characteristic of the idea that we have of sensation, insofar as it approaches this limit, is the "differential" (Maimon 2010, 33), the idea of which is drawn from the differential calculus.[10] When thought in relation to mathematics, the differential as an idea of the understanding is understood solely as a limit concept. Maimon maintains that "with differentials we do not think them in intuition, but merely have cognition of them" (Maimon 2010, 290). However, when thought in relation to an empirical intuition as an idea of sensation, a differential is brought to consciousness as an idea of reason.

This characterization of the idea of sensation as a differential is the key to Maimon's solution to the *quid juris* question. While this is only one aspect of Maimon's account of the characteristics of our experience in intuition when faced with a manifold of sensation, it is crucial for developing an understanding of how the integral calculus is deployed in Maimon's account of cognition. The characterization of an idea of sensation as a differential is an example of the application of an a priori rule of the understanding, i.e. a mathematical concept, to an empirical intuition. The differential is the pure a priori concept that is applied to sensation in order to characterize its constituents, i.e. to represent them in imagination, of which we can then have an idea. Maimon distinguishes between

> two kinds of infinitely small namely a symbolic and an intuitive infinitely small. The first signifies a state that a quantum approaches ever closer to, but that it could never reach without ceasing to be what it is, so we can view it as in this state merely symbolically. On the other hand, the second kind signifies every state in general that a quantum can reach; here the infinitely small does not so much fail to be a quantum at all as it fails to be a determined quantum. (Maimon 2010, 352)

One of the examples that Maimon gives of the first kind is the angle between parallel lines, which arises by moving the meeting point of the lines enclosing a given angle to infinity, "the angle becomes infinitely small, but it altogether ceases to be an angle" (Maimon 2010, 252. See also V289). As such, it is a limit concept, "i.e. a merely symbolic infinitely small" (Maimon 2010, 252). The second kind of infinitely small, i.e. the intuitive infinitely small, is referred to as intuitive because there is a procedure by means of which the concept is applied to sensation, rather than because it can itself be intuited. The example that Maimon gives of it is "the differential of a magnitude" (Maimon 2010, 252), which "does not signify the state where the magnitude ceases to be what it is, but each state that it can reach, without distinction, i.e. a determinable but undetermined state" (Maimon 2010, 352). The mathematical example that Maimon uses here is the differential of a differential ratio, $dx:dy = a:b$. In this example, dx is a differential of magnitude x, and Maimon argues that "we can take x to be as small or as large as we want (as long as it has some magnitude)" (Maimon 2010, 352). Maimon defines magnitude as "something such that something else larger than it or something else smaller than it can be thought; consequently what is *omni dabili majus* (greater than any given magnitude) as well as what is *omni dabili minus* (less than any given magnitude) i.e. the infinitely large and the infinitely small, is a magnitude" (Maimon 2010, 352). It therefore follows from the ratio $x{:}y$, if x is smaller than any given magnitude, that $dx{:}dy$. One explanation for how this works is to draw upon the Leibnizian syncategorematic definition of the infinitesimal in the example of the calculus of infinite series, which defines the differential as the infinitesimal difference between consecutive values of a continuously diminishing quantity.[11] If the limit of the series is zero, as it is in Maimon's example of "consciousness = 0," then the differential is defined as the difference between the consecutive values of the continuously diminishing quantity as it approaches zero. This would be the a priori rule of the understanding that is applied to sensation in order to define the idea of sensation as a differential.

The differential itself as a mathematical concept is an idea of the understanding because as a magnitude less than any given magnitude it is not a concept to which an object corresponds. However, because the concept of the differential is less than any given magnitude, it is only ever approached without being reached, and is therefore understood as a limit concept. What distinguishes differentials from the other mathematical concepts dealt with so far is that with differentials, there is no corresponding empirical intuition, they therefore cannot be constructed in intuition like lines, circles, or numbers. Nevertheless, the differential can be applied to intuition as the predicate of sensation. This is how differentials can be represented in intuition, i.e. not as differentials per se, but as the intuitive ideas of that of which they are predicated. When predicated of sensation, i.e. singling out the differential and applying it to sensation to determine it as an idea of sensation, the differential is represented by the imagination as an idea of reason.

While Maimon describes the symbolic infinitely small as "merely the invention of mathematicians that lends generality to their claims" (Maimon 2010, 352), he maintains that the intuitive infinitely small or differential can be understood to be real, and "can itself be thought as an object (and not merely as the predicate of an intuition) despite the fact that it is itself a mere form that cannot be constructed as an object, i.e. presented in intuition" (Maimon 2010, 353). When considered in relation to sensible representation, Maimon argues that "a magnitude (*quantum*) is not treated as a large quantity, but rather as a quality abstracted from quantity" (Maimon 2010, 261n1). Maimon defines quality "abstracted from all quantity" as an intensive magnitude and as the "differential of an extensive quantity" (Maimon 2010, 395). It is therefore as the intensive magnitude of a sensible representation that the differential can be thought of, and is represented by the imagination, as an object. The infinitely small can legitimately be predicated of the quality of a sensible representation because the a priori rule of the understanding that determines the differential in mathematical cognition can be applied to our understanding of the relation between quality and quantity in sensible representation. Maimon argues that, "considered in itself as a quality, every sensible representation must be abstracted from all quantity" (Maimon 2010, 26), i.e. as the differential of an extensive quantity. The differential can therefore be thought of, and is represented by the imagination, as both the idea of sensation and the corresponding object of this idea.

Maimon's explanation of the intuitive infinitely small as able to be thought of as an object is characteristic of his account of the metaphysically infinitely small as real. Maimon claims that "The metaphysically infinitely small is real because quality can certainly be considered in itself abstracted from all quantity" (Maimon 2010, 354). The example given by Maimon in which the metaphysically infinitely small is predicated of the quality of a sensible representation is his account of the representation of the color red. Maimon argues that the representation of the color "must be thought without any finite extension, although not as a mathematical but rather as a physical point, or as the differential of an extension" (Maimon 2010, 27).

The idea of the differential as a physical point, which, as outlined above, is the idea of the corresponding object of the differential as an idea of sensation, must "be thought without any finite degree of quality, but still as the differential of a finite degree," that is, every sensible representation considered as a quality "must be abstracted from all quantity" (Maimon 2010, 27) and yet still be understood as a differential of that quantity. Insofar as the differential is predicated of a quality, and is therefore understood to be a real physical point although abstracted from all quantity, each differential is understood to function as a "determinate unit" of sensation such that when they "are added to themselves successively, an arbitrary finite magnitude then arises" (Maimon 2010, 29n2). So as physical points of intuition, the differentials of one sensation can be added to one another successively to determine an arbitrary finite magnitude or a manifold of sensation.

In order to be able to distinguish one manifold of sensation from another, Maimon maintains that "we must assume that these units are different in different objects" (Maimon 2010, 29n2). So, the determinate units of different manifolds of sensation are qualitatively different differentials. This can be accounted for by Maimon's definition of the intuitive infinitely small as the undetermined quantum of "every state in general that a quantum can reach" (Maimon 2010, 352). The Leibnizian example of the calculus of infinite series provides an explanation for the qualitative difference between different differentials, or the different undetermined quantums of the different states that a quantum can reach. According to Leibniz, the differential varies with the different consecutive values of the continuously diminishing quantity, i.e. there's a differential for each quantity that the series reaches and each of these differentials can be considered to be different, and each can be predicated of a different quality as an intuitive infinitely small differential of extension or physical point. So, for Maimon, the representations of different manifolds of sensation are qualitatively different "according to the difference of their differentials" (Maimon 2010, 29).

While this explains that the different manifolds of sensation are different and distinct representations, it does not explain how each of these representations is brought to consciousness. Maimon outlines the next stage of this process by which the differential, as both an idea and unit of sensation, is brought to consciousness as follows:

> Sensibility thus provides the differentials to a determined consciousness; out of
> them, the imagination produces a finite (determined) object of intuition; out of the
> relations of these different differentials, which are its objects, the understanding
> produces the relation of the sensible objects arising from them. (Maimon 2010, 32)

Sensibility provides the differentials as ideas of sensation, and the imagination produces
a finite (determined) object of intuition from the manifold of sensation that results
from the "addition" (Maimon 2010, 29n2) or sum of the differentials as determinate
units of sensation. Before explicating how this takes place, a more detailed account of
Maimon's understanding of intuition is required.

For Maimon, intuition, like sensation, is also "a modification of the cognitive
faculty," however it is "actualized within that faculty in part passively and in part
actively" (Maimon 2010, 168). The passive part is termed its matter, and is supplied
by sensation. The active part is its form, which is supplied by the a priori intuitions
of space and time. What has been accounted for so far in this explication is only the
passive part of intuition. As regards the active part, Maimon maintains that

> consciousness first arises when the imagination takes together several homogeneous
> sensible representations, orders them according to its forms (succession in time
> and space), and forms an individual intuition out of them. (Maimon 2010, 30)

Each homogeneous sensible representation that Maimon is referring to is the product
of having taken together, or having added together successively, the differentials
as ideas or objects of a particular sensation to form a manifold of sensation. This
correlates with the successive addition of the differentials as determinate units of
sensation that determines an "arbitrary finite magnitude" (Maimon 2010, 29n2), or
"finite (determined) object of intuition" (Maimon 2010, 32). However, it is only when
manifolds of sensation are ordered according to the a priori intuitions of space and
time that an arbitrary finite magnitude, or finite (determined) object of intuition is
formed and brought to consciousness as an individual empirical intuition.

The example that Maimon gives of the way that two different homogeneous sensible
representations, or manifolds of sensation, are ordered in space and time to form
distinct individual empirical intuitions is the way a distinction is made between the
perception, or passive intuition, of a red and a green manifold of sensation.

> When a perception, for example red, is given to me, I do not yet have any
> consciousness of it; when another, for example green, is given to me, I do not yet
> have any consciousness of it in itself either. But if I relate them to one another (by
> means of the unity of difference), then I notice that red is different from green, and
> so I attain consciousness of each of the perceptions in itself. If I constantly had the
> representation red, for example, without having any other representation, then I
> could never attain consciousness of it. (Maimon 2010, 131–2)

It is therefore only insofar as individual empirical intuitions are related to one another
that they are brought to consciousness, and it is by means of what Maimon refers to
as the "unity of difference" that they are able to be related to one another. In the case

of the representation of red and green, Maimon refers to this unity of difference as a relation between differentials:

> For example, if I say that red is different from green, then the pure concept of the understanding of the difference is not treated as a relation between the sensible qualities (for then the Kantian question *quid juris?* remains unanswered), but rather either (according to the Kantian theory) as the relation of their spaces as *a priori* forms, or (according to my theory) as the relation of their differentials, which are *a priori* ideas of reason. (Maimon 2010, 33)

In the "Notes & Clarifications" to the *Essay*, Maimon provides an account of how individual intuitions are brought to consciousness by means of the relations between their differentials, which he refers to in this passage initially as "elements":

> the pure concepts of the understanding or categories are never directly related to intuitions, but only to their elements, and these are ideas of reason concerning the way these intuitions arise; it is through the mediation of these ideas that the categories are related to the intuitions themselves. Just as in higher mathematics we produce the relations of different magnitudes themselves from their differentials, so the understanding (admittedly in an obscure way) produces the real relations of qualities themselves from the real relations of their differentials. So, if we judge that fire melts wax, then this judgment does not relate to fire and wax as objects of intuition, but to their elements, which the understanding thinks in the relation of cause and effect to one another. (Maimon 2010, 355–6)

The mathematical rules of the understanding and the categories are solely related to the elements of individual empirical intuitions, i.e. to their differentials, which are ideas of reason, rather than to the intuitions themselves. And just as with "higher mathematics," here Maimon is referring to the operations of the calculus, where the ratios or relations of different magnitudes, for example $x{:}y$, can be produced from the ratio of their differentials, $dx{:}dy$. So too can the understanding apply this a priori rule to the elements of sensation to produce, "admittedly in an obscure way," the real relations of qualities themselves from the real relations of their differentials.

The specific mathematical operation, or concept, being referred to is integration. As has already been discussed in relation to the work of Leibniz, the mathematical concept of integration can be understood both as the inverse operation of differentiation and also as a method of summation in the form of series.[12] The method of integration in general provides a way of working back from the differential relation to the construction of the curve whose tangent it represents. The problem of integration is therefore that of reversing the process of differentiation. That is, given a relation between two differentials, dy/dx, the problem of integration is to find a relation between the quantities themselves, y and x.

Given that the elements of sensation Maimon is working with are modeled on differentials, and that, as determinate units of sensation, they are characterized as being "added to themselves successively" to determine an arbitrary finite magnitude or manifold of sensation, the method of integration that Maimon applies as a rule of the understanding to the elements of sensation should be understood implicitly to be the method of summation. The application of the mathematical rule of the understanding, which is the operation of integration, to the elements of sensation, which are modeled on differentials, brings the manifolds of sensation to consciousness as sensible objects of intuition. In the first step of the process, two different manifolds of sensation characterized by different differentials are brought into consciousness by virtue of the application of integration as a rule of the understanding to the elements of sensation that models the real relation between the two qualities themselves, as sensible objects, on the real relation between their differentials. This happens as follows: Each manifold of sensation is brought to consciousness as a sensible object by virtue of the relation between their respective differentials, dy/dx, and the application of the operation of integration to this relation. In integration, the differential relation dy/dx gives the slope of the tangent to the graph of a function, or curve, where the tangent is a straight line that touches a curve at only one point. Let's call this point b. It is important to note that at this stage of the operation there is no curve, the only information available is that consciousness = 0 at a point, let's call this point a, and that a point b can be determined as a potential point of tangency by virtue of the contingent nature of the relation between two differentials of sensation.

The method of integration as a summation that Maimon deploys is the method of approximation of a differentiable function around a given point provided by a Taylor series or power series expansion.[13] This method is appropriate for Maimon because the coefficients of the function depend solely on the relations between the differentials at that point. The power series expansion can be written as a polynomial, the coefficients of each of its terms being the successive differential relations evaluated at the given point. The sum of such a series represents the differentiable function provided that any remainder approaches zero as the number of terms becomes infinite; the polynomial then becomes an infinite series which converges with the function around the given point. Given the differential relation, dy/dx, what can be determined at this point is the power series expansion of this differential relation. As the number of terms of the power series expansion approaches infinity, the polynomial of the power series converges with the function, which is therefore its limit.

For Maimon, the differentiable function would therefore be the materially completed concept of the polynomial of the power series expansion of this particular differential relation, which we can only understand as a limit concept. Therefore the operation of integration that Maimon has in mind, and which is the rule of the understanding for how sensible objects are brought to consciousness, is the process of determining the polynomial of the power series expansion of the differential relation at the given point b to an arbitrary finite number of terms. It is common practice to use a finite number of terms of the series to approximate the function in the immediate neighborhood of the given point.[14] The finite polynomial of the power series expansion would be the formally complete concept of this particular relation. At the given point b of tangency to the curve, y can be approximated as a function of x in the immediate neighborhood of the given point by expanding the polynomial of the power series expansion to an arbitrary finite number of terms. x can therefore also be approximated as a function of *y* in the immediate neighborhood of the given point. *x* and *y* then function as the empirical correlates to which the concept of the differentiable function as a limit concept is applied. The result of applying this limit concept to *x* and *y* is that both the limit concept and *x* and *y* are brought to consciousness as ideas of reason, and *x* and *y* are represented to consciousness as sensible objects.[15]

When Maimon refers to the understanding as producing these real relations between sensible objects "admittedly in an obscure way," what he means is that the concept of the sensible object that is obtained in this process is "merely" formally complete and therefore is an idea of reason, rather than materially completed and an idea of the understanding. Maimon also refers to the operation of integration as producing a "synthetic unity" between the representations of sensible objects. In this instance, Maimon argues that an individual empirical intuition "becomes a representation only by being united with other intuitions in a synthetic unity, and it is as an element of the synthesis that the intuition relates itself to the representation (that is, to its object)" (Kant 1967, 176).[16] The synthetic unity is between the individual empirical intuitions that are determined in relation to one another, by means of the operation of integration, and the elements of the synthesis are the different differentials as determinate units of sensation of each respective manifold of sensation that is a party to the differential relation and therefore to the synthetic unity. Maimon characterizes each component of the synthetic unity as a "determined synthesis," which correlates with the finite solution to the polynomial of the power series expansion to an arbitrarily finite number of terms. He then contrasts each determined synthesis with an "undetermined synthesis," which correlates with the polynomial of the power series expansion with infinite terms. Maimon argues that

> the determined synthesis to which the representation is related is the represented object; and any undetermined synthesis to which the representation could be related is the concept of an object in general. (Kant 1967, 176)

The idea that we have of the represented object is obscure because it is related to the "determined synthesis" which is the formally complete synthesis or "complete synthesis," rather than the "undetermined synthesis," which would be the materially complete synthesis or the "completed synthesis." The former correlates with the finite solution to the polynomial of the power series expansion, the latter with the convergence of the polynomial of the power series expansion with the differentiable function. Both the determined and the undetermined synthesis are considered by the imagination to be representations, since the imagination is only ever conscious of things as representations, the former as the sensible object itself and the latter as the limit concept of the former, which is represented as an object in general that is outside of thought and therefore unknowable in order to be able to relate the former sensible object itself to it as its cause. The imagination does this because the production and the mode of production of the sensible object "escapes consciousness" (Gueroult 1929, 64). This explains the illusion that sensible objects appear as external objects to us when in fact they are the product of our understanding. Of both the differential and the completed synthesis as limit concepts, Maimon argues that

We should note that both *the* primitive consciousness of a constituent part of a synthesis (without relating this part to the synthesis) as well as *the* consciousness of the complete synthesis *are* mere ideas, i.e. they are the two limit concepts of a synthesis, in that without synthesis no consciousness is possible, but the consciousness of the completed synthesis grasps the infinite itself, and is consequently impossible for a limited cognitive faculty. (Maimon 2010, 349–50)

Maimon here distinguishes between the two ideas of the understanding, the differential and the completed synthesis, which exceed our consciousness, and the two "mere" ideas of reason, by means of which the former are brought to consciousness: the differential as the determinate unit or element of sensation, and the completed synthesis as the limit concept of the synthesis, i.e. of the polynomial of the power series expansion in which the differential is integrated. What is brought to consciousness is between these two limits. So Maimon can conclude that "we start in the middle with our cognition of things and finish in the middle again" (2010, 350).

Noumena, phenomena, and regulative ideas

The clearest statement in the *Essay* of how these components of Maimon's system displace those of Kant's first *Critique* is as follows:

These differentials of objects are the so-called *noumena*; but the objects themselves arising from them are the *phenomena*. With respect to intuition = 0, the differential of any such object in itself is $dx = 0$, $dy = 0$ etc.; however their relations are not = 0, but can rather be given determinately in the intuitions arising from them. These *noumena* are ideas of reason serving as principles to explain how objects arise according to certain rules of the understanding. (Maimon 2010, 32)

Maimon is referring to the relation between dy and dx in the differential relation dy/dx, which despite the terms equaling zero, does not itself equal zero. In mathematics, while the terms between which the relation is established are neither determined nor determinable, the relation between the terms is determined,[17] and is the basis for determining the real relation between the qualities themselves by means of the operation of integration as a method of summation. The Kantian *noumena* is displaced by the metaphysical infinitely small as it operates in intuition as a rule of the understanding applied to sensation. And Kantian *phenomena* is displaced by the sensible objects produced by the synthetic unity which is determined by the operation of integration on these infinitely small elements.

To return to the example of the judgment that fire melts wax that Maimon gives in the *Essay* (2010, 356), two steps are required to make this judgment. The first involves the application of the mathematical rule of the understanding, which is the concept of integration as a method of summation, to the elements of sensation, i.e. differentials, which brings the manifolds of sensation to consciousness as sensible objects of intuition that are then ordered in space and time. The second is the judgment that involves the application of the pure concept of cause to the intuited relation between the sensible objects, which are determined by the relation between their elements, i.e. their respective differentials. However, pure concepts of the understanding, whether mathematical or categorical, "never relate to intuitions, but only to their elements and these are ideas of reason concerning the way these intuitions arise" (Maimon 2010, 355) because it is the relation between these elements that gives rise to the sensible intuitions in the first place. Maimon describes a similar judgment in relation to the elements of heat and presumably frozen water as follows: "there is a necessity connected with the actual perception of fluidity following heat . . . from which I judge that heat makes the water fluid (is the cause)" (Maimon 2010, 129). The judgment in the case of the wax applies the pure concept of cause to the elements of the intuited relation between fire and wax, i.e. to their differentials as qualities of magnitudes. The judgment that fire (as the cause) melts wax is then made in accord with the "necessity connected with the actual perception of fluidity following heat." The application of mathematical rules of the understanding to sensation determines the objects of sensation and makes them available to be ordered in space and time and therefore available as the objects of categorical judgments.

When it comes to regulative ideas, Maimon distinguishes himself from Kant by proposing "a single Idea (of an infinite understanding)" to displace Kant's three Transcendental Ideas: God, the World, and the human Soul. Maimon attributes an

> objective reality to this idea (not, it is true, viewed in itself – for this is contrary to the nature of an idea – but only in so far as it acquires objective reality for us in so many ways by means of objects of intuition). And also the other way around, i.e. intuitions acquire objective reality only because they must eventually resolve into this idea . . . Now the understanding . . . insists on absolute totality in these concepts so that this totality belongs as much to the essence of the understanding as concepts in general even if we cannot attain it. (Maimon 2010, 367)

The regulative use of the concept of the infinite understanding does not make Maimon's system theocentric. Nor does Maimon presuppose the infinite understanding as an absolute reality the realization of which we gradually approach. The infinite understanding for Maimon is only an idea of reason that functions as an ultimate limit concept that our understanding continuously approaches without ever reaching. The limit concept is applied to the intuition of a totality of objects, where the thought of the element of each is perceived as conditioned by the thought of all the others. This is a totality that approaches the infinite; however, it is not a privileged reality projected as external to us like an object.

When discussing the totality of sensible objects that constitute the world as we know it, Maimon distinguishes between the way the understanding thinks objectively about sensible objects and the way those objects are represented subjectively to consciousness. He argues that, objectively, "the understanding can only think objects as fluent" (Maimon 2010, 33). Maimon is drawing here upon the dynamic characteristic of Newtonian calculus, which deals with the rate of change, or fluxion, of continuously varying quantities, called fluents (such as lengths, areas, volumes, distances, temperatures).[18] The understanding, which brings unity to the manifold of sensation can only think an object by specifying the way it arises or the rule by which it arises: this is the only way that the manifold of an object can be brought under the unity of the rule, and consequently the understanding cannot think an object as having already arisen but only as arising, i.e. as fluent. (Maimon 2010, 33. Translation modified.)

The rules according to which the understanding thinks the object, and this includes both the mathematical rules applied to sensation and the categorical judgments made about individual intuitions determined by the former, are not themselves thought as fluent, but the production of the sensible object according to these rules is conceived as fluent.

An object requires two parts. First, an intuition given either *a priori* or *a posteriori*; second, a rule thought by the understanding, by means of which the relation of the manifold in the intuition is determined. This rule is thought by the understanding not as fluent but all at once. On the other hand, the intuition itself (if it is *a posteriori*), or the particular termination of the rule in the intuition (if it is *a priori*), is such that the object can only be thought of as fluent. (Maimon 2010, 33. Translation modified)

What this means is that the dynamic account of the calculus given by Newton is characteristic of what is represented by the imagination as the operation of the calculus in sensible representation, i.e. the application of rules of the understanding to the determinate units of sensation. It is therefore the Newtonian fluent that functions as the idea of reason of the differential. However, the concept of the differential as an idea of the understanding, and the rule of the understanding by which it is thought as a limit concept, is the conceptualizable character of Leibniz's concept of the differential as an infinitely small magnitude. This is the reason that Leibniz's syncategorematic definition of the differential in the calculus of infinite series has been used as the example of the mathematical rule that is applied to sensation to determine the differential as the idea of sensation on the one hand, and as the object of this idea, i.e. as a physical point, on the other.

In contrast to the understanding, which thinks objectively about the production of sensible objects as "fluent," Maimon argues that these objects are brought to consciousness as static and fixed products of intuition:

the faculty of intuition (that certainly conforms to rules but does not comprehend rules) can only represent the manifold itself, and not any rule or unity in the manifold; so it must think its objects as already having arisen not as being in the process of arising. (Maimon 2010, 34. Translation modified)

As an example, Maimon distinguishes between how the understanding thinks a line synthetically, i.e. how the imagination represents to the understanding the process of the application of the rule of the understanding to sensation, and how a line is presented statically in intuition: "For the understanding to think a line, it must draw it in thought, but to present a line in intuition, it must be imagined as already drawn" (Maimon 2010, 35). So there is a dynamism in the way rules of the understanding are applied to sensation which is not reflected either in the intuitions themselves or in the rules of the understanding themselves, whether mathematical or categorical.

The main difficulties that Maimon has with Kant's system include the presumption of the existence of synthetic *a priori* judgments; the question *quid juris*, i.e. how can *a priori* concepts be applied to *a posteriori* intuition?; and the question *quid facti*: whether the fact of our use of *a priori* concepts in experience is justified? Maimon deploys mathematics, specifically arithmetic, against Kant to show how it is possible to understand objects as having been constituted by the relations between them, and he proposes an alternative solution to the question *quid juris*, which relies on the concept of the differential. For Kant, the *quid juris* problem consists in legitimizing the claim that the subjective conditions of thought provide the conditions of the possibility of experience, and thus provide the ground for all objective value. The problem with this for Maimon is that Kant simply assumes that experience exists, just as he assumes that synthetic *a priori* judgments exist, and the task that Kant sets himself in the first *Critique* is simply to give an account of how both are possible. Maimon is critical of Kant for this assumption. Maimon rejects the assumption that it is possible to use synthetic *a priori* judgments to link *a priori* concepts to *a posteriori* intuitions via the schematism, as Kant proposes. For Maimon, the nature of the synthesis is different. Rather than there being a sensible intuition belonging to the faculty of the imagination that represents the concept in the faculty of the understanding, and which is necessary for its construction, for Maimon, the intuition, as an image or mark of the concept, is itself conceptual, although only a limited version of the conceptual. So for Maimon, the synthesis is between different conceptual components of the proposition, rather than between a concept and a heterogeneous intuition. For Kant, the representation in intuition is necessary for the construction of the mathematical concept, whereas for Maimon it merely brings the concept to consciousness.

The hypothesis that Maimon adopts in order to render the connection between pure a priori concepts and their intuitions comprehensible is that both are modifications of the same cognitive faculty. The question *quid juris* is thus resolved because the understanding does not subject something given in a different faculty, the faculty of the imagination, to its rules *a priori*, as is the case with the Kantian schematism. What Maimon proposes instead is that the understanding produces this something as an intuition that conforms to its rules by virtue of being of the same faculty.

What then do we learn from Maimon's critique of Kant's approach to mathematics? For Kant, mathematics requires the form of temporal intuition for the construction of arithmetic concepts, and the form of spatial intuition for geometric ones. Kant therefore upholds the indispensability of intuition in mathematical proof. The corollary to this is that mathematics cannot be held to be a formal discipline. Maimon, on the contrary, maintains that the use of diagrams in mathematical demonstrations is shown to be superfluous when the intuition, or idea of reason, is reducible to a more abstract concept. Regardless of whatever shortcomings there may be with the concept of the infinite intellect,[19] Maimon demonstrates a profound understanding of the implications of the developments of the mathematics of his time, and this is reinforced by the relation that his account of mathematics has to subsequent developments in the discipline. One of the conditions of the exercise of the understanding in bringing sensible objects of intuition to consciousness is the prior existence of difference (as intrinsic, between intensive magnitudes, and not simply numerical difference). Maimon's idealism therefore accounts for representation without recourse to the thing in itself. Instead he uses the model of the differential as the means of solving the problem of explaining the intellectual character of the content that is given to us. The production of the phenomenal world according to the model of differentials and their relations is made in the same way that mathematical figures are determined in intuition, i.e. according to the rule that expresses the image of this figure. However, sensible representations in themselves, considered as mere differentials, do not yet result in consciousness. What is required to bring sensible representations to consciousness is the integration of the differentials by means of the process of summation. From the point of view of the finite understanding, i.e. from the point of view of sensibility or of intuition, the consciousness of sensible representation is not reflected upon as happening according to the application of a mathematical rule of the understanding, but rather is (erroneously) considered to actually be produced by the differentials.[20]

As for the question *quid facti*, however, Maimon defers to Hume (See Maimon 2010, 9, 215, 371). Maimon doesn't doubt that sensation is presented to us, he rather considers the presentation of sensation and the identities inferred in its mode of presentation to be produced in accordance with the mathematical rules of the understanding applied to sensation, i.e. the rule according to which the understanding thinks the object. However, because of our limited understanding we can only assume that the world is a product of reason and of the regulative idea of the infinite intellect, but this cannot be proved. The rational principle that matter flows from the understanding is merely a *hypothesis*. Therefore, the gap between the given sensation and the *a priori* rule is still not bridged. Maimon's rational dogmatism is therefore tested and skepticism is not fully eradicated from the system.

Bordas-Demoulin on the differential relation as "the universal function"

Salomon Maimon, Hoëné Wronski, and Jean Bordas-Demoulin are the three post-Kantians that Deleuze refers to as the three bright stars that shine forth in "the esoteric history of the differential philosophy" (DR 170). Each demonstrates "a great deal of heart and a great deal of truly philosophical naivety" in taking the differential, *dx*, seriously and in deploying it in their responses to Kant. What interests Deleuze in the work of these figures is one specific aspect of each of their respective deployments of the differential, which he extracts from their work and redeploys as a component in his own project of responding to Kant and of constructing a philosophy of difference.

From Bordas-Demoulin, Deleuze extracts the notion of the differential relation as "the universal function" in order to further characterize the nature of the relation between the singular and the universal. Bordas-Demoulin attributes Leibniz with having "seized upon the universal" and with having "adapted a symbol for it" (Bordas-Demoulin 1843, 385), by which he means the differential relation, *dy/dx*. However, he considers it "surprising that Leibniz, who knew how to distinguish general ideas from particular ideas, had not seen, in the essential relation of a function [or curve], the general idea; and in the successive values of variables of the function, the particular ideas of this function" (Bordas-Demoulin 1843, 666).

The problem with Leibniz, for Bordas-Demoulin, is that he attributes a value to differentials, which, despite Leibniz's claim that they are fictional, ruins the exactitude of the calculation. (See Bordas-Demoulin 1843, 410). Deleuze's gloss of this argument is that "Leibniz's mistake is to identify them with the individual or with variability" (DR 172). Bordas-Demoulin is also critical of Newton's approach to the calculus. He argues that "with Newton, one is obliged to annul the differentials, such that there is no longer anything to consider" (Bordas-Demoulin 1843, 410). Again Deleuze's gloss of this argument is that "Newton's mistake, therefore, is that of making the differentials equal to zero" (DR 172).

Bordas-Demoulin changes the focus of the debate about whether differentials are real or fictive and instead considers dy/dx, as 0/0, to be the symptom of a qualitative difference or change of function insofar as it excludes that which "individualizes the function" in favor of the "universal." By that which individualizes the function he means the "fixed quantities of intuition [*quantum*]" (DR 171), i.e. the general representation of the curve in intuition, and the "variable quantities in the form of concepts of the understanding [*quantitas*]" (DR 171), i.e. the particular changeable values of the function and its property of variation. The object of the differential calculus for Bordas-Demoulin is "to bring to the fore the relations that constitute the universal of the functions, by eliminating the part of the relation constitutive of the individual, which hide them, and which particularize the functions" (Bordas-Demoulin 1843, 415). In this respect, the universal, which is the differential relation, differs in kind from the function or curve, and from the primitive function. Instead it represents "the immutable along with the operation which uncovered it" (DR 172), i.e. the operation of differentiation. It is not the differentials that are canceled in the differential relation, but rather the general and the particular, i.e. the *quantum* and the *quantitas*.

While Leibniz privileged the singular over the particular, Bordas-Demoulin allows Deleuze to characterize the nature of the relation between singular and universal as that between distinctive points on a curve and the differential relation of that curve. Deleuze argues that in this respect Bordas-Demoulin is "close to the modern interpretation of the calculus" insofar as "the limit no longer presupposes the idea of a continuous variable and infinite approximation" (DR 177), but instead grounds "a new, static and purely ideal definition of continuity" (DR 177). Deleuze draws here upon the concept of the Dedekind cut to characterize the nature of the distinction between the function of the curve and the differential relation. Just as the Dedekind cut constitutes the real numbers insofar as it designates the irrational numbers as real on the number line, and as differing in kind from the series of real rational numbers, so too does the differential relation, a straight line that represents the slope of the curve at any point, constitute the function insofar as it cuts the curve or the function at any specific point. Deleuze argues that the differential relation operates as "a genuine cut [*coupure*], a border between the changeable [that is, the successive values of the variable of the function] and the unchangeable [differential relation] within the function itself" (DR 172).

Bordas-Demoulin claims that this is "the true metaphysics of the differential calculus," which is not found in "the principles of mathematical operations," but rather "in the nature of ideas" (Bordas-Demoulin 1843, 418). It is to the work of Spinoza that Bordas-Demoulin turns in order to give an example of the operation of the metaphysics of the calculus in relation to the nature of ideas, an example that Deleuze cannot but have been struck by. Bordas-Demoulin writes that "According to this metaphysic, it can be said, by means of comparison, that the God of Spinoza is the differential of the universe, and the universe the integral of the God of Spinoza" (Bordas-Demoulin 1843, 418). This account of the metaphysics of the calculus and its connection with Spinoza represents one of the main guiding threads to the way that Deleuze deploys this aspect of Bordas-Demoulin's work in his project of constructing a philosophy of difference. However, Deleuze is quite explicit in stating that "this is only a first aspect" (DR 172) of this difference, i.e. characterizing the differential relation as universal in relation to the function or curve. For an account of the second aspect of this difference, it is necessary to return to some of the developments made by the earlier figures in the esoteric history of the differential philosophy and to again update these developments in relation to subsequent developments in the history of mathematics.

Maimon's infinite intellect is displaced by a theory of problems

Deleuze next extracts what is useful to his project from the work of Salomon Maimon. It is Maimon's reformulation of Kant's critique and of the heterogeneous duality between concept and intuition that Deleuze redeploys; however, this aspect of Maimon's work is redeployed with significant qualifications that take into account the subsequent developments in mathematics and in the esoteric history of the differential philosophy, notably Bordas-Demoulin's concept of the differential relation as universal and of the metaphysics of the calculus as found in the nature of ideas.

With respect to what Deleuze extracts from Maimon's work, rather than one term of the difference between concept and intuition being conditioned by the other via the intermediary of the schematism, as Kant proposes in the first *Critique*, Deleuze draws upon what he describes as "Maimon's genius" to show that "both terms of the difference must equally be thought" (DR 173), and that it is "the reciprocal synthesis of differential relations" that operates as both "the source of the production of real objects" and "the substance of Ideas" (DR 173).

Deleuze's claim that "physical judgment tends to ensure its primacy over mathematical judgment" (DR 173) is a restatement of the illusion that sensible or real objects appear as external objects to us, when in fact they are the product of our understanding, i.e. the application of the mathematical rule of the understanding, which I have argued can be understood implicitly to be the operation of integration as a method of summation in the form of series, to the elements of sensation, of which the differentials serve as a model and about which a primary physical judgment in relation to sensation is made. What this amounts to is that all physical judgments whatsoever are predicated on a prior mathematical judgment, which "escapes consciousness" (Gueroult 1929, 64). It is important to keep in mind here that what appear to us as external objects are constructed as such, and the explanation of the construction is that it is the result of the application of a mathematical rule of the understanding to the elements of sensation.

Deleuze distances himself from the naivety of Maimon's approach by not extracting the concept of the infinite intellect from Maimon's work. Instead Deleuze displaces this concept with a theory of problems drawn from subsequent developments in the history of mathematics that render it, and the ensuing skepticism, redundant. There are then two preliminary steps that Deleuze makes in order to begin the process of updating the mathematics that I have argued Maimon implicitly deploys in his work that effect this displacement.

The first is to draw upon the work of Jules Houël (1867) to make explicit what remains implicit in Maimon's analytic proof about the nature of the straight line as the shortest distance between two points (See DR 174). Maimon argues "that one line (between two points) must be shorter than several lines (between the same points)" (Maimon 2010, 65), on the basis of the Euclidean proposition that "In any triangle two sides taken together in any manner are greater than the remaining one" (Euclid 1956, 293). But then he claims that this proof can be extended to "several lines that lie . . . between the same points" (Maimon 2010, 66). Houël maintains that "The straight line is the shortest of all those lines that have the same extremities, including both rectilinear and curvilinear lines," and thus that the proof is not Euclidean at all, but rather Archimedean (Houël 1867, 67), i.e. based on the approximation of a curve by a polygon in the Archimedean approach to geometrical problems by means of the method of exhaustion. Houël argues that "this Archimedean method of exhaustion for determining the length of the curve does not contain the definition of the straight line, but rather serves to define, by means of the straight line, the length of the curved line" (Houël 1867, 68).

The rigorous algorithm of Wronski's transcendental philosophy

The second is to draw upon the work of Hoëné Wronski (1817) to make explicit what I have argued remains implicit in Maimon's account of the operation of integration, i.e. it being a method of summation in the form of series. To do so, Deleuze draws upon Wronski's objection to Lagrange's presentation of Taylor's series (Lagrange 1797). As explained above, a Taylor or power series expansion can be written as a polynomial, the coefficients of each of its terms being the successive differential relations evaluated at a given point. The coefficient of the first term of the power series expansion is the differential relation, and each subsequent term in the series repeats the operation of differentiation such that the successive coefficients of each of its terms are the successive differential relations evaluated at that point. What Wronski's objection amounts to is that Lagrange is more intent on characterizing the nature of the relation between the coefficients of the evolution function, or power series expansion, i.e. that each is comparable because each contains the differential relation despite having been successively differentiated in each successive term of the series, and therefore that Lagrange presupposes the nature of the differential calculus itself. Whereas for Wronski, the whole problem "lies precisely in determining this first coefficient" (DR 175), which is itself independent of the undetermined quantity or variable of the polynomial of the power series expansion, which is denoted by the symbol i because the variables being referred to are on the complex plane.

From the point of view of "the rigorous algorithm," with which Wronski characterizes "transcendental philosophy" (DR 175), the discontinuous coefficients, or different successive terms of the series, "assume a signification only by virtue of the differential functions which compose them" (DR 175), where "differential functions" refers to the successively differentiated differential relations of each successive term of the power series expansion. Therefore the differential relation of the first coefficient must first be determined before "Lagrange's undetermined quantity," i.e. the variable of the polynomial of the power series expansion, can "carry out the determination expected of it," i.e. before the power series expansion can be understood to converge with the function around the given point. Wronski characterizes each of the differentials of the differential relation as an "ideal difference," which "constitutes an unconditioned rule for the production of knowledge of quantity" (DR 175). He characterizes the different successive terms of the power series expansion as providing the understanding with a "discontinuous summation" which thereby constructs the "matter for the generation of quantity" (DR 175). And, the function that the power series expansion converges with by "graduation or continuity" constitutes "the form" of these quantities, "which belongs to Ideas of reason" (DR 175). The matter/form distinction is therefore mapped by Wronski onto an adjusted account of Lagrange's presentation of the Taylor series, which, on Wronski's account, emphasizes instead the constitutive nature of the differential relation.

What Deleuze has done in this passage is map the elements of the rigorous algorithm of Wronski's transcendental philosophy onto Maimon's reformulation of Kant's first *Critique*. Wronski's characterization of the differential as an ideal difference maps onto Maimon's account of the differential as an intensive quantity. The role of the understanding in Wronski's account of "discontinuous summation" as constituting the matter for the generation of quantitas maps onto the role of the understanding in Maimon's account of the illusion of the externality of objects. What Wronski characterizes as the form of these quantities, which is constituted by the gradual and continuous convergence of the power series expansion with the function, belongs to Ideas of reason. The Ideas of reason to which Wronski refers should therefore be understood to be those ideas of reason which are distinct from ideas of the understanding as explicated in the work of Maimon. What is effectively achieved in this passage is the making explicit of the role of the operation of integration as a method of summation in the form of series in Deleuze's redeployment of this aspect of Maimon's work.

A "problematic" is "the ensemble of the problem and its conditions"

Deleuze's next move is to incorporate into this picture the subsequent developments in the differential calculus made by Weierstrass.

> [I]t is only here that the serial form within potentiality assumes its full meaning: it even becomes necessary to present what is a relation in the form of a sum. For a series of powers with numerical coefficients surround one singular point, and only one at a time. The interest and the necessity of the serial form appear in the plurality of series subsumed by it, in their dependence upon singular points, and in the manner in which we can pass from one part of the object where the function is represented by a series to another where it is expressed in a different series, whether the two series converge or extend one another or, on the contrary, diverge. (DR 176)

Deleuze here provides an eloquent description of Weierstrassian analytic continuity which he thereby incorporates into his discussion of the operations of the differential calculus. With this move, Deleuze displaces Maimon's infinite intellect as the limit of Ideas of reason with the Bordas-Demoulin inspired Ideas as concrete, rather than abstract, universals, which are characterized by the differential relations of the coefficients of the terms of the power series expansions at the distinctive points of a curve or function, i.e. its turning points or singularities.

The way that Deleuze connects this Weierstrassian development with Poincaré's qualitative theory of differential equations is through the work of Carnot, which has already been presented by Deleuze as the object of Wronski's criticism for having proposed that differentials cancel each other out in "a strict compensation of errors" (DR 177). While endorsing this criticism of Wronski, Deleuze argues that by proposing that differential equations express "the conditions of the problem to which responds a desired equation" (DR 177), Carnot invokes the notions of "problem" and "problem conditions" that "opened up for metaphysics a path which [goes] beyond the frame of his own theory" (DR 177).[21] It is to the work of Leibniz and Poincaré that Deleuze turns to further characterize these notions, and the metaphysics that they imply.

Deleuze refers in this instance to Leibniz's interest in transcendent problems in mathematics. A specific example of which would be the square or quadrature of the circle and hyperbola, i.e. the process of constructing with a compass and straight edge a square with an area equal to that of a circle or of another figure bounded by a curve, such as the hyperbola. Curves such as these have resisted all attempts at quadrature because their quadratrices cannot be constructed by finite geometrical or algebraic means. Because they could not be constructed, they were not considered to constitute solutions to the problem but rather to be mathematically unintelligible. It is for this reason that they were referred to as transcendent problems. However, Leibniz maintained that the fact that they are transcendent does not make them "any less real than the curves they square" (Mahoney 1990, 471).[22] Instead, these examples bring to the fore the question of solvability rather than that of solution, i.e. they introduce "the idea of determining the nature of a problem without necessarily solving it" (Mahoney 1990, 465). Leibniz demonstrated that his methods of analysis by means of the differential calculus did have a capacity for clearly stating the nature of the problems without expressly finding the solutions. While the problems could not be solved, they could at least "show what sort of solution or what limits of solution" (Mahoney 1990, 465) the problems involved.

The structure of the notions of "problem" and "problem conditions" that Deleuze develops is drawn from Poincaré's qualitative theory of differential equations, which, as presented in Chapter 1, involves the construction of essential singularities from two divergent local polynomial functions. Deleuze distinguishes between, on the one hand, the four types of essential singularities—nodes, saddles, foci, and centers (DR 177. Translation modified).—which are constructed when the two local functions are presented as numerator and denominator of a meromorphic function, and, on the other hand, the solution curves, which are only represented by the trajectories of variables across the domain of the potential function[23] and are determined by "the field of vectors defined by the equation itself" (DR 177), i.e. by the power series expansion of the meromorphic function. Deleuze argues that the complementarity of these two aspects—essential singularities and solution curves—"does not obscure their difference in kind – on the contrary" (DR 177). The specification of the essential singularities "already shows the necessary immanence of the problem in the solution," i.e. the involvement of the problem "in the solution which covers it," which "testifies to the transcendence of the problem and its directive role in relation to the organization of the solutions themselves" (DR 177).

Poincaré's approach was radically different to the work of Cauchy and Weierstrass, which "was conducted primarily in the *complex plane* and was mostly of a *local* nature, i.e. the behavior of the solutions was studied in a neighborhood of an individual point" (Kolmogorov and Yushkevich 1998, 173). Instead, Poincaré "looked beyond the confines of a local analysis and brought a global perspective to the problem, undertaking a qualitative study of the function in the whole plane" (Barrow-Green 1997, 30). And unlike his predecessors, "who had studied singular points without the constraint of distinguishing between the real and complex case, Poincaré considered only real values" (Barrow-Green 1997, 31). What was new and important in Poincaré's qualitative theory of differential equations is the "idea of thinking of the solutions in terms of curves rather than functions" (Barrow-Green 1997, 30). To get around the problem posed by the difficulty of the construction of curves with infinite branches that Weierstrass had encountered, Poincaré first projected the x-y plane onto the surface of a sphere. Poincaré was then able to show that these four types of essential singularity necessarily existed by analyzing the solutions both in terms of the particular geometrical features of the projected image, i.e. whether nodes, saddles, foci, or centers, and in terms of their number and distribution (See Barrow-Green 1997, 32).

One of the problems that motivated Poincaré's work on the qualitative theory of differential equations was his interest in the fundamental questions of celestial mechanics related to the stability of the solar system. The question of the long-term stability of the solar system—i.e. whether the movements under gravity of the sun and planets will cause them to remain in periodic, more or less "stable", orbits, or whether these movements are unstable and therefore whether the planets are liable to depart from their existing orbits—is one of the big questions in celestial mechanics that remains in general unresolved to this day (See Laubenbacher and Pengelley 1998, 43). Poincaré recognized the need for a qualitative theory of differential equations, specifically the importance of considering the global properties of *real*, as opposed to complex solutions, for furthering our understanding of this type of problem.

Despite the meromorphic function used by Poincaré having no direct application in celestial mechanics, by using only one of the essential singularities, a center, and curves presented in the form of closed cycles around it as the basis for characterizing the problem, Poincaré was able to "extend and elaborate his results to include more complex systems" (Barrow-Green 1997, 31). That is, specifically, the study of the problem of the movements of three celestial bodies, the sun, the earth, and the moon, subject to their mutual gravitational attractions, which is known as the three body problem. The movements of these three celestial bodies can be represented as spirals that approach the limit of a closed cycle around a center asymptotically. By continuously varying the initial conditions, Poincaré was able to demonstrate that in certain situations stable solutions exist. In fact, Poincaré's demonstration of solutions to the three body problem represents an application of a mathematical rule or model, Poincaré's qualitative theory of differential equations, to an empirical observation for the purposes of providing a more rigorous and predictive account of the movement of celestial bodies, in much the same way as Maimon's use of the differential calculus is as a mathematical rule of the understanding or model applied to empirical experience to provide an account of its genesis.

While the three body problem represents a well-known application of Poincaré's qualitative theory of differential equations, Deleuze's interest in Poincaré's theory is broader than simply in this application of it as a model. Indeed, Deleuze is specifically interested in the implications of the mathematical developments in the qualitative theory of differential equations for determining a metaphysics of the calculus oriented around the notions of problem and problem conditions. While essential singularities and solution curves are different in kind, the complete determination of a problem, which is characteristic of what Deleuze refers to as the "solution-instance" (DR 178), is inseparable from the existence, the number, and the distribution of the essential singularities, "which precisely provide its conditions" (DR 177), which Deleuze refers to as the "problem-instance" (DR 177). Describing the structure of the meromorphic function that Poincaré utilizes, Deleuze emphasizes that "one singular point" or essential singularity "gives rise to two condition equations," the two polynomials of the meromorphic function, which he claims are "constitutive of the problem," i.e. of the essential singularity, "and of its synthesis" (DR 177). This leads Deleuze to define a "problematic" as "the ensemble of the problem and its conditions" (DR 177), of the essential singularity and its two condition equations.

Abel and Galois on the question
of the solvability of polynomial equations

Deleuze concedes that "from a technical point of view, differential calculus" is not "the only mathematical expression of problems as such" (DR 179). Both the method of exhaustion and Cartesian analytic geometry played this role before the development of the differential calculus. And more recently, this role has been fulfilled by other mathematical procedures better than it had been by the differential calculus. The mathematical procedures that Deleuze is referring to here are those developed respectively by Niels Henrik Abel (b. 1802–1829) and Évariste Galois (b. 1811–1832) on the question of the solvability of polynomial equations. The introduction of their work is an important move by Deleuze that serves a crucial purpose in his argument, namely the formalization of the mathematical expression of problems as such. So the work of Abel and Galois is not simply an alternative mathematical expression of problems, but a formal restatement of it. Deleuze maintains that "Abel was perhaps the first to break" the "circle in which the theory of problems was caught" (DR 179). The circularity consisted in the following: thinking that "a problem is solvable only to the extent that it is 'true',", when the very criterion of truth is itself defined in terms of solvability (DR 179). What Abel brings to this circularity is a method that reverses the problem-solution relation, according to which solvability follows "from the form of the problem" (DR 180). Rather than basing the extrinsic criterion of solvability, i.e. truth, upon the internal character of the problem as an Idea, Deleuze proposes to make the internal character of the problem as an Idea dependent upon the "simple external criterion" (DR 180), i.e. upon the very conditions of the problem itself.

Abel is important to Deleuze because it was he who in 1824 provided the first accepted proof of the insolubility of the quintic, or fifth degree polynomial equations, for example $x^5 + 1$. To do so, Abel used the ideas about the permutations of roots that were introduced by Lagrange (1770, 205–421).[24] Mathematicians had previously thought that all polynomial equations could be solved by finding the roots as expressions of the coefficients involving only the elementary algebraic operations (addition, subtraction, multiplication, and division) and the extraction of radicals (square roots, cube roots, etc). The method for determining the roots of a polynomial equation was known as solving by radicals. Formulas to solve polynomial equations of first, second, third, and fourth degree had been developed; however, mathematicians had been unable to discover similar formulas for higher degree polynomial equations. Lagrange analyzed the general formulas for determining solutions of cubics and quartics—i.e. third and fourth degree polynomial equations, for example $x^3 + 1$ and $x^4 + 1$, respectively—by considering the polynomial equations in terms of the symmetries among their roots, which formed a set of permutations. In this way he was able to derive respectively the general cubic and quartic formulas from the elementary expressions of their symmetric roots as polynomial equations or symmetric functions. This provided a unified understanding of the general formulas for determining the solutions to polynomial equations of degree less than or equal to four. However, Lagrange was unable to do the same for quintics, and suggested that they might not be solvable in this way.[25] Abel provided the first conclusive proof of this conjecture. He proved that, despite some specific quintics actually having solutions, it was impossible to construct an algebraic formula that solved all quintics using the method of solving by radicals. This result also holds for polynomial equations of higher degree. What Abel's proof shows is that even though a solution can be provided in certain special cases, a solution to a special case is not generalizable, i.e. a general formula for a solution with the same form as the solution for special cases does not exist. What this means is that rather than the solvability of a higher order polynomial equation being determinable by a general formula, its solvability is determinable solely by the specific permutations of the roots of the polynomial equation, which are the conditions of the problem itself.

What Deleuze extracts from Abel's proof is "the necessity of recognizing . . . an alternative to abstraction by generalization" (Vuillemin 1962, 216), which, as a rule developed by the ancient geometers, was sufficient to solve polynomial equations of degree less than or equal to four. Vuillemin describes this new alternative as "abstraction by formalization" (Vuillemin 1962, 216), which is irreducible to abstraction by generalization. What is required instead is "first bringing to light the general conditions of a problem, and as a consequence, the postulates on which a theory depends" (Vuillemin 1962, 216). To determine whether or not a given equation is solvable, it is necessary to "determine the conditions of the problem which . . . specify the fields of solvability in such a way that the statement" of the conditions of the problem "contains the seeds of the solution" (DR 180). Deleuze maintains that this reversal of the problem-solution relation is "a more considerable revolution than the Copernican" (DR 180). He argues that Abel "inaugurated a new *Critique of Pure Reason*, in particular going beyond Kantian '*extrinsicism*'" (DR 180). Kant doesn't question the validity of the extrinsic nature of synthetic a priori judgments as he conceives them, i.e. as judgments with reference to the relation between intuitions and concepts. The project of the first *Critique* is an attempt to prove their possibility based upon the presumption of their validity. There is a truth about the nature of the relation between intuitions and concepts and it is the job of the critical philosopher to provide an account of how such judgments are possible. Maimon argues that this is a false presumption on Kant's part, and that rather than synthetic a priori judgments providing a ground for resolving the problem of the relation between the content of sensation and the concept under which it is subsumed by means of the schematism, synthetic a priori judgments, on Maimon's account, are internal to products of the understanding, insofar as intuitions, as images of concepts, are always already conceptual though of limited degree. He maintains that it is this relation that functions as a model for the way empirical intuitions are understood to relate to the objects of which they are the ideas, via the account of the differential. What Abel's proof provides is a formal restatement of the reversal of the problem-solution relation that is figured in Maimon's critique of Kant.

Having emphasized the importance of Abel's work to his own project, Deleuze then turns to Galois, who developed a novel technique for determining whether a given polynomial equation could be solved by radicals. He combined Abel's work with his own ideas to develop what is considered to be a more complete theory on the solvability of higher degree polynomial equations by radicals. What Galois showed is that "a simpler proof of Abel's result could be found along purely group-theoretic lines" (Birkhoff 1937, 263).

Galois's basic idea was that the question of the solvability of any polynomial equation was related to the structure of a group of permutations of the roots of that equation, which is now known as the Galois group. The Galois group, which consists of all the permutations that preserve the relations among the roots, shows to what extent the roots of the polynomial equation are permutable or interchangeable. Galois was able to demonstrate that this group provides an effective measure of whether or not the polynomial equation is solvable by radicals. Indeed, a polynomial equation is solvable by radicals if and only if its Galois group is solvable. A Galois group is said to be solvable if it can be demonstrated to have a certain structure. Galois noted that certain subsets of the members of the Galois group satisfied the requirements of being a group, and therefore constituted a subgroup of the Galois group, and that these subgroups could also have subgroups of their own. The number of elements, or order, in any subgroup of a finite group must divide evenly into the number of elements in the group, or be a divisor of the order of the group. By dividing the order (number of members) of the parent group by the order of the subgroup Galois obtained the *composition factor* of the group. In this way, a genealogy of subgroups can be constructed, which generates a corresponding sequence of *composition factors* (See Livio 2006, 168–71). Given this structure, a Galois group is said to be solvable if it contains a sequence of subgroups "such that each subgroup is normal of prime index in the preceding one" (Tignol 2001, 265). A subgroup is said to be "normal" if it consists of permutable roots that are invariant under every permutation, and a subgroup is said to be "of prime index" if the composition factor of the subgroup is a prime number.

Deleuze's account of Galois's theory draws explicitly upon its field theoretic presentation, which is only implicitly posed by Galois, and is rather the result of subsequent developments in mathematics by Leopold Kronecker (b. 1839–1891), who explicitly defined the mathematical concept of a "field of adjunction," and Emil Artin (b. 1898–1962), who first developed the relationship between groups and fields in detail. Indeed, Galois's theory is now presented predominantly in field theoretic terms, according to which the solvability of a Galois group is able to be determined by "describing the behavior of the group under extension of the base field" (Tignol 2001, 233). If the Galois group of a polynomial equation is solvable, then a radical extension of the base field containing all the roots of the polynomial equation can be obtained by the sequential extraction of its roots, where each extraction of a root consists of a "successive adjunction to this field" (DR 180). Insofar as there is a one-to-one correspondence between subgroups of the Galois group and subfields of a base field, the sequence of subgroups of the Galois group corresponds to the successive adjunctions to the base field. Essentially, Galois's theory shows that the solvability of a polynomial equation was related to the structure of the permutations of its roots and that this could be measured by means of determining the structure of the subgroups of the Galois group or by describing the behavior of the group under extension of the base field.

Deleuze draws three significant conclusions from the development represented in Galois's theory. First, he notes that "The theory of problems is completely transformed and at last grounded" (DR 180). By this he means that Galois's theory is not simply another example or expression of the mathematical theory of problems, but rather a formal restatement of the theory of problems as such, in purely group theoretic terms. Second, Deleuze notes that because the sequence of subgroups, or the successive adjunctions to the base field, are determined progressively, the question of whether or not the polynomial equation is solvable is also discerned progressively. From this, Deleuze argues that "Galois's 'progressive discernibility' unites in the same continuous movement the processes of reciprocal determination and complete determination" (DR 180), which he then characterizes in group theoretical terms as the products of relations between permutable roots: "pairs of roots and the distinction between the roots within a pair" (DR 180). What Deleuze means by this is that Galois's theory unites in one formal theory those aspects of the theory of problems represented in Weierstrass's theory of analytic continuity and Poincaré's qualitative theory of differential equations.

Third, he notes that this progressive discernibility represents the formal introduction of "time" into "the total figure of sufficient reason" (DR 180) that the theory constitutes. Deleuze argues that the "adjunct fields . . . form the synthetic progression of a sufficient reason" (DR 181). So, in addition to the 'three principles which together form a sufficient reason'" (DR 171), which Deleuze has discussed previously solely in terms of developments in the differential calculus—namely, the principle of determinability that "corresponds to the undetermined as such (dx, dy)," the principle of reciprocal determination that "corresponds to the really determinable (dy/dx)," and the principle of complete determination that "corresponds to the effectively determined (values of dy/dx)" (DR 171)—Galois's theory allows a formal group theoretic concept of time to be incorporated into the formal presentation of the figure of sufficient reason that Deleuze deploys in his work. This progressive discernibility is formal because it is the formal presentation of a temporal feature that remains only intuitive in Poincaré's qualitative theory of differential equations, namely the leap of the variable across the cut of the potential function in the diagrammatic representation of essential singularities, which are determined in relation to the problem of the representation of meromorphic functions, where more formal solutions remain elusive.

Having just showcased Galois's theory as the formal restatement of the mathematical expression of problems as such, Deleuze now moves to reintroduce the role of the differential calculus back into the discussion. He does this by distinguishing between an understanding of modern mathematics which is "regarded as based upon the theory of groups and set theory" and the broader understanding of mathematics that includes those developments in mathematics that fall outside of these programs, such as the subsequent developments in the differential calculus to which I have been referring. The work of Abel is significant for Deleuze in this respect. Deleuze maintains that "it is no accident that Abel's method concerned above all the integration of differential formulae" (DR 180). Abel's formal proof of the mathematical expression of problems is no less formal simply because it employs elements of the differential calculus. Deleuze argues that:

> What matters to us is less the determination of this or that break [*coupure*] in the history of mathematics (analytic geometry, differential calculus, group theory. . .) than the manner in which, at each moment of that history, dialectical problems,

their mathematical expression and the simultaneous origin of their fields of solvability are interrelated. (DR 180–81)

While I will return to the question of the dialectic and "dialectical problems" after discussing the role of Albert Lautman's work in Deleuze's argument in Chapter 4, Deleuze's discussion of the work of Abel and Galois provides an account of how developments in the problem of the solvability of polynomial equations of higher degree are interrelated with subsequent developments in the differential calculus by means of the question of the mathematical expression of problems. Deleuze takes this claim to interrelatedness further by arguing that:

> From this point of view, there is a continuity and a teleology in the development of mathematics which makes the differences in kind between differential calculus and other instruments merely secondary. (DR 181)

Again the question of how this continuity and teleology operate in relation to mathematics will be addressed in relation to the work of Lautman in Chapter 4. But for the moment, the important point to take from this passage is that the differences in kind between differential calculus and both group theory and set theory, namely, the formalization of the latter versus the informal collection of intuitive results of the former, are "merely secondary" on Deleuze's reckoning. What is important is that they are each characterizations of the mathematical expression of problems as such. This distinction between formal and informal characterizations of the mathematical expression of problems as such is important for determining how Deleuze's approach to the relation between mathematics and philosophy differs from that of Badiou, which is the focus of Chapter 5.

The final major development in the history of mathematics with which Deleuze engages is the differential geometry of Bernhard Riemann. Deleuze redeploys the conceptual characteristics of Riemann's mathematics in relation to the work of Henri Bergson in order to reconfigure Bergson's concept of duration. The details of this engagement between Deleuze, Bergson, and Riemann are the focus of the following Chapter.

Bergson and Riemann on Qualitative Multiplicity

Henri Bergson (b. 1859–1941) is one of the major influences on Deleuze, as is evident by the number of concepts that Deleuze has drawn from his work. While much research has been done on the importance of these concepts to the development of Deleuze's philosophy, very little research has been done on Bergson's relation to mathematics and the importance of this relation for understanding Deleuze's engagement with Bergson. It is well known that the differential calculus plays an explicit role in Bergson's work; however, exactly what function it has remains obscure. What I propose to do in this chapter is negotiate the fine line between clarifying the role of mathematics in Bergson's work, isolating those aspects of it that are of interest to Deleuze, and then indicating Bergson's shortcomings when it comes to realizing the potential of some of these developments for his own project. Bergson remains important to Deleuze despite this. Deleuze's engagement with Bergson can be understood to be an attempt to rehabilitate and extend Bergson's work by taking full advantage of the potential of these developments in mathematics. So, in addition to examining the explicit role played by the infinitesimal calculus in Bergson's philosophy, this chapter examines the implicit role of the work of Bernhard Riemann (b. 1826–1866) in the development of Bergson's concept of multiplicity. While Bergson only draws upon one aspect of Riemann's work, specifically the implications of the concept of qualitative multiplicity for the development of his concept of duration, Deleuze rehabilitates and extends the Bergson's work by clarifying and drawing upon the full potential of Riemann's mathematical developments. The most important aspects of which are the implications of the concept of qualitative multiplicity for reconfiguring the concept of space in a way that does all of the work required by Bergson's concept of duration.

Before developing this argument, it is necessary to set up one of the other important connections that there is in Bergson's work to the development of Deleuze's philosophy. Bergson's account of sensation and its role in the determination of extensive magnitudes has important resonances with the work of Maimon, in particular, the illusory way in which sensible objects of the intuitions are represented to the understanding as being extracognitive, when in fact they are the product of our understanding.[1]

The role of judgment in the determination
of the idea of an extensive magnitude

When discussing the "intensity of a sensation" in *Time and Free Will* (1910), Bergson argues that it "bears witness to a more or less considerable work accomplished in our organism" (TF 6); however, he is quick to point out that "it is the sensation which is given to us in consciousness, and not this mechanical work" (TF 7). Indeed, he stresses that intensity is only "apparently" a property of sensation, and that it is rather the product of a judgment: "it is by the intensity of the sensation that we judge of the greater or less amount of work accomplished" (TF 7).

This judgment is made on the presumption that "cause is extensive and therefore measurable" (TF 42). So we take a constant experience that gives "us a definite shade of sensation" and assume that it corresponds "to a definite amount of stimulation" (TF 42). In doing so, Bergson argues that "we . . . associate the idea of a certain quantity of cause with a certain quality of effect" (TF 42). This idea of the quantity of the cause is transferred into the sensation, i.e. into the quality of the effect. Bergson notes that it is at this very moment that "the intensity, which was nothing but a certain shade or quality of the sensation, becomes a magnitude" (TF 42). So, it is from this idea of intensity that "the idea of extensive magnitude" is derived (See TF73).

The problem Bergson has with intensity in *Time and Free Will* is with the way that it is implicated in the determination of extensive magnitude, i.e. insofar as intensity is reduced to a quantity or magnitude. According to Bergson, "the projection of our psychic states into space" influences these states themselves and gives them a new form, as extensive magnitudes, in reflective consciousness, "which immediate perception did not attribute to them" (TF 90).[2] In *Mélanges*, Bergson comments upon and clarifies the critique of intensity that appeared in his early work (See TF 84ff; MM 206–7) by describing this idea of intensity as "the notion of intensity in psychology." He argues that "In *Time and Free Will*, I criticized the notion of intensity in psychology not as false but as demanding to be interpreted. No one can deny that a psychological state has an intensity" (1972, 491).[3] In order to respond to this demand for interpretation and to thereby bring a greater degree of explanatory purchase to this distinction between intensity reduced to its psychological state, from which the idea of extensive magnitude is derived, and intensity as a certain shade or quality of sensation, Bergson turns to the distinction between two kinds of multiplicity: one quantitative and discrete, or numerical; the other qualitative and continuous.

It is by means of the concept of quantitative or numerical multiplicity that Bergson is able to distinguish the character of extensive magnitudes or material objects from the multiplicity of states of consciousness. The character of extensive magnitudes or material objects, to which the conception of number or some symbolical representation is immediately applicable and in which space is a necessary element, is distinguished from the multiplicity of states of consciousness, which is characteristic of a qualitative magnitude, and in which qualitative discrimination or differentiation is made "without any further thought of counting the qualities or even of distinguishing them as several" (TF 122). Space is a necessary element of numerical multiplicity because it enables a number of identical and simultaneous sensations to be distinguished from one another. Bergson therefore characterizes space as "a principle of differentiation other than that of qualitative differentiation" (TF 95), and he describes space so characterized as "a reality with no quality" (TF 95). However, Bergson insists that the idea of discrete multiplicity cannot even be formed without the simultaneous consideration of a qualitative multiplicity (See TF 123). Indeed he maintains that "it is through the quality of quantity that we form the idea of quantity without quality" (TF 123). Consider the so-called successive states of the external world, each of which can be understood as a discrete or numerical multiplicity, and each of which exists independently of all others. The numerical multiplicity of each of these worlds "is real only for a consciousness that can first retain them and then set them side by side by externalizing them in relation to one another" (TF 120). This can only be achieved by considering each of the successive states of the world together under the form of a "qualitative multiplicity" (TF 124). Consciousness carries out a synthesis between the actual states of the external world and what the memory refers to as the former states of the external world, and causes these images to "permeate, complete, and . . . to continue one another" (TF 124) in much the same way that the motion of a body through space is consciously perceived. The motion of a body through space is perceived consciously by virtue of the synthesis by consciousness of the actual position of the body and the memory of the former position of the body. The wholly qualitative multiplicity that this entails incorporates each of the successive states of the external world, each of which is heterogeneous. The qualitative multiplicity of heterogeneous states of the world is characteristic of what Bergson refers to as "duration" (TF 229). In *The Creative Mind* (1992), Bergson further characterizes this qualitative multiplicity of heterogeneous states of the world as "the idea of an indistinct and even undivided multiplicity, purely intensive or qualitative, which, while remaining what it is, will comprise an indefinitely increasing number of elements, as the new points of view for considering it appear in the world" (CM 28), and he refers to it as "a duration in which novelty is constantly springing forth" (CM 28).

Deleuze points out that this distinction is drawn from the work of Bernhard Riemann, and he argues that "It is clear that Bergson, as a philosopher, was well aware of Riemann's general problems" (B 39). Before providing an account of the degree to which Bergson's treatment of the distinction draws upon the mathematical developments made by Riemann and the importance of this connection for understanding the degree to which Deleuze draws upon the work of Bergson, I'd like to examine the way that mathematics features as an important touchstone in Bergson's work and to provide a framework for understanding the nature of this engagement. In order to do so, the subsequent developments in Bergson's account of perception require further elaboration.

In *Matter and Memory* (1911a), Bergson refines his account of perception by distinguishing between "the perceptive faculty of the brain and the reflex functions of the spinal cord" (MM 110). The spinal cord transforms the stimulation received into movements that "remain inseparably bound up with the rest of the material world" (MM 12), whereas the brain has the capacity to delay or prolong the stimulations received into "reactions which are merely nascent" (MM 110). Bergson argues that the brain appears to be "an instrument of analysis in regard to the movement received, and an instrument of selection in regard to the movement executed" (MM 20). For this reason, perception appears at the precise moment when a stimulation received by matter is not transformed into an action, and conscious perception consists in mainly the "practical discernment" (MM 46) of this interval. The brain therefore doesn't manufacture representations, but only complicates the relationship between a received stimulation or excitation and an executed action or response. There is what Bergson refers to as an "indetermination" (MM 24) in the effect of the stimulation when it is prolonged by the brain, insofar as there are "multiple probabilistic outcomes of the stimulation" (MM 24). And it is precisely from this "indetermination" that "the necessity of a perception" is inferred (MM 24), "that is to say, of a *variable* relation between the living being and the more or less distant influence of the objects which interest it" (MM 24).

What Bergson sets out to explain in *Matter and Memory* is "not how perception arises" (MM 34), which was already the focus of *Time and Free Will*, but rather "how it is limited" (MM 34). Rather than providing what Bergson refers to as "the image of the whole," perception, by virtue of the process of analysis and selection by the perceptive faculty of the brain, "is in fact reduced to the image of that which interests you" (MM 34). In *Creative Evolution* (1911b), Bergson presents this argument as follows:

> The cerebral mechanism is arranged just so as to drive back into the unconscious almost the whole of this past, and to admit beyond the threshold only that which can cast light on the present situation or further the action now being prepared— in short, only that which can give *useful* work. (CE 5)

Just as Bergson characterized sensation, in *Time and Free Will*, as a certain shade or quality of sensation into which the idea of the quantity of cause is transferred, so too, in *Matter and Memory*, is the "unextended" (MM 52) quality of all sensation emphasized, and the process of perception is characterized as consisting in an "exteriorization" (MM 52) of those unextended sensations that are not transformed into action. What this means is that "extensity is superimposed upon sensation" (MM 52).

The important addition to this story that is furnished by *Matter and Memory* is that the mechanism by means of which this exteriorization takes place and by virtue of which the brain acts as an instrument of analysis and selection is intimately bound up with the memory. Bergson argues that "there is no perception which is not full of memories" (MM 24), and that "In most cases these memories, supplant our actual perceptions, of which we then retain only a few hints, thus using them merely as 'signs' that recall to us former images" (MM 24). Bergson insists that every perception "prolongs the past into the present, and thereby partakes of memory" (MM 325). From the moment when the past is imported into a present sensation, Bergson argues that the recollection is "actualized," that is, "it ceases to be a recollection and becomes once more a perception" (MM 320). While Bergson argues that between the perceptive faculty of the brain and the reflex function of the spinal cord there is "only a difference of degree" and "no difference in kind" (MM 110); the same does not hold for the relation between perception and memory. "Memory," he argues, "is something other than a function of the brain" (MM 315), and he insists that "there is not merely a difference of degree, but of kind, between perception and recollection" (MM 315).

During perception, "We become conscious of an act *sui generis* by which we detach ourselves from the present in order to replace ourselves, first in the past in general, then in a certain region of the past by a work of adjustment, something like the focusing of a camera" (MM 133–4). This process of adjustment is represented in the figure of the inverted cone. Between the present, figured by the inverted apex of the cone, and the totality of the memories, disposed in the horizontal slice that is the base of the cone, Bergson maintains that "there is room . . . for a thousand repetitions of our psychical life" (MM 212), figured by as many parallel horizontal sections as can be cut between the apex and the base of the same cone (See MM 212). Each of the horizontal sections is a repetition of all of the others and is distinguished from them only by the order of the relations and the distribution of what Bergson refers to as "dominant recollections," or "shining points" (MM 223), and which Deleuze refers to as remarkable, distinctive, or singular points (See B 62; DR 212). Each section is a different level or adjustment in the process of focusing the memory on a specific recollection, represented by the apex. Once a specific memory is isolated, it still remains virtual, as a memory. As Bergson argues, "Virtual, this memory can only become actual by means of the perception which attracts it" (MM 163). The specific memory is actualized by means of the perception which attracts it as a present perception, i.e. "from the virtual state it passes into the actual" (MM 133–4) as a present perception. By importing the past into the present, Bergson argues that perception thereby contracts many moments of duration into a single intuition (See MM 80). In this way, "The whole of our past psychical life conditions our present state, without being its necessary determinant" (MM 191). In *The Creative Mind*, Bergson further characterizes present perception as a perception of both the immediate past, insofar as it is perceived, and the immediate future, insofar as it is being determined as an action or movement. He argues that "duration . . . grasps a succession which is . . . the uninterrupted prolongation of the past into a present which is already blending into the future" (CM 35).

Mechanical explanation as a method or as a doctrine?

There is an often overlooked complexity with the way that Bergson engages with the scientific discourse of his day. The explicit aim that underpins his entire body of work is to overturn the dogmatic tendency in nineteenth century science for the generalization of the fruits of reduction. What is not adequately appreciated is that this opposition does not at all entail dispensing with the more epistemically modest approach of science that was also operative at the time. This tension is most clearly expressed in Bergson's discussion of the distinction between mechanistic explanation as a "method," and mechanistic explanation as a "doctrine" (CE 366). As a method, Bergson argues that "the mechanistic explanation might have remained universal in this, that it can indeed be extended to as many systems as we choose to cut out in the continuity of the universe" (CE 366). Mechanistic explanation as a method, he maintains, "would have expressed the fact that the function of science is to scan the rhythm of the flow of things and not to fit itself into that flow" (CE 366). As a doctrine, the impetus of mechanistic explanation is "to convert a general rule of method into a fundamental law of things"

(CE 368). The result is what Bergson refers to as "radical mechanism" (CE 41). "The essence of" radical "mechanical explanation," Bergson argues, "is to regard the future and the past as calculable functions of the present, and thus to claim that *all is given*. On this hypothesis, past, present and future would be open at a glance to a superhuman intellect capable of making the calculation" (CE 40). Contrary to the epistemic modesty of the former approach, radical mechanism "implies a metaphysic in which the totality of the real is postulated complete in eternity, and in which the apparent duration of things expresses merely the infirmity of a mind that cannot know everything at once" (CE 39). Bergson rejects such a radical mechanism and the universal mathematic that it entails. He argues that our inability to subject organic *creation*, or "the evolutionary phenomena which properly constitute life," (CE 21) to a mathematical treatment is not "due only to our ignorance" (CE 21), i.e. relative to a super human intellect. He maintains rather that "the mathematical order is nothing positive," and that "there is no definite system of mathematical laws at the base of nature" (CE 232). However, he also argues that "There is no reason . . . why a duration, and so a form of existence like our own, should not be attributed to the systems that science isolates" (CE 12), the proviso being that "such systems are reintegrated into the Whole," and he insists that "they must be so reintegrated" (CE 12). Bergson even refers to his own approach in *Matter and Memory* as making use of a scientific understanding for the convenience of study, which he then "reintegrates into the whole":

> we have, to begin with, and for the convenience of study, treated the living body as a mathematical point in space and conscious perception as a mathematical instant in time. We then had to restore to the body its extensity and to perception its duration. (MM 310)

One of the examples of this tension in Bergson's work between mechanical explanation as a method and mechanical explanation as a doctrine is in his treatment of the relation of modern to ancient geometry. Bergson describes ancient geometry as having worked with figures that were "given to it at once, completely finished, like Platonic Ideas," that is, with figures that are purely static. Whereas modern geometry studied "the continuous movement by which the figure is described" (CE 33) and thereby introduced time and movement into the consideration of figures. While rigor in mathematics calls for the elimination of all considerations of motion from mathematical processes, Bergson maintains that "the introduction of motion into the genesis of figures is nevertheless the origin of modern mathematics" (CE 34) and that this constitutes "the first of the great transformations of geometry in modern times" (CE 353).

Modern geometry regarded every plane curve as being described by the movement of a point that is expressed by the equation of the curve, although Bergson stresses that Descartes' geometry did not give it this form because his metaphysics is more closely correlated with that of radical mechanism. What modern geometry did in relation to ancient geometry was "to substitute an equation for a figure" (CE 353). Bergson views this as "the directing idea of the reform by which both the science of nature and mathematics, which serves as its instrument, were renewed" (CE 354). So, on the one hand, Bergson praises modern science and argues that "modern science must be defined pre-eminently by its aspiration to take time as an independent variable"

(CE 355). Indeed, Bergson casts the relation that modern geometry has to ancient geometry as a model for the kind of transformation that he has undertaken to bring about in biology:

> We believe that if biology could ever get as close to its object as mathematics does to its own, it would become, to the physics and chemistry of organized bodies, what the mathematics of the moderns has proved to be in relation to ancient geometry. (CE 34)

However, on the other hand, he also argues that modern science is unable "to lay hold" of "the flux itself of duration," and the prime reason he gives for this is that modern science is "bound . . . to the cinematographical method" (CE 364). The significance of this description of modern science as being bound to the cinematographic method and its implications for Deleuze's engagement with the work of Bergson will be returned to in the following lines. Bergson maintains that "real time, regarded as a flux, or, in other words, as the very mobility of being, escapes the hold of scientific knowledge" (CE 355), including that of modern geometry.

The appraisal that Bergson offers of this shortcoming on the part of modern geometry is directly related to its doctrinal or radical mechanistic incarnation. Modern geometry, on this reading, reduces "real time" to the expression of time as an independent variable in the equation of a curve by the interval dt. Bergson argues that only "the present state of the system is defined by equations into which differential coefficients enter, such as" the rates of change of distance, or ds/dt, which provides a measure of the "*present* velocities," and the rates of change of velocities, or dv/dt, which provides a measure of the "*present* accelerations" (CE 23). What distinguishes the systems science works with from those that are "reintegrated into the whole" is that the scientific systems are "in an instantaneous present that is always being renewed" (CE 23). According to Bergson, "such systems are never in that real, concrete duration in which the past remains bound up with the present" (CE 23).

Referring to the mathematician who has adopted the doctrinal or radical mechanistic approach to the role of science, Bergson argues that "When the mathematician calculates the future state of a system at the end of" the interval, dt, "there is nothing to prevent him from supposing that the universe vanishes from" one moment to the next (CE 23).

> If he divides the interval into infinitely small parts by considering the differential dt, he thereby expresses merely the fact that he will consider accelerations and velocities [,which enables] him to calculate the state of the system at a given moment. But he is always speaking of a given moment—a static moment, that is—and not of flowing time. In short, *the world the mathematician deals with is a world that dies and is reborn at every instant—the world which Descartes was thinking of when he spoke of continued creation.* (CE 23)

This is the reason why Bergson distinguishes Descartes's geometry, which represents an early form of radical mechanism that retains the remnants of the static thinking of the Greeks, from those developments of modern geometry that do fall rather under the rubric of mechanical explanation as a method. However, later in *Creative Evolution*, when describing "the procedure by which we should then pass from the definition of a certain vital action to the system of physico-chemical facts which it implies" (CE 34), Bergson again draws upon the more epistemically modest approach to modern science as a model and to the recent developments in mathematics that serve as its instruments. The particular development in mathematics that Bergson refers to is the differential calculus. Rather than just measuring the rates of change of the present state of the system, as just elaborated, he maintains that this procedure of passing from the definition of a certain vital action to the system of physico-chemical facts that it implies "would be like passing from the function to its derivative, from the equation of the curve (*i.e.* the law of the continuous movement by which the curve is generated) to the equation of the tangent giving its instantaneous direction" (CE 34). Using the differential calculus as a model, vitality is characterized by Bergson as being "tangent, at any and every point, to physical and chemical forces" (CE 33). Bergson maintains that "such a science would be a *mechanics of transformation*" (CE 34).

A similar argument appears in *Matter and Memory* when Bergson is discussing the distinction between immediate and useful perceptions as marking the dawn of human experience. However, rather than using simple differentiation as a model, which involves passing from the function to its derivative, this example starts with infinitely small elements and poses the problem of reconstituting from these elements the curve itself.

> To give up certain habits of thinking, and even of perceiving, is far from easy: yet this is but the negative part of the work to be done: and when it is done. . ., there still remains to be reconstituted, with the infinitely small elements which we thus perceive of the real curve, the curve itself stretching out into the darkness behind them. In this sense the task of the philosopher, as we understand it, closely resembles that of the mathematician who determines a function by starting from the differential. The final effort of philosophical research is a true work of integration. (MM 241–2)

This example draws upon the problem in the differential calculus of integration as a process of summation in the form of series.[4] The "useful" perceptions are characterized as infinitely small elements, and the task of the philosopher, like that of the mathematician, is to reconstitute the real curve from these differential elements by means of the "true work of integration," which, when attempting to determine the function by starting from the differential, is a process of summation in the form of a series.

However, in *Creative Evolution*, when Bergson next refers to the work of integration, he seems to contradict this positive characterization of the potential for mathematics to function as a model for philosophical research. In the chapter entitled "Biology, Physics and Chemistry," Bergson insists that "such an integration can be no more than dreamed of" (CE 34) and he adds that "we do not pretend that the dream will ever be realized" (CE 34). These statements call for careful explication. First of all, Bergson has returned to his criticism of mathematics when understood solely from the point of view of mechanical explanation as a doctrine. This is clear in the following remarks in which he refers to radical mechanism as "pure" mechanism. Bergson maintains that he is "only trying, by carrying a certain comparison as far as possible, to show up to what point" his "theory goes along with pure mechanism, and where they part company" (CE 34–5). When understood from the point of view of pure or radical mechanism, there is no dreaming of such an integration because the points to which vitality would be tangent are only "views taken by a mind which imagines stops at various moments of the movement that generates the curve" (CE 33). However, when understood from the point of view of mechanical explanation as a method, in particular using integration as a process of summation in the form of a series as a model, differentials remain of primary concern and are not reduced to their representation in straight line segments, which form the minimal elements of a curve for the pure or radical mechanist. As Bergson argues, "In reality, life is no more made of physico-chemical elements than a curve is composed of straight lines" (CE 33). While such an "integration can be no more than dreamed of" for Bergson, it can indeed be dreamed of when considered from the point of view of mechanical explanation as a method. The problem for Bergson is not that the relation between a curve and its differential elements serves as a poor model for the relation between the vitality of life and its physico-chemical elements, but rather that the reductive understanding of a curve solely in terms of the straight line segments of which it is composed is equally as problematic as conceptualizing life solely in terms of its physico-chemical elements. Whether or not the dream of such an integration between vital life and its physico-chemical elements can ever be realized is also addressed by the mathematics when understood from the point of view of mechanical explanation as a method. Just as in mathematics, where the polynomial function generated by the operation of integration as a process of summation in the form of a series only approaches the function of the curve and therefore remains an approximation, so too in life, the characterization of life in physico-chemical terms only approaches an expression of its vitality and remains only an approximation. In both cases the integration can only be dreamed of and therefore the expression of the problem in mathematics serves well as a model for the expression of the problem in terms of the theory of the vitality of life that Bergson is articulating.

Further clarifying the point where his theory parts company with pure or radical mechanism, Bergson argues that "The mechanistic explanations . . . hold good for the systems that our thought artificially detaches from the whole. But of the whole itself and of the systems which, within this whole, seem to take after it, we cannot admit *a priori* that they are mechanically explicable" (CE 39). While Bergson cannot admit a priori that they are mechanically explainable, this doesn't rule out the possibility of *a posteriori* mechanical explanations of those "systems which, within this whole, seem to take after it," i.e. of explanations based on mechanical explanation as a method and the mathematical modeling that this entails. Indeed, as already noted, Bergson makes frequent use of this kind of explanation, particularly in terms of the differential calculus. Further evidence for this is provided in *The Creative Mind* when Bergson argues that "the idea of differential, or rather of fluxion, was suggested to science by a vision of this kind" (CM 37). The vision referred to is that above and beyond the "systems which belong to the realm of science and to which the understanding can be applied" (CM 37), there is an "intuition" of "all the real change and movement" that the universe in its entirety "contains" (CM 37). So the differential calculus and the idea of the differential that it entails are characterized by Bergson as one of the systems which, within the whole, seems to take after it. Such a vision is characterized by Bergson as "Metaphysical in its origins," however, "it became scientific as it grew more rigorous, i.e. expressible in static terms" (CM 37). Bergson here maintains that there is a relation between the idea of the differential and its metaphysical origins, "if one considers the notion such as it was to begin with" (CM 39) rather than reducing it solely to static terms. The problem of integration as a process of summation in the form of a series maintains such a relation to the differential. Bergson's consistent objection is not to the form of mechanical explanation that operates as a method nor to the mathematical modeling that this entails, but rather to the dogmatic presumption of pure or radical mechanism that is eliminative of the metaphysical, reducing it solely to static terms.

Further evidence for this more favorable approach to mechanical explanation as a method rather than as a doctrine is provided by Bergson when he argues that "it might have been possible for mathematical science not to take originally the form the Greeks gave it" (CM 44). The ancient Greeks, who considered figures to be purely static, represent the earliest form of the radical mechanistic approach to science. While Bergson acknowledges that whatever form mathematics takes it is largely made up of convention and thus "must . . . keep to a strict use of artificial signs" (CM 44); he also maintains that "prior to this formulated mathematics . . . there is another, virtual or implicit, which is natural to the human mind" (CM 44). The argument that Bergson presents in CE in support of such a virtual or implicit mathematics that is natural to the human mind recasts the judgments made about the shade or quality of sensation in perception from which the idea of extensive magnitude is derived. Bergson maintains that "it is a latent geometry, immanent in our idea of space, which is the main spring of our intellect and the cause of its working" (CE 222). The argument he provides is as follows: "prior to the science of geometry, there is a natural geometry whose clearness and evidence surpass the clearness and evidence of . . . deductions" made about already existing or static magnitudes. Unlike the latter, the deductions made on the basis of this prior natural geometry "bear on qualities, and not on magnitudes purely" (CE 223). Bergson then claims that the deductions made about already existing magnitudes "are, then, likely to have been formed on the model of the first" (CE 223), i.e. on the virtual or implicit natural geometry. He maintains that the former "borrow their force from the fact that, behind quality, we see magnitude vaguely showing through" (CE 223). What he means here is that judgments made about the shade or quality of sensation in perception determine what is then seen of these qualities, i.e. they are seen as magnitudes "vaguely showing through" the quality experienced in sensation.

Affirming this argument about a prior natural geometry, and the argument in CM referred to above, that the idea of the differential was suggested to science by a vision of the real changes and movement in the whole, Bergson, in IM, again makes explicit the role of model played by the differential calculus in his work. He refers to the "infinitesimal calculus" as "the most powerful of methods of investigation at the disposal of the human mind" (IM 52). And he characterizes modern mathematics as "precisely an effort . . . to follow the generation of magnitudes, to grasp motion no longer from without and in its displayed result, but from within and in its tendency to change; in short, to adopt the mobile continuity of the outlines of things" (IM 52).

Because mathematics is only the science of magnitudes, and its processes are applicable only to quantities, it would seem that it is confined to solely characterizing the outline of things. However, drawing upon the point of view of mechanical explanation as a method rather than as a doctrine, Bergson argues to the contrary that "it must not be forgotten that quantity is always quality in a nascent state" (IM 52). Indeed he maintains that, insofar as quantity is derived from the quality of sensation, "it is . . . the limiting case of quality" (IM 52).

The definitive statement that clearly articulates Bergson's intentions with regard to the role of the mathematics that inspired the idea of the differential in his philosophy is presented in the concluding statement to this discussion of modern mathematics in *An Introduction to Metaphysics* (1999a): "It is natural, then, that metaphysics should adopt the generative idea of our mathematics in order to extend it to all qualities; that is, to reality in general" (IM 52–3). Here, Bergson claims that the metaphysics of "reality in general" and of the relation between all the qualities of which it is composed should be modeled on the generative idea of the mathematics of the differential calculus. This is an understanding of mathematics that is different to that held by the proponents of radical mechanism. It is a mathematics understood from the point of view of mechanical explanation as a method, rather than as a doctrine.

Bergson is quick again to point out that what he is advocating here is not a "universal mathematics," the kind proffered by proponents of radical mechanism, which considers the past and future to be calculable functions of the present. He considers this "dream" to be "a survival of Platonism" (IM 58). The kind of problem solving that Bergson is proposing here is much more contingent than that proffered by a universal mathematics. Rather than thinking of the world from the point of view of pure or radical mechanism as given all at once for all eternity, the sole problem from this point of view being that of adequately grasping this eternity, Bergson maintains that

> in reality we are obliged to consider problems one by one, in terms which are, for that very reason, provisional, so that the solution of each problem will have to be corrected indefinitely by the solution that will be given to the problems that will follow: thus, science as a whole is relative to the particular order in which the problems happen to have been put. (CE 218–19)

This approach to problems is consistent with that followed by the approach to mechanistic explanation as a method.

What distinguishes the point of view of mechanical explanation as a method from the point of view of radical mechanism is that the former "will at least have begun by getting into contact with the continuity and mobility of the real, just where this contact can be most marvelously utilized" (IM 53). Bergson argues that this approach "will have seen with greater clearness what the mathematical processes borrow from concrete reality," (IM 53) that is, how mathematical processes function as models for an understanding of concrete reality, rather than the processes of mathematics providing a complete and exhaustive explanation of them. And this approach to mathematical explanation will engage with problems as they arise, looking to mathematics for more adequate models, rather than retreating from concrete reality solely into the abstract deliberations of the discipline of mathematics itself.

Bergson's concluding statement about the role of mathematics in his work makes explicit reference to the problem of integration as a process of summation in the form of a series, which Poincaré refers to as qualitative differentiation. Reflecting upon the framework that he has established to distinguish between dogmatic pure or radical mechanical explanation as a doctrine and mechanical explanation as a method, Bergson says the following:

> Having then discounted beforehand what is too modest, and at the same time too ambitious, in the following formula, we may say that *the object of metaphysics is to perform* qualitative *differentiations and integrations.* (IM 53)

Bergson here explicitly correlates the object of metaphysics with the mathematical procedures that are the instrument of mechanical explanation as a method.

Bergson therefore moves between, on the one hand, his aim of overturning a dogmatic tendency in nineteenth century science, which he characterizes as radical or pure mechanism, and on the other hand, using recent developments in science, and the mathematics which is its instrument, to characterize what he refers to as "the mechanics of transformation" (CE 34). Despite what appear to be arguments to the contrary—but which are quite specifically arguments against "radical" or "pure" mechanism, rather than against mechanistic explanation when understood as a method—Bergson does quite explicitly draw upon mathematical models to characterize the theory of the vitality of life that he is proposing.

Bergson's problem with the cinematographical method overcome

The reason that Bergson gives for what he refers to as a "choice" on the part of "the new science" for radical mechanism, as opposed to the more epistemically modest approach, is that the mind has a tendency to follow what he refers to as "the cinematographical method" (CE 323). Bergson has already characterized perception as involving causal judgments about unextended sensations, and claimed that this is the origin of extensive magnitudes. The primary function of perception is precisely to grasp a series of qualitative changes; however, perception "only manages to solidify the fluid continuity of the real into discontinuous images," which provides "only a snapshot view of a transition" (CE 319). Because of this, Bergson concludes that "the mechanism of our ordinary knowledge is of a cinematographical kind" (CE 323). The "choice" that he ascribes to science, understood from the point of view of radical mechanism, is that it settled for explanations that operate solely at the level of "ordinary knowledge" (CE 323) and that it did so because the cinematographical method, which is the mechanism of this kind of knowledge, is "a method so natural to our intellect, and so well adjusted also to the requirements of our science" (CE 366). Science, so conceived, he concludes, "must" therefore "proceed after the cinematographical method" (CE 366). Bergson goes on to claim that this provides two reasons to renounce it as speculatively impotent. First, by virtue of this choice, it is constrained to working with problems posed by ordinary knowledge and the cinematographic constraints that this poses on an account of perception, and, second, it is constrained to working within the limits of ordinary knowledge, and thus of finding solutions that are compatible with it.

Bergson is critical of all attempts to characterize movement solely in terms of the space traversed by an object, i.e. by adding together instantaneous immobile sections within the framework of an abstract time. In addition to the procedures of radical mechanism, Bergson is also critical of the new art form of the cinema, which he condemns as one of these illusory attempts because he considers it to present immobile images of movement. Indeed Bergson considers the cinema to be the technological apotheosis of this illusion, which he therefore dubs the cinematographical method. While being sympathetic to much of Bergson's work, Deleuze goes to great lengths to defend the cinema from being characterized in this way. He argues that Bergson doesn't recognize the novelty of this art form. Rather than considering cinema to be just "the perfected apparatus of the oldest illusion," Deleuze maintains that it is possible to understand the cinema as being characteristic of "the new reality" (CI 8) that Bergson is attempting to describe. Deleuze does concede that the history of the cinema includes some more or less primitive states of development, and that it is at these primitive states that Bergson's critique was directed (See CI 24). However, rather than solely considering what happens in the apparatus itself, which was the focus of Bergson's critique—the camera apparatus simply recomposes movement with the procession of images as instantaneous immobile sections—Deleuze argues that the apparatus of the cinema is eminently capable of characterizing movement between these sections. This can be effected in two ways, either by "the movement of the camera, or by the editing of the stills" (Sem. 12 Apr 1983). Each of these techniques "relates the objects or parts to the duration of a whole which changes, and thus expresses the changing of the whole in relation to the objects" (CI 11). The example that Deleuze gives is "when the camera leaves a character, and even turns its back on him, following its own movement at the end of which it will rediscover him" (CI 23). Deleuze argues that "the cinematographic image does this, but Bergson didn't know this, he couldn't know this" (Sem. 12 Apr 1983) because cinema as an art form was still in its early stages of development. Deleuze therefore characterizes the cinematographic image as "itself a *mobile section* of duration" (CI 11). This move on Deleuze's part to disburden the cinema of the accusation of being the perfected apparatus of this illusion in no way diminishes the strength of Bergson's arguments against the dogmatic tendency in science to mechanical explanation as a doctrine, i.e. to pure or radical mechanism.

The Riemannian concept of multiplicity and the Dedekind cut

In addition to the explicit role played by the infinitesimal calculus in Bergson's philosophy, there are two other examples in his work where he implicitly draws upon particular mathematical developments to characterize the continuity of duration that I'd like to draw attention to. Neither of these is directly acknowledged by Bergson;

however, by virtue of the terminology used when describing these examples, it is readily discernable that they are drawn from recent developments in mathematics that Bergson would have been aware of to some degree. The specific developments that Bergson implicitly draws upon are the concept of multiplicity developed by Bernhard Riemann (b. 1826–1866) in 1854, published in 1868 (Riemann 1963), and the idea of the Dedekind cut advanced by Richard Dedekind (b. 1831–1916) in 1872 (Dedekind 1963).

Before giving an account of the importance of Riemann's work on multiplicity to Bergson's concept of duration, which I foreshadowed above, I'd first like to briefly characterize the importance of the idea of the Dedekind cut to Bergson's ontology. The Dedekind cut demonstrates how the real numbers can be constructed from the rational numbers. It resolves the apparent contradiction between the continuous nature of the number line and the discrete nature of the numbers themselves by combining an arithmetic formulation of the idea of continuity with a rigorous distinction between rational numbers—such as m/n—and irrational numbers, which can't be expressed in a ratio—such as π, e, and $\sqrt{2}$. The idea of the Dedekind cut is rooted in Euclidean geometry and characterizes the point at which two straight lines, one of which is the real number line, cross, or "cut," one another. At that one point on the number line, if there is no rational number, then an irrational number is constructed. Wherever a cut occurs on the number line that is not a rational number, an irrational number is constructed. The result is that a real number, whether rational or irrational, is constructed at every point on the number line. The Dedekind cut therefore proves the completeness or continuity of the real number line.

Bergson employs the imagery of the Dedekind cut to characterize the way that extensive magnitudes or objects are extracted from the dynamic flux of experience which, he argues, is in constant change. In CE, Bergson speaks of "objects cut out by our perception" (CE 12) and claims that "Things are constituted by the instantaneous cut which the understanding practices, at a given moment, on a flux of this kind" (CE 262). In *The Creative Mind*, he maintains that "For intuition the essential is change: as for the thing, as intelligence understands it, it is a cutting which has been made out of the becoming and set up by our mind as a substitute for the whole" (CM 39). Just as the cut is constitutive of a real number on the number line in mathematics, so too is the cut constitutive of an extensive magnitude in perception in relation to the continuous dynamic flux of experience.

One of the novel moves that Bergson makes in his work is to characterize the opposition between a philosophical conception of duration and a scientific conception of space in terms of two different kinds of multiplicity. The concept of multiplicity does not correspond to one of the terms of the One-Multiple couple. Indeed, Deleuze argues that Bergson's use of the concept of multiplicity "exposes the traditional theme of the one and the multiple as a false problem" (B 110). Deleuze argues that "In fact for Bergson it is not a question of opposing the Multiple to the One but, on the contrary, of distinguishing two types of multiplicity" (B 39). If Deleuze's hypothesis that Bergson was "aware of Riemann's general problems" is taken seriously, then the question of how closely the concept of multiplicity that appears in Bergson's work correlates with that developed by Riemann arises. In order to be able to address this question, what I propose to do is to provide an account of Riemann's mathematical concept of multiplicity, and then to demonstrate to what degree Bergson's concept can be understood to be drawn from it and to characterize those points where Bergson's concept can be understood to depart from the Riemannian concept.

In his *Habilitationsvortrag* (Riemann 1963), written on the suggestion of his supervisor Carl Friedrich Gauss (b. 1777–1855), Riemann distinguishes between two concepts of magnitude according to whether or not a "continuous path" exists from one of the magnitudes in question to another. If there is a "continuous path," the magnitudes are called "points" and form a "continuous manifold" or multiplicity. Whereas if there is n't a "continuous path," the magnitudes are called "elements" and form a "discrete manifold" or multiplicity. In order to get an idea of what Riemann has in mind by a "continuous path" between two points, the example of the Dedekind cut can be used. If each real number on the real number line is created by a Dedekind cut, the path between any two real numbers, or "points," determined by such a cut will have a continuous segment of the real number line, which is itself continuous, between them. Riemann refers to the magnitudes that comprise a continuous multiplicity as "points" because, as with Dedekind cuts, the points qua points appear solely in relation to some continuous ambient background, whether actual or implied, such as a line or a plane.[5] One of the examples that Riemann gives of the "points" of a "continuous manifold" or multiplicity "are the positions of perceived objects," which he refers to as "a multiply extended manifoldness" (Riemann 1963, 1.1).

A discrete manifold is composed of single isolated elements. The principle of its metrical relations is determined by the number of elements belonging to it, i.e. it is determined "a priori, as a consequence of the concept of number" (Weyl 1921, 98). In other words, the elements of a discrete manifold are compared to one another with regard to quantity by "counting." In the case of the points of a continuous manifold, they are compared to one another with regard to quantity by measuring. That is, the principle of the metrical relations of a continuous manifold is determined by a measure relation. The measure of the points of a continuous manifold consists in the superposition of the magnitudes to be compared either by using one magnitude as the standard for the other, or, when one magnitude is a part of the other, by determining solely whether it is "more or less than the other and not the how much" (Riemann 1963, 1.1), i.e. not by how much. Such magnitudes are not regarded as existing independently of position nor as expressible in terms of a unit, but rather as "regions in a manifoldness" or multiplicity (Riemann 1963, 1.1). Riemann characterizes the nature of these regions in a continuous manifold or multiplicity by drawing upon the work of Gauss in differential geometry concerned with the curvature of surfaces in three-dimensional Euclidean space. Gauss showed that curvature is an intrinsic property of a surface that depends solely on how distances are measured on the surface itself rather than on the particular way in which the surface is embedded in space. Gauss's "Theorema Egregium" states that the Gaussian curvature of a surface embedded in three-dimensional space may be understood intrinsically to that surface. The Gaussian curvature can be determined by measuring how the arc lengths of small circles on the surface differ to what they would be on a flat surface or plane. If the arc length on the surface is smaller than it would be on a plane, then the surface is positively curved, if it is larger then the surface is negatively curved, and if it is the same then the surface has zero curvature. Riemann generalizes Gauss's work on the differential geometry of surfaces into higher-dimensions by developing the idea of the curvature tensor of a space of three or more dimensions. The curvature tensor is a collection of numbers at every point of the space that describe how much the space is curved. Euclidean geometry, which investigates the straight line and the plane, doesn't hold in higher dimensions because of the different nature of the spaces being dealt with, i.e. the spaces are not necessarily flat. Riemannian "space has a definite curvature at every point in the normal direction of every surface," whereas "the characteristic of Euclidean space is that its curvature is nil at every point and in every direction" (Weyl 1921, 96). Euclidean space is therefore homogenous, whereas Riemannian space, by virtue of having a definite and potentially different curvature at any point, is on the contrary devoid of any kind of homogeneity.

   While Euclidean "finite" geometry holds for three-dimensional linear point-configurations, curved three-dimensional spaces, for example, require a different approach. What Riemann did was to extend Euclidean geometry to spaces that are not necessarily flat. He does this on the premise that these spaces still resemble Euclidean space in the infinitesimal neighborhood of each point. By considering the infinitesimal neighborhood around each point as a small bit of Euclidean space, the entire space can then be constructed by the step by step juxtaposition, or accumulation, of these infinitesimal neighborhoods. In addition, there is no restriction on how connections are made from one neighborhood to the next. Deleuze argues that "It is therefore possible to define this multiplicity . . . in terms of the conditions of frequency, or rather accumulation, of a set of neighborhoods" (TP 485). The resulting Riemannian space can be defined as an assemblage of local spaces, each of which can be mapped onto a flat Euclidean space, without this determining the structure of the manifold or multiplicity as a whole. Riemann's geometry is therefore Euclidean geometry formulated to meet the requirements of continuity. By virtue of this formulation, Riemann's geometry is inclusive of and much more general in character than Euclidean geometry. With the move from Euclidean "finite" geometry to Riemannian "infinitesimal" or differential geometry, Riemann provides what Weyl describes as "a true geometry, a doctrine of space itself and not merely . . . a doctrine of the configurations that are possible in space" (Weyl 1921, 102). Rather than operating solely according to a geometry of local spaces, as Euclidean geometry does, Riemannian geometry operates according to a conception of space that is global, and this global Riemannian space is constituted by an assemblage of local spaces. Lautman describes the most general Riemann space "as an amorphous collection of juxtaposed pieces that aren't attached to one another" (Lautman 2011, 98). Deleuze describes it as "pure patchwork" (TP 485). It is these characteristics that give a Riemannian space heterogeneity; each piece of the patchwork, each local Euclidean space, while being continuous globally, is locally discrete and therefore heterogeneous.

   In the final section of his *Habilitationsvortrag*, Riemann reflects upon the limitations of the nature of the continuous manifolds or multiplicities that he has described in contrast to those of discrete manifolds or multiplicities. What is at stake in this contrast is the development of a definition of space in terms of a continuous manifold or multiplicity, rather than in terms of Euclidean geometry. Riemann writes that:

The question of the validity of the hypotheses of geometry in the infinitely small is bound up with the question of the ground of the metric relations of space. In . . . a discrete manifoldness, the ground of its metric relations is given in the notion of it, while in a continuous manifoldness, this ground must come from outside. Either therefore the reality which underlies space must form a discrete manifoldness, or we must seek the ground of its metric relations outside it, in binding forces which act upon it. (Riemann 1963, III.3)

If the reality which underlies space forms a discrete manifold or multiplicity, then this reality would be bound by a Euclidean concept of geometry and the three dimensional concept of space that it implies. At the time this was the orthodox view, and this is the view that Bergson was mobilizing against. The other option would be to consider the reality which underlies space as forming a continuous manifold or multiplicity. If this were the case, then the ground of the metrical relations of space would not be given in the notion of the manifold or multiplicity, but must rather be sought "outside it, in binding forces which act upon it" (Riemann 1963, III.3).

Riemann doesn't provide any further reflections as to the nature of these binding forces. Indeed, it is generally accepted that a solution wasn't provided until Albert Einstein developed his theory of gravitation. Einstein affirmed that the ground of the metric relations of space, considered as a continuous manifold or multiplicity, is to be found in the binding forces of gravitation.[6] According to Einstein's theory of general relativity, the laws according to which the metrical structure of space is determined, where space is considered as a continuous manifold or multiplicity, are the laws of gravitation. While Einstein is generally considered to be the first to grasp the full purport of Riemann's ideas, it is little remarked upon that Bergson was also responding to the open ended nature of this passage in Riemann, and that Bergson also proposes a solution to the question of the binding forces which act upon and provide the ground of the metrical relations of a continuous multiplicity. Rather than settling for a solution in a theory of gravity, Bergson goes further to propose a theory of duration as a more general solution. This represents a considerable shift in focus on the Riemannian distinction to that utilized by Einstein. Bergson considers continuous multiplicities to belong essentially to the sphere of duration, and his project was to bring "a 'precision' as great as that of science" (B 40) to the multiplicity proper to duration. With this shift, Bergson gives the notion of multiplicity a "renewed range and distinction" (B 40).

In *Duration and Simultaneity*, Bergson is generally understood to have been refuting Einstein on special relativity; however, by introducing the concept of duration he should in addition be understood to have been attempting to give the theory of general relativity and the multiplicities that it entails the metaphysics it lacked. For Bergson, science "demands a metaphysics without which it would remain abstract, deprived of meaning or intuition" (B 116). Deleuze argues that "Scientific hypothesis and metaphysical thesis are constantly combined in Bergson in the reconstitution of complete experience" (B 118). What Bergson is critical of in Einstein's work is that the two types of multiplicity, as Bergson understands them, have been confused. While the theory of general relativity represents a new abstract way of spatializing time, Bergson argues that the kind of abstract specialized time represented in the theory of general relativity is a composite of space and duration, i.e. of an actual spatial multiplicity and of a virtual temporal multiplicity. To the degree that this theory, as a composite, is the product of the failure to adequately reflect upon duration, which Bergson maintains is one of its components, it is a poorly analyzed composite. According to Bergson, experience is given to us as composite mixtures, and composite mixtures unite their different components in conditions such that the differences between the two cannot be grasped in the composite. In composites, continuous multiplicity is reduced to, or confused with, discrete multiplicity. While this is the rubric for Bergson's criticism of the dogmatism of radical mechanism, it is also applicable to Einstein's theory of general relativity as it too, in Bergson's eyes, is the product of the failure to adequately reflect upon duration as one of its components, and therefore risks being understood not as a general rule of method, but rather as a fundamental law of things or doctrine.

Bergson provides what he considers to be an adequate analysis of this composite by decomposing it into an actual spatial multiplicity that is numerical and discrete, and a virtual temporal multiplicity that is qualitative and continuous. The principle of the metrical relation of a discrete multiplicity is determined by the elements belonging to it and the numerical relations between those elements. As demonstrated above, the curvature of all of the points of a three-dimensional Euclidean space is nil in every direction. Euclidean space is therefore homogenous and is able to be mapped numerically with Cartesian coordinates, such that a finite geometry holds for all three-dimensional linear point configurations or shapes. Discrete multiplicities such as three-dimensional Euclidean space are therefore numerical, and because number "is the model of that which divides without changing in kind" (B 41), discrete multiplicities have only differences in degree. While discrete multiplicities therefore divide without changing in kind, a continuous multiplicity "does not divide without changing in kind, in fact it changes in kind in the process of being divided" (B 42). It is for this reason that it is a nonnumerical multiplicity. When a division is made in a continuous multiplicity, the nature of the measure relations between its magnitudes changes. This is because the magnitudes of a continuous multiplicity are only themselves determined when the measure relations in which that magnitude is itself implicated are determined. There is therefore always a change in kind of a continuous multiplicity in the process of dividing or separating out any of the magnitudes of which it is constituted. This holds for global Riemannian spaces. A global Riemannian space is a continuous multiplicity that has a definite curvature at every point and is therefore heterogeneous. It is constituted by an assemblage of local spaces, each of which can be mapped onto a flat three-dimensional Euclidean space. Each local space, as a magnitude of a continuous multiplicity, is only able to be determined in relation to, divided, or separated out from the whole global Riemannian space. Each local space is heterogeneous to the global space from which it is divided and to the other local spaces that are able to be divided from the global space. There is therefore always a change in kind of the global space in the process of dividing or separating out any of the local spaces of which it is constituted.

This can be illustrated in relation to Bergson's concept of duration, which he defines as virtual or continuous multiplicity. The divisions that occur in a qualitative multiplicity are characteristic of the divisions that occur when a virtual memory is isolated from the totality of ones memories of the past, which is then able to be actualized by means of the perception that attracts it as a present perception. When the process of isolation occurs, the nature of the totality of memories of the past changes relative to the virtual memory that is isolated from it. Each time this occurs, each virtual memory, and the totality of memories of the past from which it is isolated, and which are condensed and contracted in it, is heterogeneous to the next. There is therefore a difference in kind between them. So the process of dividing or separating out any of the magnitudes of which duration is constituted always involves a change in kind.

While at first glance this appears to correlate quite closely with the Riemannian account, however, upon closer inspection it is apparent that what Bergson leaves out of his account is the very spatial nature of Riemann's qualitative multiplicity. The more general solution that Bergson offers to the question of the ground of the metrical relations of space posed by Riemann, more general than Einstein's theory of gravity, is his theory of duration, which for Bergson is "purely temporal" (B 43).[7] Bergson's agenda of decomposing the composite mixture of space and time that he sees as operating in Einstein's response to Riemann means that he is intent on dividing the composite into duration, on the one hand, which is pure, and space, on the other hand, which is an impurity that denatures it. (See B 38) Despite drawing upon Riemann's account of qualitative multiplicity as a model for his concept of duration, Bergson fails to appreciate the implications of Riemann's work for reassessing the concept of space. Instead, Bergson continues to characterize space as a form of exteriority along Kantian lines, rather than as being based on things and on the relations between things as Gauss and Riemann demonstrated. This is one of the shortcomings of Bergson's work that Deleuze undertakes to redress in his engagement with it.

Deleuze's rehabilitation and extension of Bergson's project

Deleuze characterizes his engagement with Bergson not simply as a "return to Bergson," but rather as "an extension of his project today . . . in parallel with the transformations of science" (B 115). While Deleuze makes explicit reference to molecular biology of the brain as one potential area for continuing Bergson's project today, my focus here will be on the mathematical developments that Deleuze rehabilitates in relation to Bergson's work and the subsequent developments in mathematics that Deleuze draws upon to extend the Bergsonian project in the context of his own project of constructing a philosophy of difference.

Deleuze is quite aware of the significance of Riemann's work for reassessing the question of space on new foundations, (B 49) and he undertakes to rehabilitate Bergson's work with this in mind. Distancing himself from Bergson's intent to read duration as purely temporal, Deleuze argues that "Bergsonian duration is, in the final analysis, defined less by succession than by coexistence" (B 60). That is, duration, as Deleuze understands it, is defined less by time, as Bergson suggests, than by space, as suggested by Riemann's work on qualitative multiplicity. Deleuze recognizes that "the heart of Bergson's project is to think differences in kind independently of all forms of negation" (B 46), whether understood as simple limitation or as the negative of opposition. So, by rehabilitating Bergson's work with respect to its relation to Riemannian space, Deleuze is able to continue to develop this central problematic in relation to a number of key subsequent developments in mathematics.

Before discussing the importance of Riemann space for Deleuze's engagement with Bergson, I'd like to introduce another important development in mathematics by Riemann that Deleuze draws upon to rehabilitate and extend Bergson's project. The development in question is a Riemann surface, which is distinct from, although interestingly related to, a Riemann space. A Riemann surface is a mathematical object that has a surface-like configuration and can be referred to in two different ways. On the one hand, it is a one-dimensional complex manifold or multiplicity. What this means is that it is a topological space, at every point of which there is a neighborhood that is mappable onto the complex plane, i.e. it covers the complex plane with several, and in general infinitely many, "sheets," which can have very complicated structures and interconnections (Knopp 1996, 98–99). It is one-dimensional because the location of a point in the complex plane can be specified by a single complex number, which is denoted by $a + bi$, where $i^2 = -1$. Every complex number can be represented as a point in the complex plane. On the other hand, because a single complex number is composed of two real numbers, a and b, a Riemann surface can also be referred to as a two-dimensional real manifold or multiplicity, hence the term surface. In this respect, a "complex function" and a "real surface" can both refer to the same mathematical object, a Riemann surface (See Cohn 1967, 3–4). What Riemann imagines a Riemann surface to be is a two-dimensional real surface composed of different sheets that are mappable onto the complex plane. Riemann introduced these surfaces to try to make sense of "many-valued functions," such as the square root and the logarithm. Because these functions are many-valued, there is more than one way of defining them. Each possible definition is referred to as a branch of the function and is represented as a sheet mappable onto the complex plane. Riemann surfaces are constructed by combining the sheets of these different branches geometrically, i.e. by joining the sheets of the different branches of the function together, such that the sheet of one branch of the function joins continuously with that of another branch of the function, to obtain a geometric surface on which the function is well-defined and single valued. When represented in this way, the function appears to have many values at a single point. This is because there is no distinction between different points on the Riemann surface which project to the same point on the complex plane. This obviates the need to try to solve the function for different values at several points (See Knopp 1996, 99).

Riemann's intuitive cut-and-paste procedure for constructing Riemann surfaces was eventually given a rigorous formulation by Hermann Weyl, using topological techniques based upon Weierstrass's theory of analytic continuation by power series, which have been dealt with at length in Chapter 1 (Weyl 1913, 34). Rather than proceeding with Riemann's complicated superposition of sheets, Weyl appeals to the existence of a local uniformization in the neighborhood of each point on the surface, such that if the function of one of these points is an analytic function in the neighborhood of the point, then it can be represented in the form of a power series in the local uniformization (See Lautman 2011, 133–7).[8] Uniformization is concerned with obtaining a global representation of a Riemann surface by mapping it onto one of three domains: the Riemann sphere in spherical geometry, the complex plane in

Euclidean geometry, or the open unit disk in the complex plane in hyperbolic geometry. What this means is that Riemann surfaces are, respectively, either elliptic, parabolic, or hyperbolic. As it turns out, most of them are hyperbolic. Local uniformizations exist in the neighborhood of each point of a Riemann surface because of such a mapping procedure. Weyl considered Riemann surfaces to be constituted by the juxtaposition of neighborhoods in which such local uniformizations are defined. This is the connection that Weyl makes between Weierstrass's theory of analytic continuity and Riemann surfaces. In fact Weyl argues that "In the theory of uniformization the ideas of Weierstrass and of Riemann grow into a complete unity" (Weyl 1913, 159).[9]

Recall that an analytic function can be expanded in a convergent power series in any neighborhood that is contained in the domain of the function. If a power series expansion only represents the function in a neighborhood or circular part of its domain, then the goal of Weierstrass's principle of analytic continuity is to define the function in larger domains without losing the analytic character of the function. Weyl describes analytic continuity as follows: "if continuation along a given curve c is possible, then one can get from the initial element to the last element by a finite number of applications of immediate analytic continuation. If the continuation of the initial element along c is impossible, then there exists a definite point on the curve, the 'critical point,' at which the process finds its necessary end" (Weyl 1913, 3). It turns out that there is only one way for such a function to be defined. Weyl therefore presents Weierstrass's definition of an analytic function as "the totality G of all those function elements which can arise from a given function element by analytic continuation" (Weyl 1913, 4), whereby "function element" Weyl is referring to each of the power series expansions generated in the process of analytic continuity. Weyl then distinguishes between Weierstrass's concept of analytic function and that of analytic form. The concept of analytic form arises when one considers, in addition to the points at which the analytic function is regular, those "critical points" at which it has an infinite branch or pole. The analytic function and the analytic form therefore differ only insofar as, in addition to regular function elements, the latter includes these irregular function elements, and unlike the analytic functions, which can be extended to larger domains, the analytic form cannot be further extended.

"By the gradual reworking of Weierstrass's formulation" Weyl argues that "we will arrive at Riemann's formulation, in which the totality G of function elements, appear as uniform analytic functions . . . not in the complex plane but on a certain two-dimensional manifold, the so-called Riemann surface" (Weyl 1913, 4). The first step of this reworking that Weyl undertakes is to provide a description of how the Weierstrassian domain of analytic continuity, starting with points in three-dimensional space, is able to be mapped onto Riemann surfaces. The next step is to characterize the nature of the relation between Riemann surfaces and n-dimensional Riemann spaces, because the Riemann surfaces onto which Weierstrass's analytic forms are mapped are in n-dimensional space. He presents the scenario whereby "the Weierstrass function element plays the same role in function theory as the *point* plays" (Weyl 1913, 11) in regard to three-dimensional space in geometry. Initially, the function element can be considered to be analogous to the point, so that just as there is a concept of three-dimensional space of points, so too is there a concept of the "space (i.e. the totality) of function elements" (Weyl 1913, 11). And by extension, an "analytic chain of function elements," constructed by the process of analytic continuity, "corresponds exactly to a continuous curve in point space" (Weyl 1913, 11). However, because each function element is an infinitely expanding power series that depends on infinitely many continuous parameters, the space of a function element must be ascribed infinite dimension. The analogy here breaks down because "the space of function elements possesses a structure essentially different from that of the familiar three-dimensional space" (Weyl 1913, 11). The difference being that "the infinite dimensional space of function elements falls apart into infinitely many (two-dimensional) 'layers'" (Weyl 1913, 11). The concept of infinitely many two-dimensional "layers," "sheets," or "surfaces" can no longer be associated with points in three-dimensional space, but rather requires a much more general abstract idea. It is to Riemann that Weyl turns for this idea, more specifically to the concept of Riemann surfaces and their relation to Riemann space. Weyl argues that each analytic chain of function elements constitutes an individual layer, and that "these 'layers' are precisely the analytic forms" (Weyl 1913, 11). Weyl's approach was to regard each "layer," each analytic form, as a two-dimensional manifold or multiplicity, i.e. as a Riemann surface. Riemann surfaces "represent each function element of the analytic form by a single point of the surface so that the analytic chains of function elements appear as continuous curves on the surface" (Weyl 1913, 12).

Weyl concedes that "This formulation of the concept of a Riemann surface . . . is more general than the formulation which Riemann himself used in his fundamental work on the theory of analytic functions" (Weyl 1913, 33). However, he maintains "that the full simplicity and power of Riemann's ideas become apparent only with this general formulation" (Weyl 1913, 33), which was "first developed in intuitive form by F. Klein (1882)" (Weyl 1913, 33). The striking feature of Weyl's formulation is that he points to Riemann's work on n-dimensional multiplicities in differential geometry, defined in the infinitesimal neighborhood of each point, i.e. to Riemann space, as providing the inspiration and laying the foundations for the juxtaposition of neighborhoods in which local uniformizations are defined, and which constitute Weyl's general formulation of Riemann surfaces. While this comparison is only possible thanks to the new definition of a Riemann surface proposed by Weyl; Weyl does suggest that, for Riemann, the ideas developed in his *Habilitationsvortrag* were "closely related to his investigations in function theory" (Weyl 1913, 34). However, he maintains that there is nothing explicit in Riemann's writings to suggest that he had established the connection between the spaces that he introduced in geometry and the surfaces that he introduced in analysis.[10] One essential difference between Riemann spaces and Riemann surfaces is that Riemann spaces are defined in a purely local way by the formula that gives the distance between two infinitely near points, the entire space being constructed by the step by step juxtaposition of infinitesimal neighborhoods, whereas the principal characteristic of the Riemann surface of an algebraic form is to possess a global structure, by the global juxtaposition of neighborhoods in which local uniformizations are defined.

While the discussion so far has centered on the reformulation of Weierstrass's account of the generation of analytic functions by analytic continuity, up to and including the poles of the function, which are defined as analytic forms, Riemann surfaces are by no means solely restricted to the representation of the fruits of analytic continuity. Riemann surfaces can also be used, and in fact are primarily used, to represent meromorphic functions, which are generated by the discontinuous relation between the poles of two analytic forms in the same surface. Recall that a meromorphic function is determined by the quotient of two arbitrary analytic functions, or more specifically analytic forms, which have been determined independently on the same surface by the point-wise operations of Weierstrassian analysis. Such a function is defined by the differential relation:

$$\frac{dy}{dx} = \frac{Y}{X}$$

where X and Y are the polynomials, or power series of the two analytic forms.[11] In fact, Weyl goes so far as to say that "Weierstrass's concept of an analytic form . . . arises only when one combines two functions on one surface" (Weyl 1913, 43). Weyl argues that "With an analytic form we are given not merely a Riemann surface, but at the same time two functions . . . on the surface, regular except for poles" (Weyl 1913, 38), i.e. any analytic form implies the existence of another analytic form on the same surface. If two functions, F and G, are regular except for poles on a Riemann surface, then the meromorphic function of these two analytic forms is given by "the quotient F/G, since the quotient of the two power series . . . may be written as a power series" (Weyl 1913, 38). When expressed in this way, i.e. as the power series expansion of the quotient F/G, "the uniform functions, regular except for poles on a Riemann surface, will be called *meromorphic functions* or *'functions' on the surface*" (Weyl 1913, 43). The main reason Riemann surfaces are interesting is that meromorphic functions can be defined in terms of functions "on" Riemann surfaces. A function on a Riemann surface is therefore meromorphic if it is expressible locally as a ratio of analytic functions.

Recall that the representation of meromorphic functions posed a problem for Weierstrass, which he was unable to resolve, and that this remained a problem until Poincaré proposed "the qualitative theory of differential equations." According to Poincaré, the divergent branches of a power series expansion of a meromorphic function may furnish a useful approximation to a function if they can be said to represent the function asymptotically. However, this requires the determination of a new kind of singularity, an essential singularity, of which Poincaré distinguished four types: the saddle point; the node; the focus; and the center, and which he classified according to the topological behavior of the solution curves in the neighborhood of these points. Weyl's work means that the topological behavior of each of these solution curves is mappable onto a Riemann surface, i.e. that the solution curves of Poincaré's essential singularities are mappable onto Riemann surfaces.[12] The global topological structure of a Riemann surface confers on its analytic forms the cuts and the potential functions, discussed in Chapter 1, whose consideration is essential to the problem of the representation of the meromorphic function.

According to Weierstrass's algebraic function-theoretic point of view, "the analytic form . . . is described at each individual point by a particular representation" (Weyl 1913,

159), i.e. the power series expansion, such that explicit construction reigns. Whereas from the Riemannian point of view, which is "topological," a *global* representation of the whole form is obtained. According to this Riemannian point of view, which Weyl follows, "it is always the Riemann surface, not the analytic form, which is regarded as the given object" (Weyl 1913, 157). And, given an arbitrary Riemann surface, "the construction of an associated analytic form is a principal component of the problem to be solved" (Weyl 1913, 157–8). Weyl argues that "an arbitrary Riemann surface becomes an analytic form if we single out two functions . . . on it, regular except for poles" (Weyl 1913, 39). The main point of Riemann surfaces is that meromorphic functions can be defined "on" them. Riemann surfaces are nowadays considered the natural setting for studying the global behavior of these functions.

Weyl is important both for understanding what Bergson would not have been privy to about Riemann, and for understanding why and how Deleuze rehabilitates and extends Bergson's work by returning to the concept of space in Riemann. On the one hand, Weyl is important because there is no indication that Riemann connected the concept of Riemann space and Riemann surface in the way suggested by Weyl, and on the other hand, it is because Weyl sets up the relation between Poincaré's qualitative theory of differential equations and Riemann surfaces. Weyl is not unfamiliar with Bergson's work, indeed in *The Continuum* (1918), he credit's Bergson with having "pointed out forcefully this deep division between the world of mathematical concepts and the immediate experience of continuity of phenomenal time (*la durée*)" (Weyl 1918, 90). In fact Weyl goes on to argue that "The conceptual world of mathematics is so foreign to what the intuitive continuum presents to us that the demand for coincidence between the two must be dismissed as absurd. Nevertheless, those abstract schemata supplied by mathematics must underlie the exact sciences of domains of objects in which continua play a role" (Weyl 1918, 108). So Weyl endorses that aspect of Bergson's project that problematizes the dogmatic tendency to reduce the intuitive continuum to the mathematical in nineteenth century science, which Bergson characterizes as radical or pure mechanism. However, Weyl also recognizes the potential of Riemann's mathematics to give an account of continua in relation to objects within mathematics. It is precisely this relation within mathematics that Deleuze draws upon as a model for the relation between objects of sensation, or extensive magnitudes, and the continuity within which they are perceived. Far from reducing one to the other, Deleuze deploys Riemann's mathematics as a model in order to displace Bergson's concept of duration. Rather than duration, Deleuze deploys the full potential of a concept of the virtual modeled on Riemann space, where Riemann space is composed of sheets, each of which is a Riemann surface.

While Riemann surfaces provide a new way of conceiving the power series expansions of meromorphic functions, which are representations of essential singularities, Riemann space provides a new way of conceiving the relations between Riemann surfaces, or between the meromorphic functions and the essential singularities they represent. What is characterized in Duffy 2006a according to the logic of different/ *c*iation, as the actually infinitely composite multipli–differen*c*iated assemblage of global integrations, which is determined by both the differen*c*iations of the differen*t*iated and the differen*c*iations of the differen*c*iated,[13] can now be given its full mathematical treatment. Indeed, the resources are now available to provide a thorough account of the role of mathematics in Deleuze's work. The logic of differen*t*iation is characterized by Weierstrassian analytic continuity and the problem of the representation of meromorphic functions. The logic of differen*c*iation was initially characterized in Chapter 2 by Poincaré's qualitative theory of differential equations, which proposed the construction of essential singularities as a solution to the representation of the power series expansions of meromorphic functions. However, because of Weyl's work, these essential singularities and the power series expansions of the meromorphic functions that they represent can now be mapped onto Riemann surfaces. The logic of differen*c*iation, which involves generating differen*c*iations of the differen*t*iated, can now be understood to be about relations that generate Riemann surfaces. And, the differen*c*iations of the differen*c*iated, which, in Duffy 2006a, may have seemed to be more like speculative extrapolations on Deleuze's part, can now be understood mathematically to characterize relations between Riemann surfaces. Weyl understood these relations between Riemann surfaces to occur within the context of a Riemannian conception of space, i.e. a Riemann space.[14] Recall that there are no restrictions on how connections are made from one sheet of Riemann space, i.e. a Riemann surface, to the next. This mathematical model displaces Bergson's descriptions of duration in Deleuze's work.

In *Matter and Memory*, Bergson gives an account of duration by clarifying the distinction between recollection and perception using the figure of the inverted cone as a model, the apex of the cone being a specific recollection, and each of the horizontal sections of the cone being a different level or adjustment in the process of focusing the memory on or condensing it to a specific recollection. Each section is determined by a particular distribution of dominant recollections or "shining points" (MM 223) that order the relations between memories on that section. Once a specific recollection is isolated, it remains virtual as a memory; however, it can be actualized by means of the perception which attracts it and which serves as the principle that orders the memories in this conic arrangement. It is in this way that Bergson figures the past as a condition of the present, which then also anticipates the future. The past is a condition of the present insofar as the specific recollection, which is virtual, is actualized as a present perception. In this way, it is determined as an action or movement. The present anticipates the future insofar as it has the potential to become a dominant memory in ordering the past for future perceptions.

On Deleuze's model, utilizing Riemann space, each horizontal section of the cone is a Riemann surface, and the dominant recollections, or shining points, of each of these Riemann surfaces, is an essential singularity, which condenses the remarkable, distinctive, or singular points (See B 62; DR 212) of the analytic functions on that Riemann surface.[15] Each Riemann surface relates to the other Riemann surfaces not as different horizontal sections of a cone, but rather as different sheets of a Riemann space. The relations between Riemann surfaces in Riemann space are determined by the logic of differen*c*iation, according to which Riemann surfaces, as differen*c*iations, are further differen*c*iated in relation to one another generating differen*c*iations of the differen*c*iated.[16] These relations between Riemann surfaces are determined by the nature of the essential singularities of each surface and the relations between them.

While with Bergson, a specific recollection is isolated in relation to a present perception from a series of horizontal sections of past memories which are ordered according to the dominant memory of each section, with Deleuze, the Riemann surfaces are nested in relation to one another, according to the logic of differenciation, in terms of the relative dominance of the memory to which the essential singularity of each respective Riemann surface correlates. This relative order is determined with respect to the specific memory that is being isolated. And, just as with Bergson, this specific memory remains virtual until it is actualized by means of the perception that attracts it in a present perception. So the model of Riemann space that Deleuze uses to displace Bergson's concept of duration also models the virtual and the process of actualization.[17] Rather than the past being represented in the figure of a cone, for Deleuze the past, or the virtual, is much more a "patchwork" (TP 485) of sheets, or Riemann surfaces, and the dominant Riemann surface has the potential to be actualized in a present perception. This process of actualization can be of two different kinds. On the one hand, if what transpires is simply a rearrangement of the patchwork of surfaces, either in relation to one another or because different Riemann surfaces are put into relation with them, thus changing the patchwork assemblage specific to the dominant memory, then what is registered is a change understood as simple consequence or modification. However, on the other hand, if what has transpired is the result of a new configuration between different analytic functions, and a new essential singularity and therefore a new Riemann surface has been constructed, then what is registered is a change understood as innovation or novelty.[18]

A little caution is required when thinking through Deleuze's relation to Bergson in order to avoid reducing Deleuze to Bergson by emulating the distinction that Bergson imposed between duration and space. What I have tried to do in this chapter is negotiate the fine line between clarifying the role of mathematics in Bergson's work, isolating those aspects of it that are of interest to Deleuze, and indicating Bergson's shortcomings when it comes to realizing the full potential of these developments. Despite these shortcomings, Deleuze rehabilitates and extends Bergson's work by drawing upon the full potential of Riemann's concept of qualitative multiplicity in order to reconfigure the concept of space in a way that does all of the work required by Bergson's concept of duration. This model of Riemann space that Deleuze develops is now also available as a subsequent development in the history of mathematics that allows the developments in mathematics that Deleuze deploys in his reading of Kant and Maimon to be updated directly in relation to the work of Bergson. The concept of Riemann space, composed of Riemann surfaces that are the generalization of the representation of essential singularities, displaces the pure intuition of space in Kant and the infinite intellect in Maimon. It is therefore an instrumental concept in the development of Deleuze's post-Kantian philosophy, which is one of the features of his philosophy of difference. Chapter 2 can now be read retrospectively in accordance with this new mathematical generalization of essential singularities in Riemann surfaces, which are understood to be sheets of a Riemann space.[19]

The first stage of the development of the mathematical resources that Deleuze draws upon in his philosophy extends from Leibniz's concept of the infinitesimal, through Weierstrass's concept of analytic continuity, to Poincaré's qualitative theory of differential equations. The next stage, which neatly dovetails with the first[20] thanks to Weyl, includes both Riemann space and the Riemann surfaces of which it is composed. Together with the myriad of steps from one development to the next and from one stage to the next, which have been chartered in the chapters of this book, these are the mathematical resources that Deleuze draws upon in his project of constructing a philosophy of difference. Having provided an account of these mathematical resources and of how they operate in Deleuze's philosophy, what is now required is a more thorough account of the broader framework that Deleuze draws upon in order to adequately deploy these resources within his philosophy. This framework is drawn largely from the work of Albert Lautman, with a number of important qualifications, an account of Lautman's work and of Deleuze's engagement with it is the focus of the next chapter.

Lautman's Concept of the Mathematical Real

Albert Lautman (b. 1908–1944) was a philosopher of mathematics who postulated a conception of mathematics that is both formalist and structuralist in the Hilbertian sense. The reference to the axiomatic structuralism of Hilbert is foundational for Lautman, and it is because of this that his views on mathematical reality and on the philosophy of mathematics parted with the dominant tendencies of mathematical epistemology of the time. Lautman considered the role of philosophy, and of the philosopher, in relation to mathematics to be quite specific. He writes that "in the development of mathematics, a reality is asserted that mathematical philosophy has as a function to recognize and describe" (Lautman 2011, 87). He goes on to characterize this reality as an "ideal reality" that "governs" the development of mathematics. He maintains that "what mathematics leaves for the philosopher to hope for, is a truth which would appear in the harmony of its edifices, and in this field as in all others, the search for the primitive concepts must yield place to a synthetic study of the whole" (Lautman 2011, 87).

One of the challenges that Lautman set himself, but never carried through with, was the task of deploying the mathematical philosophy that he developed in other domains. The commentator that shows the most assiduity in his engagement with Lautman by taking up this challenge is Gilles Deleuze. The philosophy of mathematics that is drawn upon and that plays a significant role in Deleuze's philosophical project is that of Lautman. Indeed, the philosophical logic that Deleuze constructs as a part of his project of constructing a philosophy of difference retains certain aspects of the structure of Lautman's dialectics of mathematics. The aim of this chapter is to give an account of this Lautmanian dialectic, of how it operates in Lautman's work, and to characterize what Deleuze does to Lautman's dialectic when it is incorporated into his project of constructing a philosophy of difference.

Lautman's axiomatic structuralism

What is quite clear in Lautman's work is that he was not concerned with specific foundational questions in mathematics, neither with those relating to its origins, to its relationship to logic, or to the problem of foundations. What he is interested in rather is shifting the ground of this very problematic by presenting an account of the nature of mathematical problematics in general.

Lautman, along with Cavaillès, is one of the introducers of the German axiomatic into the French context that at the time was dominated by the "intuitionisms" of Poincaré, Borel, Baire, and Lebesgue (Petitot 1987, 83). The two main ideas that are foregrounded in his primary theses in the philosophy of mathematics (Lautman 1938a; 1938b) and which dominate the development of his subsequent work are "the concept of *mathematical structure* and the idea of the essential *unity* underlying the apparent multiplicity of diverse mathematical disciplines" (Dieudonné 1977, 16). It should be noted that, "in 1935, the concept of structure" in mathematics "had not yet been made completely explicit" (Dieudonné 1977, 16). Lautman's project is therefore novel. Lautman was inspired by the work of Hilbert on the axiomatic concept of mathematics to deploy the potential of an axiomatic-structuralism in mathematics. The essential point that motivated this move was Lautman's conviction "that a mathematical theory is predominantly occupied with the relations between the objects that it considers, more so than with the nature of those objects" (Dieudonné 1977, 16).

Lautman considers the understanding that there is "an independence of mathematical entities compared to the theories in which they are defined" (Lautman 2011, 186) to be steeped in the analysis and geometry of the nineteenth century. Lautman on the contrary championed the modern algebra, and maintains that "if classical mathematics was constructivist . . . modern algebra is on the contrary axiomatic" (Loi 1977, 13). The introduction of the axiomatic method[1] into mathematics means that there is an "essential dependence between the properties of a mathematical entity and the axiomatic of the domain to which it belongs" (Lautman 2011, 186). The isolation of "elementary mathematical facts" that would function as building blocks is ruled out. Lautman can therefore claim that "the problem of mathematical reality arises neither at the level of facts, nor at that of entities, but [rather] at that of theories" (Lautman 2011, 187). This, of course, is not to put mathematical facts per se into question. Lautman considered mathematics to be constituted like physics: "the facts to be explained were throughout history the paradoxes that the progress of reflection rendered intelligible by a constant renewal of the meaning of essential notions" (Lautman 2011, 88). Rather than being isolatable elementary objects, mathematical facts, such as the "irrational numbers, the infinitely small, continuous functions without derivatives, the transcendence of e and of π, and the transfinite," "were admitted by an incomprehensible necessity of fact before there was a deductive theory of them" (Lautman 2011, 88). He argues that mathematical and physical facts "are thus organized under the unity of the notion that generalizes them" (Lautman 2011, 184).

Lautman's "axiomatic structuralism" was the new mathematics that inspired the Bourbaki project which was influential in mathematics for a number of the decades that followed,[2] notably in the figure of Jean Dieudonné, who wrote the foreword to Lautman's collected works (Dieudonné 1977). The structuralist point of view has been so influential on the development of mathematics since 1940 that it has become rather commonplace.[3] However, this was not yet the case when Lautman was writing (Dieudonné 1977, 16).

The first move that Lautman makes to develop his structural conception of mathematics is against the logical positivism of the Vienna Circle logicists. Lautman considered their effort "to construct all mathematical notions from a small number of notions and from primitive logical propositions" to be in vain, because it loses sight of what he refers to as "the qualitative and integral character of the constituted theories" (Lautman 2011, 87). He argues that "it is impossible to consider a mathematical 'whole' as resulting from the juxtaposition of elements defined independently of any overall consideration relative to the structure of the whole in which these elements are integrated" (Lautman 2011, 108). For Lautman, this impoverishment of logical positivism is the consequence of its conception of mathematics in propositional terms, as "nothing more than a language that is indifferent to the content that it expresses" (Lautman 2011, 87).

Lautman also protests against the use made of Hilbert by the Vienna Circle logicists. Despite their claims to endorse the Hilbert program,[4] Lautman is critical of the logicist interpretation of the term "formalism," which he considers to be unrepresentative of Hilbert's thought (Lautman 2011, 17). While the logicists are deriving theorems in a formal system, such that the theorems are genetic or constitutive of the system, for Lautman, Hilbert is rather looking for theorems about formal systems, such as consistency or noncontradiction, completeness, decidability etc.[5] Rather than confounding mathematical philosophy with the study of the different logical formalisms, Lautman considered it necessary to try to characterize mathematical reality "from the point of view of its own structure" (Loi 1977, 9). Lautman considered this to be a more accurate characterization of Hilbert's metamathematical program, which, he argued, "internalized the epistemological problem of foundations by transforming it into a purely mathematical problem" (Petitot 1987, 98).[6]

Against the logicist interpretation of Hilbert's work Lautman argues that "Hilbert has replaced the method of genetic definitions with that of axiomatic definitions, and far from claiming to reconstruct the whole of mathematics from logic, introduced on the contrary, by passing from logic to arithmetic and from arithmetic to analysis, new variables and new axioms which extend each time the domain of consequences" (Lautman 2011, 89). The (Hilbertian) axiomatic structural conception of mathematics that Lautman mobilizes in his work is a nonconstructivist axiomatic, and he argues that "Mathematics thus presents itself as successive syntheses in which each step is irreducible to the previous step" (Lautman 2011, 89). He continues by making the important point, again drawn from Hilbert, that "a theory thus formalized is itself incapable of providing the proof of its internal coherence. It must be overlaid with a metamathematics that takes the formalized mathematics as an object and studies it from the dual point of view of consistency and completeness" (Lautman 2011, 89–90). This dual point of view distinguishes Lautman's concept of mathematics from the formalism of the logicists, which considered the study of mathematical reality to consist in solely the demonstration of the consistency of the axioms which define it. The consequence of this "duality of plans" that Hilbert establishes between "formalized mathematics and the metamathematic study of this formalism" is that while the formalism is governed by the concepts of "consistency and completeness," these concepts are not themselves defined by this formalism (Lautman 2011, 90). Hilbert expresses this governing role of metamathematical concepts over formalized mathematics when he writes that

> The axioms and provable theorems (i.e. the formulas that arise in this alternating game [namely formal deduction and the adjunction of new axioms]) are images of the thoughts that make up the usual procedure of traditional mathematics; but they are not themselves the truths in the absolute sense. Rather, the absolute truths are the insights (*Einsichten*) that my proof theory furnishes into the provability and the consistency of these formal systems. (Hilbert 1923; 1935, 180; Ewald 1996, 1138)

So, according to Lautman, the value of a mathematical theory is determined by "the metamathematical properties that its structure incarnates" (Lautman 2011, 90).

While Lautman took a position against the version of logicism and formalism proposed by the Vienna Circle, he also distances himself from the empirico-psychologising perspective of French mathematicians such as Brunschvicg. Brunschvicg developed "the idea that the objectivity of mathematics was the work of intelligence, in its effort to overcome the resistance that is opposed to it by the material on which it works" (Lautman 2011, 88). Brunschvicg goes so far as to maintain that "any effort of a priori deduction tends . . . to reverse the natural order of the mind in mathematical discovery" (Lautman 2011, 89).[7] While Lautman follows Brunschvicg in distrusting all attempts "to deduce the unity of mathematics starting from a small number of initial principles," including "the reduction of mathematics to logic" (Lautman 2011, 88), he doesn't endorse Brunschvicg's concept of mathematical philosophy "as a pure psychology of creative invention" (Lautman 2011, 89). For Lautman, the task of characterizing the mathematical real must be undertaken rather by mediating between these two extreme positions. By extracting the minimal elements of each, the "logical rigor" of the former and "the movement of the intelligence" of the latter (Lautman 2011, 89), Lautman proposes a third alternative characterization of the mathematical real that is both axiomatic-structural and dynamic, where the fixity or temporal independence of the logical concepts and the dynamism of the temporal development of mathematical theories are combined.

The metaphysics of logic: A philosophy of mathematical genesis

In order to do this, Lautman distinguishes two periods in mathematical logic, the first he characterizes as "the naive period," which goes from "the early work of Russell until 1929," which is the "date of the metamathematical work of Herbrand and Gödel." The latter marks the beginning of what Lautman calls "the critical period."[8] He characterizes the first period as "that where formalism and intuitionism are opposed in discussions that extend those raised by Cantor's theory of sets" (Lautman 2011, 141). These involved the criticism of classical analysis and the foundational disputes which were largely characterized by the dispute over the legitimacy of the actual infinite. While the formalists, as partisans of the actual infinite, claim the right to identify a mathematical object "as a result of its implicit definition by a system of non-contradictory axioms" (Lautman 2011, 141), the intuitionists, on the contrary, maintain that "asserting the possibility of an unrealizable operation," for example, "with regard to an object whose construction would require an infinite number of steps, or a theorem that is impossible to verify" because it relies on impredicative definitions,[9] "is to assert something which is either meaningless, or false, or at least unproven" (Lautman 2011, 141–2).

Lautman's interpretation of the unity of mathematics distinguishes him from the constructivist perspective of his French intuitionist contemporaries (including Brouwer) because Lautman considered the actual infinite to be legitimate in its algebraic-axiomatic presentation. And, contrary to the intuitionists and constructivists, Lautman grants to mathematical logic all the consideration which it deserves, i.e. Lautman accepts the logical principle of the excluded middle.[10] However, he maintains that "logic is not *a priori* in relation to mathematics but that for logic to exist a mathematics is necessary" (Lautman 2011, 109). He considered the simple idea that the logicists of the "naive period" had made of "an absolute and univocal anteriority of logic in relation to mathematics" to be "out-of-date" (Loi 1977, 13).

For Lautman, the philosophy of mathematics is not reducible to a secondary epistemological commentary on problematic logical foundations, nor to historical or *a fortiori* psychosociological research, nor to reflections on marginal movements such as intuitionism.[11] It is however precisely in the research of the critical period relating to the consistency of arithmetic that Lautman considers a new theory of the mathematical real to have been affirmed, one that is "as different from the logicism of the formalists as from the constructivism of the intuitionist" (Lautman 2011, 143). Lautman claims that between the naive and critical periods there is an "evolution internal to logic," and he sets himself the task of disengaging from this new mathematical real "a philosophy of mathematical genesis, whose scope goes far beyond the domain of logic" (Lautman 2011, 143).

While Hilbert's metamathematics proposes to examine mathematical theories from the point of view of the logical concepts of noncontradiction and completeness, Lautman notes that "this is only an ideal toward which the research is oriented, and it is known at what point this ideal currently appears difficult to attain" (Lautman 2011, 90). This is an implicit reference to Gödel's second incompleteness theorem which demonstrates that any consistent formal system cannot demonstrate its completeness by way of its own axioms. Lautman concludes from this that "Metamathematics can thus envisage the idea of certain perfect structures, possibly realizable by effective mathematical theories, and this independently of the fact of knowing whether theories making use of the properties in question exist" (Lautman 2011, 90). What we have with this conception of the mathematical real is that "the statement of a logical problem is possessed without any mathematical means to resolve it" (Lautman 2011, 90). What this means for Lautman is that the critical period marks the appearance of innovation in mathematics, not only at the level of results, but also at that of the problematic (Lautman 2011, 143). Lautman proposes to characterize the problematic "distinction between the position of a logical problem and its mathematical solution" (Lautman 2011, 91) by means of an "exposé" of what he calls "the metaphysics of logic"

(Lautman 2011, 141). This takes the form of "an introduction to a general theory of the connections which unite the structural considerations" of the critical axiomatic-structural conception of mathematics with the "assertions of existence" of a particular dynamic conception (Lautman 2011, 141). The particular dynamic conception of mathematics that Lautman deploys is further characterized when he qualifies his conception of the essential nature of mathematical truth as follows: "Any logical attempt that would profess to dominate *a priori* the development of mathematics therefore disregards the essential nature of mathematical truth, because it is connected to the creative activity of the mind, and participates in its temporal character" (Lautman 2011, 187). Lautman is careful here to point out that mathematical truth is only partially related to the creative activity of the mind of the mathematician. In order to distinguish his account of dynamism from Brunschvicg's Lautman considers it "necessary to grasp, beyond the temporal circumstances of a discovery, the ideal reality which is solely capable of giving its sense and value to the mathematical experience" (Cavaillès and Lautman 1946, 39). The lynchpin of this distinction is that Lautman conceives "this ideal reality as independent of the activity of the mind." For Lautman, the activity of the mind of the mathematician "only intervenes . . . once it is a matter of creating effective mathematics," i.e. effective mathematical theories (Cavaillès and Lautman 1946, 39). This ideal reality is constituted by what he refers to as "abstract Ideas." Lautman proposes to call the relation between the independent activity of the mind of the mathematician in the development of mathematical theories and the ideas of this ideal reality "dialectical," and he refers to these ideas as "dialectical Ideas" (Lautman 2011, 199). Lautman's principal thesis is that mathematics participates in a dialectic that governs it in an abstract way. He argues that the ideas "which seem to govern [*domines*] the movement of certain mathematical theories" (Lautman 2011, 91–2), and which are conceivable as independent of the mathematics, "are nevertheless not amenable to direct study" (Lautman 2011, 92). When Lautman maintains that they are conceivable as independent of the mathematics, he means of the mathematical theories themselves, but not of the mathematical real, of which they are a component. Lautman is working with a broader concept of mathematics, that of the mathematical real, which is greater than the sum of mathematical theories. He goes on to claim that it is these dialectical ideas that "confer on mathematics its eminent philosophical value" (Lautman 2011, 92). This is why Lautman considers mathematics, and especially "modern mathematics," and here Lautman is referring to the postcritical developments in algebra, group theory, and topology, to tell, "in addition to the constructions in which the mathematician is interested, another more hidden story made for the philosopher" (Lautman 2011, 91). The gist of the story is that there is a "dialectical action [that] is always at play in the background and it is towards its clarification" (Lautman 2011, 91) that Lautman directs his research. Lautman characterizes this dialectical action as follows: "Partial results, comparisons stopped midway, attempts that still resemble gropings, are organized under the unity of the same theme, and in their movement allow a connection to be seen which takes shape between certain abstract ideas, that we propose to call dialectical" (Lautman 2011, 91). Lautman argues that the nature of the mathematical real, and indeed the nature of physical reality, "its structure and the conditions of its genesis are only knowable by ascending to the Ideas" (Lautman 2011, 193).

Lautman's Platonism

This account of Ideas does commit Lautman to a version of Platonism. It is however a Platonism that is quite distinct from what is usually called "Platonism" in mathematics, which consists in rather the practice of summarily indicating with the name Platonism any mathematical philosophy for which the existence of a mathematical object is held as assured. Lautman considers this to be only one superficial understanding of Platonism (Lautman 2011, 190). Nor does he "understand by Ideas the models whose mathematical entities would merely be copies" (Lautman 2011, 199). Lautman is here opposed to the Platonism traditionally founded on a certain realm of ideas, which interprets mathematical theories as copies, reproductions, translations, or simple transpositions of eternal ideal models or forms. Instead he wants to "remove the idea of an irreducible distance between the 'eidos' and its representation to affirm the productive power of ideas which are incarnated in the theories."[12] What Lautman wants to do is restore to ideas what he considers to be "the true Platonic meaning of the term." The role Lautman assigns to mathematics is the result of a "Platonic interpretation." "'Platonism' in mathematics is usually understood to be a simple abbreviation for the realism of Plato's ideas applied to the existence of mathematical things, or objects. This meaning corresponds to the Platonic dualism popularized in the myth of the Cave: to the Visible world of bodies is superimposed the Intelligible world of ideas. But in the Analogy of the Line which precedes it, Plato makes a double division: . . . [the Line] is initially divided into the Intelligible and the Visible [or Ontological], then the superior segment of the understandable is subdivided in turn into the distinction between visible Forms, which include mathematical objects, and Forms themselves, which are the objects of the Dialectic or 'Ideas.'"[13]

Lautman's philosophy of mathematics embraces pure and applied mathematics in a unitary theory. Applied mathematics, which is occupied with the physical real, is deployed in the "Visible" or Ontological—one of the initial divisions of the line— whereas the treatment of pure mathematics requires the "Intelligible." The intelligible is then subdivided into the inferior segment, occupied by the visible Forms of mathematics, and the superior segment by the "ideas" of the Dialectic (See Dumoncel 2008, 200). A practicing geometer or mathematician, working with visible lines and figures, is thinking about the square itself and the diagonal itself, which are not visible. The visible forms with which he works are useful as images in coming to see truths about intelligible objects. One and the same thing (a visible triangle) can therefore serve both as an original in the visible or ontological division (when compared to its shadows and reflections—the inferior subdivision of the ontological) and as an image in the intelligible (when compared to the triangle itself, which is among the contents of knowledge/understanding). This is reflected in the two attitudes one can take to the numbers, lines, angles, and figures of the mathematician:

1. One is to take them as known, as starting-points or first principles, and to reason from them without ever examining them. This is what Plato considers to be the customary attitude, which involves reasoning from hypotheses to end-points or conclusions. But then what one is entitled to conclude can be only as clear as one's

hypotheses will allow. And since they are never themselves examined, this may leave room for unclarity or doubt.
2. The other attitude is to regard hypotheses not as starting-points, but as what they really are, things set down at the beginning of an inquiry to enable one to work one's way toward something else. This is what the dialectician does. He begins with hypotheses just as the geometer does, but by subjecting these hypotheses to dialectical examination he can work his way to a clearer grasp, of even the geometer's conclusions.

The practicing mathematician takes for granted the entities with which he works and gives no account of them, but treats them as starting-points; his state or condition is thought/reasoning (Plato 1997, 510C2–D3). He may deal with forms, e.g. the square itself or the diagonal itself. But he simply takes them for granted. It is with such an attitude in mind that, after describing the mathematical curriculum in Book VII of the Republic, Plato says that the mathematical sciences are evidently dreaming about reality. There's no chance of their having a conscious glimpse of reality as long as they refuse to disturb the things they take for granted and remain incapable of explaining them. Plato is concerned to stress that one must not rely on unexamined hypotheses, but must rather subject all one's hypotheses to dialectical scrutiny. The dialectician, as distinguished from the practicing scientist or mathematician, sees things holistically, and leaves no assumption unexamined. There is thus a difference in method and attitude between the dialectician and the mathematician; however, Plato insists that knowledge can be had of those things the practicing mathematician grasps by thought/reasoning. Plato goes so far as to suggest that by diligent use of dialectic, one can work one's way to what is unhypothesized, the starting-point for everything. Having got that far, one can draw conclusions, even mathematical and geometrical ones, without using anything perceptible at all, but simply "by means of forms alone, in and of themselves, and [ending] with forms" (Plato 1997, 511B8–C2, 511C8–D2).

It is important to note that Lautman's Platonism and the dialectic that he employs do not go this far. The most important point for Lautman is that Platonic ideas are by no means reducible to "universals." The Platonic idea is moreover an Archetype or Ideal, which makes them the touch stone for the selective function which is that of the Dialectic. Lautman wants to restore the Platonic understanding of these abstract dialectical ideas, not as universal Forms, but as "the structural schemas according to which effective theories are organized" (Lautman 2011, 199).[14] Lautman characterizes these structural schemas as establishing specific connections between contrary concepts such as local–global; intrinsic–extrinsic; essence–existence; continuous–discontinuous; and finite–infinite. Lautman provides many examples of these contrary concepts, including the introduction of analysis into arithmetic; of topology into the theory of functions; and the effect of the penetration of the structural and finitist methods of the algebra into the field of analysis and the debates about the continuum.[15]

The nature of mathematical reality for Lautman is therefore such that "mathematical theories . . . give substance to a dialectical ideal" (Lautman 2011, 240). This dialectic is constituted "by pairs of opposites" and the Ideas or structural schemas of this dialectic are presented in each case "as the problem of establishing connections between opposing notions" (Lautman 2011, 240), or concepts. Lautman makes a firm distinction between concepts and dialectical Ideas: the Ideas "consider possible relations between dialectical notions" (Lautman 2011, 204), or conceptual pairs,[16] and "these connections can only be made within the domains in which the dialectic is incarnated" (Lautman 2011, 240). What Lautman is proposing is a philosophical logic that considerably broadens the field and range of the metamathematics that he adopts from Hilbert. While metamathematics examines mathematical theories from the point of view of the concepts of noncontradiction and completeness, or consistency, Lautman argues that there are "other logical notions," or concepts, "equally likely to be potentially linked to one another within a mathematical theory" (Lautman 2011, 91). These other logical concepts are the conceptual pairs of the structural schemas,[17] and Lautman argues that, "contrary to the preceding cases (of non-contradiction and completeness)," each of which is bivalent, "the mathematical solutions to the problems" which these conceptual pairs pose can comprise "an infinity of degrees" (Lautman 2011, 91).

So, for Lautman, Ideas constitute, along with mathematical facts, objects and theories, a fourth point of view of the mathematical real. "Far from being opposed these four conceptions fit naturally together: the facts consist in the discovery of new entities, these entities are organized in theories, and the movement of these theories incarnates the schema of connections of certain Ideas" (Lautman 2011, 183). For this reason, the mathematical real depends not only on the base of mathematical facts but also on dialectical ideas that govern the mathematical theories in which they are actualized. Lautman thus reconsiders metamathematics in metaphysical terms, and postulates the metaphysical regulation of mathematics. However, he is not suggesting the application of metaphysics to mathematics. Mathematical philosophy such as that Lautman conceives does not consist "in finding a logical problem of classical metaphysics within a mathematical theory" (Lautman 2011, 189). Rather it is from the mathematical constitution of problems that it is necessary to turn to the metaphysical, i.e. to the dialectic, in order to give an account of the ideas which govern the mathematical theories. Lautman maintains that the philosophical meaning of mathematical thought appears in the incorporation of a metaphysics (or dialectic), of which mathematical theories are the necessary consequence. "We would like to have shown," he argues, "that this rapprochement of metaphysics and mathematics is not contingent but necessary" (Lautman 2011, 197). Lautman doesn't consider this to be "a diminution for mathematics," on the contrary "it confers on it an exemplary role" (Lautman 2011, 224).[18] Lautman's work can therefore be characterized as metaphysical, which, in the history of modern epistemology, characterizes it as "simultaneously original and solitary."[19]

Problematic ideas and the concept of genesis

A key point for Lautman is that dialectical ideas only exist insofar as incarnated in mathematical theories. Lautman insists on this point. He argues that "the reality inherent to mathematical theories comes to them from their participation in an ideal reality

that is dominating with respect to mathematics, but that is only knowable through it"
(Lautman 2011, 30). This is what distinguishes Lautman's conception from "a naive
subjective idealism" (Petitot 1987, 86). The dialectical ideas are therefore characterized
by Lautman as constituting a problematic.[20] He argues that "while the mathematical
relations describe connections existing in fact between distinct mathematical entities,
the Ideas of dialectical relations are not assertive of any connection whatsoever that
in fact exists between notions," or concepts (Lautman 2011, 204). They constitute
rather a problematic, i.e. they are "posed problems, relating to the connections that
are [only] likely to support certain dialectical notions" or concepts (Lautman 2011,
205). As such, they are characterized by Lautman as "transcendent (in the usual
sense) with respect to mathematics" (Lautman 2011, 205). The effective mathematical
theories are constructed in an effort to bring a response to the problem posed by these
connections, and Lautman interprets "the overall structure of these theories in terms
of immanence for the logical schemas of the solution sought after" (Lautman 2011,
205–6). That is, the conceptual pairs of the logical schemas "*are not anterior to their
realization within a theory*" (Lautman 2011, 188). They lack what Lautman calls "the
extra-mathematical intuition of the exigency of a logical problem" (Lautman 2011,
188–9). The fundamental consequence is that the constitution of new logical schemas
and problematic Ideas "*depend on the progress of mathematics itself*" (Lautman 2011,
189). Mathematical philosophy such as that Lautman conceives consists in "grasping
the structure of" a mathematical "theory globally in order to identify the logical
problem that" is mathematical and is "both defined and resolved by the very existence
of this theory" (Lautman 2011, 189). "An intimate link thus exists," for Lautman,
"between the transcendence of the Ideas and the immanence of the logical structure
of the solution to a dialectical problem within mathematics" (Lautman 2011, 206). It
is in direct relation to this link that Lautman characterizes the concept of "genesis"
(Lautman 2011, 206) that he considers to be operative in the relation between the
dialectic and mathematics. However, "the order implied by the concept of genesis is
not about the order of the logical reconstruction of mathematics" as undertaken by
the logicists. For the latter, the genetic definitions or initial axioms of a theory give rise
to "all the propositions of the theory" (Lautman 2011, 203). Whereas for Lautman,
although the dialectic is anterior to mathematics, it "is not part of mathematics," i.e.
the mathematical theories and its concepts "are without relationship to the primitive
notions," or concepts, "of a theory" (Lautman 2011, 204). Nor is the genesis conceived
in the Platonic sense as "the material creation of the concrete from the Idea," but rather
as what Lautman describes as the "advent of notions relative to the concrete within
an analysis of the Idea" (Lautman 2011, 200). Lautman defines the "anteriority of the
dialectic" as that of "the 'question' with respect to the response": "it is of the nature of
the response to be an answer to a question already posed . . . even if the idea of the
question comes to mind only after having seen the response" (Lautman 2011, 204).

The dialectic therefore functions by extracting logical problems from mathematical
theories. The apprehension of the conceptual pair, i.e. the logical schema of the
problematic Idea, only comes after having extracted the logical problem from the
mathematical theory. This is the basis for Lautman's understanding of the genesis
of concepts from the concrete that is operating in the dialectic. And, it is the logical

problem itself, rather than the problematic Idea, that directly drives the development of mathematics. The problematic idea governs the extraction process that deploys the logical problem in the further development of new mathematical theories. So for Lautman, "The philosopher has neither to extract the laws, nor to envisage a future evolution, his role only consists in becoming aware of the logical drama which is played out within the theories" (Lautman 2011, 189). This effort of understanding on the part of the philosopher that is "adequate to dialectical Ideas" is itself "creative of the system of more concrete notions," or concepts, where the connections between the concepts are defined (Lautman 2011, 200). The only "a priori element" that is able to be conceived "is given in the experience of the exigency of the problems," which is anterior not only to "the discovery of their solutions" (Lautman 2011, 189), but also to the extraction of the logical problem from the mathematical theory under scrutiny.

So there are dialectical Ideas which are referred to as "problematic" because they are solely presented as the problem of establishing the connections between conceptual pairs. This relation between conceptual pairs is only recognized as being characteristic of a mathematical theory after the logical problem, which is specific to the mathematical theory, has been extracted from it. So the starting point is with a mathematical theory, and the extraction of a logical problem from it leads to the retrospective recognition that the development of the mathematical theory was governed by the problematic relation between the relevant conceptual pairs, which is representative of a particular dialectical idea.

Heidegger and the naive period in the history of mathematical logic

Lautman suggests that the anteriority of the dialectic in relation to mathematics "is a matter of an 'ontological' anteriority, to use the words of Heidegger" (Lautman 2011, 204). Lautman describes this as a "transcendental conception of the relation of governing . . . between the dialectic and mathematics" (Lautman 2011, 200), by which he means mathematical theories, and he draws conceptual support for this by analogy with Heidegger, who, Lautman argues, "independently of any reference to mathematical philosophy, . . . presented analogous views to explain how the production of notions," or concepts, "relative to concrete existence arise from an effort to understand more abstract concepts" (Lautman 2011, 200).[21]

Lautman considers such an analysis to be "masked" in *Being and Time* (1962) by the importance that Heidegger places on "the existential considerations relating to being-in-the-world" (Lautman 2011, 201). However, he claims that "in the second part of *The Essence of Reason* (1969), Heidegger relies precisely on the distinction of the ontological point of view and ontical point of view to explain the link that exists between human reality and existence-in-the-world" (Lautman 2011, 201). Heidegger describes it as "a genesis of the ontical concept of the World from the idea of human reality" (Lautman 2011, 202).[22] Lautman maintains that the "primacy of the anthropological preoccupations" in Heidegger's philosophy "should not prevent his conception of the genesis of notions," or concepts, "relating to the Entity," or to what already exists, "from having a very general bearing", despite being almost exclusively deployed by Heidegger "within the analysis of Ideas relating to Being" (Lautman 2011, 202). Lautman notes that Heidegger himself applies this analysis "to physical concepts" such as "space, locus, time, movement, mass, force and velocity" (Lautman 2011, 202).[23] However, those "questions that do not come out of the anthropology . . . remain" for Heidegger "very brief" (Lautman 2011, 203). Despite this, Lautman considers it to be "possible, in the light of these conceptions of Heidegger, to see the utility of mathematical philosophy for metaphysics in general" (Lautman 2011, 203), a move that Heidegger himself is highly skeptical of. What is encouraging in this respect with Heidegger is that in *Being and Time*, he does not collapse mathematics completely into "the mathematical," or the "theoretical attitude" that Dasein adopts as a way of being that is ostensibly inauthentic (Heidegger 1962, 408–15. See Woodard 2006, 9). Neither does he do so in the much later work *The Question Concerning Technology* [1949] (1967), when he characterizes this attitude as "Enframing," or "the mode of ordering as standing-reserve" (Heidegger 1967, 20. See Woodard 2006, 14). Heidegger's objections against modern mathematics, together with his sporadic endorsements of the intuitionist rejoinders against the principle of the excluded middle, can be presented as targeting the formalism of the logicists (See Woodard 2006, 17). However, there is nothing to indicate that these Heideggerian comments deal with anything but what Lautman has characterized as the "naive period" in the history of mathematical logic.

Lautman does however acknowledge that "the restrictions and delimitations" in Heidegger"s text "should not be conceived as an impoverishment, but on the contrary as an enrichment of knowledge, due to the increase in precision and the certainty provided" (Lautman 2011, 205). What Lautman draws from Heidegger then is the understanding that "the constitution of the being of the entity, on the ontological plane, is inseparable from the determination, on the ontic plane, of the factual existence of a domain in which the objects of a scientific knowledge receive life and matter" (Lautman 2011, 201). So when he is referring to the governing role of the problematic ideas of the dialectic over the development of mathematical theories, Lautman claims that "It then happens to be once again exactly as in Heidegger's analysis, that the Ideas that constitute this problematic are characterized by an essential insufficiency, and it is yet once again in this effort to complete the understanding of the Idea, that more concrete notions are seen to appear relative to the entity, i.e. true mathematical theories" (Lautman 2011, 204). He also claims that, "As in the philosophy of Heidegger, in the philosophy of mathematics, as we conceive it, the rational activity of foundation can be seen transformed into the genesis of notions relating to the real" (Lautman 2011, 218).

Lautman here presents the structure of Heidegger's philosophy as providing an analogy for the structure of the mathematical real, without commitment to the question of fundamental ontology. Indeed Lautman's aim is to displace the question of fundamental ontology with a structural genetic approach to the mathematical real that serves as a model for developing an understanding of ontology in general.[24] Lautman's claim of the utility of mathematical philosophy for metaphysics, indeed of the necessity of bringing metaphysics and mathematics together, runs counter to the aesthetic move that Heidegger eventually makes against the risks posed by mathematics toward the poesis of the fine arts, specifically poetry. Lautman's approach can therefore be understood to be offering an alternative point of view that champions the utility of the mathematical real and thereby challenges Heidegger's turn away from mathematics.

The virtual in Lautman

The method that Lautman uses in his mathematical philosophy is "descriptive analysis." The particular mathematical theories that he deploys throughout his work constitute for him "a given" in which he endeavors "to identify the ideal reality with which this matter is involved" (Lautman 2011, 92). That is, Lautman starts with mathematical theories that are already in circulation. For example, he incorporates all the new work in algebraic topology of the German mathematicians Alexandroff, Hopf, and Weyl, and connects it to the work of Elie Cartan in complex analysis and to that of André Weil in what was then the emerging field of algebraic geometry (Barot 2003, 22). He is also one of the first to anticipate the philosophical interest in algebraic topology, a branch of mathematics that was then under development. In relation to these mathematical theories Lautman argues that while

> it is necessary that mathematics exists, as examples in which the ideal structure of the dialectic can be realized, it is not necessary that the examples which correspond to a particular dialectical structure are of a particular kind. What most often happens on the contrary is that the organizing power of a same structure is asserted in different theories; they then present the affinities of specific mathematical structures that reflect this common dialectical structure in which they participate. (Lautman 2011, 207)

One of the examples that is developed by Lautman is the operation of the local–global conceptual pair in the theory of the approximate representation of functions (Lautman 2011, 46, 60, 95–109). The "global conception" of the analytic function that one finds with Cauchy and Riemann (Lautman 2011, 95) is posed as a conceptual pair in relation to Weierstrass's approximation theorem, which is a local method of determining an analytic function in the neighborhood of a complex point by a power series expansion that, by a series of local operations, converges around this point (Lautman 2011, 105–6).

The same conceptual pair is illustrated in geometry (Lautman 2011, 95–9), by the connections between "topological properties and the differential properties of a surface," i.e. between the curvature of the former and the determination of second derivatives of the latter, both in the "metric formulation" of geometry in the work of Hopf (Lautman 2011, 95–8), and "in its topological formulation" in Weyl and Cartan's theory of closed groups (Lautman 2011, 98–9). Distinct mathematical theories can therefore be structured by the same conceptual pair.[25]

Lautman sees in the local–global conceptual pair the source of a dialectical movement in mathematics that produces new theories. He argues that "one can follow . . . the mechanism of this operation closely in which the analysis of Ideas is extended in effective creation, in which the virtual is transformed into the real" (Lautman 2011, 203). In the case of the Cauchy and Riemann–Weierstrass example, one of the new mathematical theories that was effectively created is Poincaré's qualitative theory of differential equations.[26]

According to Lautman, the problematic nature of the connections between conceptual pairs "can arise outside of any mathematics, but the effectuation of these connections is immediately mathematical theory" (Lautman 2011, 28). As a consequence, he maintains that "Mathematics thus plays with respect to the other domains of incarnation, physical reality, social reality, human reality, the role of model where the way that things come into existence is observed" (209) This is an important point for Deleuze which shapes his strategy of engagement with a range of discourses throughout his work. Lautman's final word on mathematical logic is that it "does not enjoy in this respect any special privilege. It is only one theory among others and the problems that it raises or that it solves are found almost identically elsewhere" (Lautman 2011, 28). Lautman maintains that "For the mathematician, it is in the choice of original definitions and judicious axioms that true invention resides. It is by the introduction of new concepts, much more than by transformations of symbols or blind handling of algorithms that mathematics has progressed and will progress" (Loi 1977, 12).

Deleuze and the calculus of problems

At the time, opinion among mathematicians and philosophers was largely unfavorable to Lautman. Mathematicians were at odds with what was for them his incomprehensible "philosophical speculation" and its "subtleties" (Petitot 1987, 99). While the philosophers reproached him for what they considered to be a certain inaccuracy in his use of the term "dialectical" (Lautman 2011, 28): was it Socratic, Kantian or Hegelian?[27] It wasn't for another 30 years before an adequate account of the dialectic proposed by Lautman was able to be given. This was done by Deleuze in his major work *Difference and Repetition*. Despite Deleuze's work, the confusion over the nature of the dialectic in Lautman remains pretty much intact, with quite recent commentators such as Jean Petitot—a French mathematician and philosopher of mathematics who, contrary to Lautman's peers, considers Lautman to be one of the most inspiring philosophers of the twentieth century (Petitot 1987, 80)—suggesting that the dialectic proposed by Lautman is a Hegelian one (Petitot 1987, 113).[28] It is only in recent work on Deleuze's engagement with mathematics that the significance of Lautman to the development of Deleuze's philosophy, and of Deleuze to the recent reception of Lautman's work, is being recognized.[29] Even Petitot proclaims that "with Ferdinand Gonseth and very recently Jean Largeault, Gilles Deleuze is one of the (too) rare philosophers to have recognized the importance of Lautman" (Petitot 1987, 87n14). Jean-Michel Salanskis acknowledges that it was Deleuze's *Difference and Repetition* that led him to read Lautman's work and to appreciate its significance to the subsequent developments in mathematics, in particular to the Bourbaki project.[30] And both Petitot and Salanskis draw attention to the "visionary and profound character of Deleuze's presentation of the notion of structural multiplicity" (Salanskis 1996, 64) in *Difference and Repetition*. (DR 182–84).

It is in the chapter of *Difference and Repetition* entitled "Ideas and the synthesis of difference" that Deleuze mobilizes mathematics to develop a "calculus of problems" (TP 570n61) that is based on Lautman's work.[31] Following Lautman's general theses, a problem has three aspects: its difference in kind from solutions, its transcendence in relation to the solutions that it engenders on the basis of its own determinant conditions, and its immanence in the solutions which cover it, the problem being the better resolved the more it is determined. Thus the ideal connections constitutive of the problematic (dialectical) idea are incarnated in the real solutions which are constituted by mathematical theories and carried over into problems in the form of solutions (DR 178–9). Deleuze explicates this process by referring to the operation of certain conceptual pairs in the field of contemporary mathematics: most notably the continuous and the discontinuous, the infinite and the finite, and the global and the local. The two mathematical theories that Deleuze draws upon for this purpose are the differential calculus and the theory of dynamical systems, and Galois' theory of polynomial equations. For the purposes of this chapter I will only treat the first of these,[32] which is based on the idea that the singularities of vector fields determine the local trajectories of solution curves, or their "topological behavior" (Salanskis 1998). These singularities can be described in terms of the given mathematical problematic, i.e. for example, how to solve two divergent series in the same field, and in terms of the solutions, as the trajectories of the solution curves to the problem. What actually counts as a solution to a problem is determined by the specific characteristics of the problem itself, typically by the singularities of this problem and the way in which they are distributed in a system (Salanskis 1998). Deleuze understands the differential calculus essentially as a "calculus of problems," and the theory of dynamical systems as the qualitative and topological theory of problems, which, when connected together, are determinative of the complex logic of differen*t*/*c*iation. (DR 209).[33] Deleuze develops the concept of a problematic idea from the differential calculus, and, following Lautman, considers the concept of genesis in mathematics to "play the role of model . . . with respect to all other domains of incarnation" (Lautman 2011, 209). While Lautman explicated the philosophical logic of the actualization of ideas within the framework of mathematics, Deleuze (along with Guattari) follows Lautman's suggestion and explicates the operation of this logic within the framework of a multiplicity of domains, including for example philosophy, science, and art in *What is Philosophy?* (1994), and the variety of domains which characterize the plateaus in *A Thousand Plateaus* (1987). While for Lautman, a mathematical problem is resolved by the development of a new mathematical theory, definition, or axiom, for Deleuze, it is the construction of a concept that offers a solution to a philosophical problem, even if our understanding of the genesis of this newly constructed concept is modeled on the Lautmanian account of the mathematical real.

One of the differences between Lautman and Deleuze is that while Lautman locates the ideas in a specifically Platonic and idealist perspective, the ideas that Deleuze refers to are not Platonic in any traditionally conceived way,[34] not even the softer version of Platonism that Lautman endorses, because of the presumed ontology of perceived things. Ideas for Deleuze are rather Kantian, or more specifically post-Kantian, and it is to Maimon's critique of Kant that one should look to characterize Deleuze's post-Kantianism, which, I have argued in Chapter 2, Deleuze updates by means of a number of subsequent developments in mathematics. It should now be clear that in doing so, Deleuze is drawing specifically on the work of Lautman.

Another difference that follows from the first is that Lautman's idealism is displaced in Deleuze's work by an understanding of the Lautmanian Idea as "purely" problematic, i.e. where the exigency is immanent to problems themselves. Deleuze shares the reservations expressed by Jean Cavaillès (b. 1903–1944) in regard to positing something beyond the exigency of the problems themselves. In a presentation to the *Société française de philosophie* in 1939, at which Lautman was also invited to speak, Cavaillès says that "Personally I am reluctant to posit something else that would govern the actual thinking of the mathematician, I see the exigency in the problems themselves. Perhaps this is what he calls the Dialectic that governs; if not I think that, by this Dialectic, you would only arrive at very general relations" (Lautman 2011, 224). In consonance with these reservations, Deleuze recasts Lautman's concept of real mathematics on the basis of problems, rather than Dialectical ideas. There are therefore no overarching governing ideas in Deleuze, but rather ideas are constituted by the purely problematic relation between conceptual pairs. Deleuze defines the "Idea" as a structure that is "a system of multiple, non-localizable connections between differential elements which is incarnated in real relations and actual terms" (DR 183). The real relations in which the problematic Idea is incarnated are the relations between conceptual pairs, and the actual terms are the solutions that can be offered to such problematic relations. For Deleuze, it is the problematic nature of the connections between differential elements that characterize problematic ideas and which govern the kinds of solutions that can be offered to them.

What Deleuze specifically draws from Lautman is a relational logic that designates a process of production, or genesis, which has the value of introducing a general theory of relations that unites the structural considerations of the differential calculus to the concept of "the generation of quantities" (DR 175). The process of the genesis of mathematical theories that are offered as solutions to mathematical problems corresponds to the Deleuzian account of the construction of concepts as solutions to philosophical problems. The mathematical problematics that Deleuze extracts from the history of mathematics, following Lautman's lead, are directly redeployed by Deleuze as philosophical problematics in relation to the history of philosophy. This is achieved by mapping the alternative lineages in the history of mathematics onto corresponding alternative lineages in the history of philosophy, i.e. by isolating those points of convergence between the mathematical and philosophical problematics extracted from their respective histories. The redeployment of mathematical problematics as philosophical problematics is one of the strategies that Deleuze employs in his engagement with the history of philosophy. Deleuze actually extracts philosophical problematics from the history of philosophy and then redeploys them either in relation to one another, or in relation to mathematical problematics, or in relation to problematics extracted from other discourses, to create new concepts, which Deleuze and Guattari (1994) consider to be the task of philosophy (WP 5).

Deleuze is therefore very much interested in particular kinds of mathematical problematics that can be extracted from the history of mathematics, and in the relationship that these problematics have to the discourse of philosophy. He can therefore be understood to redeploy not only the actual mathematical problematics that are extracted from the history of mathematics in relation to the history of philosophy, but also the logic of the generation of mathematical problematics, i.e. the calculus of problems, in relation to the history of philosophy, in order to generate the philosophical problematics which are then redeployed in his project of constructing a philosophy of difference. It is in relation to the history of philosophy that Deleuze then determines the logic of the generation of philosophical problematics as that characteristic of a philosophy of difference.

The logic of the calculus of problems

This logic, the logic of the calculus of problems, is determined in relation to the discipline of mathematics and the mathematical problematics extracted from it. It is not simply a logic characteristic of the relation between the history of mathematics and its related mathematical problematics, or between axiomatics and problematics,[35] or between what Deleuze and Guattari characterize as Royal science and nomad science. It is rather a logic of the generation of each mathematical problematic itself, or of nomad science itself. Deleuze writes that:

> It is sufficient to understand that the genesis takes place in time not between one actual term, however small, and another actual term, but between the virtual and its actualization – in other words, it goes from the structure to its incarnation, from the conditions of a problem to the cases of solution, from the differential elements and their ideal connections to actual terms and diverse real relations which constitute at each moment the actuality of time. This is a genesis without dynamism. (DR 183)

It is this logic that Deleuze redeploys in relation to the history of philosophy as a logic of different/ciation in order to generate the philosophical problematics that he then uses to construct a philosophy of difference.

Lautman refers to this whole process as "the metaphysics of logic" (Lautman 2011, 141), and, in *Difference and Repetition*, Deleuze formulates a "metaphysics of logic" that corresponds to the local point of view of the differential calculus. He endorses Lautman's broader project, if not some of its specific details, when he argues that "we should speak of a dialectics of the calculus rather than a metaphysics" (DR 178), since, he continues, "each engendered domain, in which dialectical Ideas of this or that order are incarnated, possesses its own calculus. . . . There is no metaphor here [and] . . . It is not mathematics which is applied to other domains but the dialectic," or the structure of the problematic idea, "which establishes for its problems, by virtue of their order and their conditions, the direct differential calculus corresponding or appropriate to the domain under consideration" (DR 181). It is not mathematical theories that are applied to other domains of investigation, or other discourses, but rather the structure of the purely problematic Idea, which is modeled on the local point of view of the differential calculus, and which establishes the differential elements,[36] that generate the calculus which serves as a model for the domain under consideration.

It is only in this sense then that Deleuze refers to his project as developing a "*mathesis universalis*" (DR 181). Like Bergson, Deleuze doesn't consider there to be a definite system of mathematical laws at the base of nature. Mathematics is not privileged in this way over other discourses. There is however a peculiarity about the discourse of mathematics that remains a sticking point in other discourses, and that is the nature of the relation between the objects of the discourse and the ideas of those objects as expressed within the discourse. Mathematics is peculiar because all of its objects are actually constructed by the discourse itself. The ideas of the objects of mathematics are therefore directly and unproblematically related to the objects themselves. It is for this reason that mathematics is figured as providing a model for our understanding of the nature of this relation in other discourses, where it is far from straightforward. Deleuze takes Lautman's concept of the mathematical real, which includes the sum of all mathematical theories and the structure of the problematic ideas that govern them, and casts it as a model for our understanding of the nature of the relation between the objects of any one discourse and the structure of the problematic ideas that govern them within that discourses. Insofar as all discourses can be modeled in this way, Deleuze argues that there is a "*mathesis universalis*" (DR 181). Deleuze is not positing a positive mathematical order to the universe, but he is rather nominating the Lautmanian mathematical real as a model for our understanding of the structure of all other discourses.

There is therefore a correspondence between the logic of the local point of view of the differential calculus and the logic of the theory of relations that is characteristic of Deleuze's philosophy of difference, insofar as the latter is modeled on the former. The manner by means of which an idea is implicated in the mathematical theory that determines it serves as a model for the manner by means of which a philosophical concept is implicated in the philosophical problematic which determines it. There are "correspondences without resemblance" (DR 184) between them, insofar as both are determined according to the same logic, i.e. according to the logic of different/ciation, but without resemblance between their elements. The philosophical implications of this convergence, or modeling relation, are developed by Deleuze in *Expressionism in Philosophy* (1990) in relation to his reading of Spinoza's theory of relations in the *Ethics*,[37] and in *Bergsonism* (1988), and *Cinema 1* and *2* (1986, 1989) in relation to his understanding of Bergson's intention "to give multiplicities the metaphysics which their scientific treatment demands" (B 112).[38]

The problematic ideas that "it is possible to retrieve in mathematical theories," and that are "incarnated in the very movement of these theories" (Lautman 2011, 83), are characterized retrospectively by virtue of the relations between conceptual pairs. The solutions to these problematic Ideas are recast by Deleuze as philosophical concepts. Together these are used to develop the logical schema of a theory of relations characteristic of a philosophy of difference. It is in the development of this project that Deleuze specifically draws upon Lautman's work to deploy a logic that, in *Difference and Repetition*, is determined in relation to the history of the differential calculus as the logic of different/ciation; in *Expressionism in Philosophy*, is determined in relation to Spinoza's theory of relations as the logic of expression; and in *Bergsonism*, and *Cinema 1* and *2*, is determined in relation to the work of Bergson as a logic of multiplicities.

Lautman outlined a "critical" program in mathematics that was intended to displace the previous foundational discussions that were occupied with the criticism of classical analysis. Against the logicist claim that the development of mathematics is dominated a priori by logic, Lautman proposes a "metaphysics of logic," and calls for the development of a "philosophy of mathematical genesis." Deleuze responds to this call. His Lautmanian inspired preoccupation with mathematics is primarily focused on locating what Lautman characterizes as "dialectical" or "logical Ideas," which are recast by Deleuze as problematic ideas to develop the logical schema of a theory of relations characteristic of a philosophy of difference. Lautman's work on mathematics provides the blue print for adequately determining the nature not only of Deleuze's engagement with mathematics, but also of Deleuze's metaphysics, the metaphysics of the logic of different/ciation.

Deleuze is not the only recent French philosopher to express their admiration of the work of Lautman. Indeed, in *Being and Event*, Alain Badiou openly declares that what he owes to Lautman's writings, "even in the very foundational intuitions for this book, is immeasurable" (Badiou 2005, 482). One of the crucial differences in their respective approaches to the work of Lautman hinges on the relation that each establishes to Lautman's Platonism. While Deleuze draws upon the Lautmanian concept of a dialectic of ideas stripped of both its Platonic and ideal elements and deployed solely as a calculus of problems, Badiou follows Lautman's lead in characterizing his position as Platonist and undertakes to develop a Platonism that is capable of responding to the demands of a post-Cantorian set theory. In the chapter that follows, this distinction will be developed to more adequately characterize the difference between the respective engagements with mathematics undertaken by Badiou and Deleuze.

Badiou and Contemporary Mathematics

Rather than getting drawn into a debate about the adequacy of Alain Badiou's presentation of Deleuze's engagement with mathematics,[1] the alternative approach to assessing the nature of the relation between the respective interpretations of mathematics by Deleuze and Badiou that is undertaken in this chapter is to read their respective interpretations of mathematics, and the role that they each assign to mathematics in the development of their respective philosophical projects, together, alongside of one another. This strategy entails examining those points of convergence between their respective philosophical projects, in order then to determine what sets them radically apart. It is in the difference of approach to the relation between mathematics and philosophy in their respective philosophies that this radical difference is manifested, and it is by means of the determination of this difference in approach that the difference in their respective philosophical projects in general is able to be determined.

The difference between the respective philosophical engagements with mathematics of Deleuze and Badiou is primarily due to their different attitudes to the question of the nature of the relation between mathematics and philosophy. One attempt to formulate a response to this question would be "to make an inventory of all of the major historical developments in philosophy to examine whether or not a complicity with mathematics can be established with any regularity" (Salanskis 2008, 10). The outcome of such an enquiry would be that in an overwhelming majority of cases these developments take place in proximity to and with an essential affinity with advances in mathematics; however, this does not prove the necessity of an affinity between philosophy and mathematics. A different approach is therefore required. One hypothesis would be to claim that it is mathematics that is the source of the kind of universal with which philosophy is concerned. The most elementary and the most convincing explication of this affinity is as follows: while "everyday spatio-temporal entities of average size, such as tables" (Salanskis 2008, 11), can be considered to be objects of both mathematics and philosophy, it is less clear

> whether a sentiment, an intention, a signification, or an epoch are objects in this sense. Philosophy is concerned with all of these things that only controversially merit being treated as objects because they are tainted by subjectivity, relativity, intersubjectivity or ideality. (Salanskis 2008, 12)

What then is the relation between the mathematical universal, "all objects," and the philosophical universal, "all things"? While the thought of "all things" seems to exceed the thought of "all objects," it is in fact the latter that provides the model for the former. The thought of "all things" is not possible without the thought of "all objects" (See Salanskis 2008, 12). This role of mathematics is tied to the idea of a transfer of the concept of the universal from mathematics to the horizon of things that are "moral or epistemological" (Salanskis 2008, 13). Philosophy thus appears to be dependent on mathematics in the sense that the implication of the infinite in the mathematical universal serves as a model for the inclusion of all forms of things, whatever they may be, in philosophy. The hypothesis of such an

> essential affinity between mathematics and philosophy . . . determines philosophy in its different styles and modalities . . . regardless of the object with which it is occupied. Whether philosophy is dealing with existence or art does not detract from its dependence on mathematics. (Salanskis 2008, 15)

One way of responding to this characterization of the essential relation between mathematics and philosophy is to champion the idea that mathematics must therefore provide a foundation for philosophy. The proponents of this position "privilege the primary and most general elements of the construction of the mathematical edifice" (Salanskis 2008, 29). They maintain that the best candidate for this foundational role should be drawn from the current, most advanced mathematics, given the historical developments of mathematics to date. The mathematical theory that best accounts for the above argument and that can therefore fulfill this role of providing a foundation for philosophy is set theory. Set theory seeks to resolve the problem of the infinite, i.e. the problem of conceptualizing "the existence of an infinity irreducible to any principle of totality," which "runs directly counter to any presumed existence of a closed totality," i.e. one world or one universe (Gillespie 2008, 146). The foundational role of set theory is a widely endorsed position within philosophy. Proponents of this position include philosophers in both the Anglo-American or analytic and Continental traditions of philosophy, including contemporary French philosophy, notably this is the approach endorsed by Badiou.

There is however a strong counter current among philosophers who are more concerned with mathematical practice outside the question of foundations, and who are not put out by the lack of a necessary affinity between mathematics and philosophy. This alternative point of view "goes straight to the heart of live mathematics in all its complexity" (Salanskis 2008, 29), in order to extract the ingenuity of mathematics and make it available to philosophy. According to this approach, any characterization of the relation between mathematics and philosophy should take into account the range of processes involved in the myriad developments within the discipline of mathematics itself, rather than resorting to the most recent and viable theory to fulfill the foundational role. The questions which occupy philosophers interested in exploring the relationship between mathematics and philosophy from this point of view include: What kind of relations are there between advances in mathematics and developments in philosophy? How can these advances be characterized? Can this be done using mathematics itself without resorting to the question of foundations? Is there a way of characterizing the relation of mathematics to philosophy that is not dependent on the most recent development in mathematics, and that is rather flexible enough to also apply retrospectively and if new developments overturn the appropriateness of the foundational role of set theory? Rather than defending dogmatic foundational claims, the latter approach is interested in exploring the full range of mathematical theories, practices, and developments to determine the ways in which they can be understood to be implicated in developments in philosophy. This includes not only the role played by advances in mathematics for our understanding of what underpins developments in philosophy, but also developments in other disciplines, insofar as the claims of other disciplines can themselves be understood to be bound up with specific philosophical claims of one kind or another. This latter approach brings renewed focus on the role of mathematics in philosophy, and raises the profile of mathematics and of its importance to other disciplines.

This difference in approach to the relation between mathematics and philosophy is reflected in the difference between the work of Badiou and Deleuze. While Badiou advocates the foundational role of mathematics in relation to philosophy, Deleuze is more interested in mathematical practice outside the question of foundations and in how mathematical problems or problematics that have led to the development of alternative lineages in the history of mathematics can be redeployed to reconfigure philosophical problems, and problems in other discourses. Before attempting to draw out the implications of this difference in approach to the relation between mathematics and philosophy, the specific character of Badiou's approach to mathematics requires further explication.

Badiou and the role of mathematics as ontology

Mathematics has a dual function in Badiou's philosophy. On the one hand, mathematics plays the central role in the determination of Badiou's ontology. And on the other hand, mathematics has the privileged status of being the paradigm of science and of scientific enquiry in general, and is therefore instrumental in the determination of science as what he calls a truth procedure. Science, including mathematics, proceeds by following experimental lines of enquiry that are established by new discoveries. What differentiates mathematics from science is that it is only in mathematics that a problem can be solved unequivocally. Badiou maintains that, insofar as thought formulates a problem, it is only in mathematics that it can or will definitively be solved, however long it takes. He notes that the history of mathematics is littered with examples of breakthroughs that resulted from proving or disproving conjectures first proposed by the Greeks more than two thousand years ago. What this means for Badiou is that mathematics does not acknowledge categories such as the unthinkable or the unthought, which he characterizes as spiritualist because they exceed the resources of human reason, or those according to which we cannot resolve problems nor respond to questions, such as skeptical categories. Science in general on the other hand struggles in this respect, and is deemed by Badiou not to be reliable on this point. What is distinct about mathematics as a science is its abstract axiomatic foundation. And he argues that it is this foundation that provides the infrastructure for the characterization of being qua being. According to Badiou, "mathematics teaches us about what must be said concerning what is; and not about what it is permissible to say concerning what we think there is" (Badiou 2006, 25). Badiou considers Cantor's invention of set theory to be the archetypal event that allows mathematics to henceforth and retrospectively be understood as the science of being qua being. The much debated proposition from *Being and Event* (2005), that "mathematics is ontology" (Badiou 2005, 4), is a philosophical idea that is conditioned by this event. The general ontology that Badiou develops in *Being and Event* draws upon a number of subsequent developments in mathematics that show felicity to this event, namely the Zermelo–Fraenkel axiomatization of set theory and the open series of extensions of these axioms, including in particular those by Kurt Gödel, who introduced the notion of constructible sets, and Paul Cohen, who developed the method of forcing and generic sets.

The characterization of mathematics as ontology has a direct bearing on how Badiou understands the nature of the relation between science and mathematics. For example, he considers physics to be "the investigation of matter, the very concept of matter," and he argues that "the more you decompose the concept of matter into its most elementary constituents, the more you move into a field of reality which can only be named or identified with increasingly complex mathematical operations" (Badiou 2001, 130). Badiou endorses the fact that in nearly all scientific theories, the structures of physical systems are modeled or described in terms of mathematical structures. Mathematics is generally considered to be applied in this way when the scientist postulates that a given area of the physical world exemplifies a certain mathematical structure. However, Badiou goes further than this. Rather than there being an analogical or metaphorical relation between the structure of the physical world and the mathematical theory that allows it to be modeled or reconstructed,[2] Badiou considers mathematics to actually articulate being itself. Mathematics doesn't just provide a description, representation, or interpretation of being. Mathematics itself is what can be thought of being *simpliciter*.[3] It is for this reason that Badiou maintains that axiomatic set theory is the science of being as pure multiplicity, or of "the presentation of presentation" (Badiou 2005, 27), i.e. of the presentation of what is presented in a situation. What this means is that Badiou figures mathematics itself as that which guarantees the access of the natural sciences to presented reality.

With the proposition "mathematics is ontology," Badiou consigns the task of ontology to mathematics, and in so doing liberates philosophy from the burden of the Heideggerian question of being. However, this doesn't liberate philosophy completely from dealing with the problems associated with the *Seinsfrage*, but rather recasts the role of philosophy in this respect from its historical preoccupation with ontology to the task of metaontology. One of the tasks of philosophy as metaontology is to articulate the relation to being that is displayed by the truth procedures operating in the different generic procedures, which for Badiou include science, politics, art, and love. Because mathematics, as the basis of science, itself belongs to one of these four generic procedures, philosophy must remain attentive to those truth procedures in mathematics that follow experimental lines of enquiry and that continue to develop new articulations of the presentation of being qua being. This line of research is evident in a number of Badiou's subsequent texts, including *Numbers and Number* (2008), where Badiou draws upon the development of surreal numbers to extend the universe of ordinals up to the reals, and in *Logics of Worlds* (2009), where Badiou attempts to address his dependence on set theory in *Being and Event,* by deploying a category theoretic presentation of set theory, namely topos theory.

One of the significant features of Badiou's engagement with mathematics that further distinguishes his work from that of Deleuze is that Badiou is an avowed Platonist. However, the particular nature of the Platonism that he defends is distinct from orthodox Platonic realism in the philosophy of mathematics. Plato's philosophy is important to Badiou for a number of reasons, chief among which is that Badiou considered Plato to have recognized that mathematics provides the only sound or adequate basis for ontology. The mathematical basis of ontology is central to Badiou's philosophy, and his engagement with Plato is instrumental in determining how he positions his philosophy in relation to those approaches to the philosophy of mathematics that endorse an orthodox Platonic realism, i.e. the independent existence of a realm of mathematical objects. The Platonism that Badiou makes claim to bears little resemblance to this orthodoxy. Like Plato, Badiou insists on the primacy of the eternal and immutable abstraction of the mathematico-ontological Idea; however, Badiou's reconstructed Platonism champions the mathematics of post-Cantorian set-theory, which itself affirms the irreducible multiplicity of being. Badiou in this way reconfigures the Platonic notion of the relation between the one and the multiple in terms of the multiple-without-one as represented in the axiom of the void or empty set. Rather than engaging with the Plato that is figured in the ontological realism of the orthodox Platonic approach to the philosophy of mathematics, Badiou is intent on characterizing the Plato that responds to the demands of a post-Cantorian set theory, and he considers Plato's philosophy to provide a response to such a challenge. In effect, Badiou reorients mathematical Platonism from an epistemological to an ontological problematic, a move that relies on the plausibility of rejecting the empiricist ontology underlying orthodox mathematical Platonism. To draw a connection between these two approaches to Platonism and to determine what sets them radically apart, this chapter will initially focus on the use that they each make of model theory to further their respective arguments. Once Badiou's philosophical project has been explicated, those points of convergence between the respective philosophical projects of Badiou and Deleuze will be examined, in order then to determine what sets them radically apart.

Orthodox Platonism in mathematics and its problems

Orthodox Platonism in mathematics advances an ontological realism according to which mathematical objects, such as numbers, functions, and sets, exist. These mathematical objects are considered to be abstract, causally inert, and eternal. The problem that accompanies orthodox Platonism is an epistemological one. If mathematical objects are causally inert, how do we know anything about them?[4] Any such knowledge would require epistemic access to an acausal, eternal, and detached mathematical realm.

The epistemic problem for realism in mathematics presumes something like a causal theory of knowledge, according to which claims to knowledge of particular objects are grounded in some account of the causal link between knower and object known. While this empiricist framework may account for knowledge of ordinary objects in the physical world, this sets up a problem for the orthodox Platonist as it doesn't account for knowledge of mathematical objects.

A further issue that can be raised is the question of the applicability of the abstract mathematical realm to the ordinary physical world. Generally, mathematics is applied when a given area of the physical world is postulated as exemplifying a certain mathematical structure. In nearly all scientific theories, the structures of physical systems are described or modeled in terms of mathematical structures (Shapiro 2000, 17). But this doesn't explain how the eternal, acausal, detached mathematical universe relates to the material world, which is the subject matter of science and everyday language. The challenge to the orthodox mathematical Platonist is to provide an account of how it is that mathematical knowledge is utilized or deployed in scientific discourse, and of how it seems to function as an essential part of it.

One realist approach, which begins with the latter problem of the relation between mathematics and science in order to attempt to provide a response to the epistemic problem, is that presented in the Quine-Putnam indispensability argument. Quine and Putnam considered mathematics to be indispensable for science, and, on the basis of the understanding that the best scientific theories determine what one ought to believe to exist, it follows that one ought to believe that the mathematical entities implicated in these theories exist.[5] While this approach does seem to provide a response to the epistemic problem, it fails to address the issue of exactly how mathematics can be applied to science, i.e. while noting the indispensability of mathematics for science, it fails to provide an account of the nature of this relation. The response to the epistemic problem provided by the indispensability argument can therefore not be sustained, or, from a realist perspective, at least not until an adequate response is provided to the question of the nature of this relation.[6]

One way of addressing the nature of this relation is to actually attempt to provide a uniform semantics for both mathematical and scientific languages, rather than merely presuming this to be the case, which is all that is required for the indispensability argument. This could be achieved by developing a model-theoretic framework according to which the relationship between mathematical language and mathematical reality is modeled on the relationship between a formal language and model-theoretic interpretations of it. The point is that if realism is correct, then model theory provides the picture, or "model" of how mathematical languages describe mathematical reality.

Model theory is the branch of logic developed to study (or model) mathematical structures by considering first-order sentences which are true of those structures and the sets which are definable in those structures by first-order formulas (Marker 1996, 753). In model theory, there are three different languages that are in operation: (1) the mathematical language itself, which is informal, (2) the object language, which is the set of first-order sentences of a formal language that "models" the first, and (3) the metalanguage, which is the informal or semiformalized language in which the semantics is carried out, i.e. it is the language used to describe what is happening in the object language. The assumption being that standard first-order sentences of a formal language capture something about real mathematical languages. A first-order sentence is a formula that has well-defined truth values under an interpretation. For example, given the formula P(x), which states that the predicate P is true of x, whether P(x) is true depends on what x represents, and the first-order sentence $\exists x$P(x) will be either true or false in a given interpretation. An interpretation of the set of sentences of a first-order language assigns a denotation to all nonlogical constants in that language, for example, what is denoted by P. It also determines a domain of discourse that specifies the range of the universal ($\forall$) and existential ($\exists$) quantifiers, where the domain of discourse generally refers to the set of entities that a model is based on. The result is that each term, x, is assigned an object that it represents, and each sentence, for example $\exists x$P(x), is assigned a truth value. In this way, a model-theoretic interpretation determines the satisfaction conditions for the formal sentences and thereby provides semantic meaning to the terms and formulas of the language.[7] The metalanguage, which is a "fully developed language" (Shapiro 2000, 71) must contain a faithful representation of the object language and should have the resources to make substantial assertions about the ontology that is attributed to the object language. In this way, the central notion of model theory is "truth in a model." The conditions for truth in the proposed model represent truth conditions, and it follows that truth in a model is a model of truth. What this means is that the truth of the existence of mathematical objects in the model, or in the object language, is a model of the truth of the existence of mathematical objects for the mathematical language itself. One criticism of this approach is that the best that can be achieved is that all models of a theory are isomorphic, in which case the ontology is only determined up to isomorphism, i.e. metaphysical realists do not really have any access to the correspondence they postulate.[8]

The structuralist approach to the program of realism in the philosophy of mathematics, represented in the work of Stewart Shapiro, draws upon Plato to set up a response to this criticism, a response which is an extension of the model-theoretic approach. Shapiro argues that Plato distinguishes between two different approaches to natural numbers: arithmetic and logistic. Arithmetic "deals with the even and the odd, with reference to how much each happens to be."[9] According to Plato, if "one becomes perfect in the arithmetical art," then "he knows also all of the numbers."[10] Logistic differs from arithmetic "in so far as it studies the even and the odd with respect to the multitude they make both with themselves and with each other."[11] So while arithmetic deals straight forwardly with the natural numbers, Shapiro argues that theoretical logistic concerns "the relations among the numbers" (Shapiro 2000, 73). Drawing upon the work of Klein, who argues that theoretical logistic "raises to an explicit science that knowledge of relations among numbers which . . . precedes, and indeed must precede, all calculation" (Klein 1968, 23), Shapiro argues that "the structuralist rejects this distinction between Plato's arithmetic and theoretical logistic." He maintains that "there is no more to the individual numbers 'in themselves' than the relations they bear to each other" (Shapiro 2000, 73). Shapiro turns to the *Republic* to find the ultimate Platonic endorsement of this move. He argues that "in the *Republic* (525C–D), Plato said that guardians should pursue *logistic* for the sake of knowing. It is through this study of the *relations* among numbers that their soul is able to grasp the nature of numbers as they are in themselves. We structuralists agree" (Shapiro 2000, 73).

In order to overcome the criticism of the problem of isomorphism in the model-theoretic framework, the structuralist program of realism in the philosophy of mathematics deploys the model-theoretic framework in relation to the problem of mathematical structures, which it can more directly address. In this respect, as Shapiro argues, "Structure is all that matters" (Shapiro 2000, 56). Mathematical objects are defined as structureless points or positions in structures that have no identity or features outside of a structure. And a structure is defined as the abstract form of a system, which highlights the interrelationships among its objects.[12] The aim of Shapiro's structuralist approach is to develop a language in which to interpret the mathematics done by real mathematicians, which can then be used to try to make progress on philosophical questions.

Badiou's "modern Platonist" response and its reformulation of the question

Another avowedly Platonic approach that redeploys the model-theoretic framework is that provided by Alain Badiou in *Being and Event*, and subsequently elaborated upon in *Logics of Worlds*. The main point of distinction between the approaches of Badiou and Shapiro that sets their projects apart and at odds with one another is that Badiou rejects the empiricist framework that characterizes the epistemic problem for the orthodox Platonist.

Badiou considers himself to be a "modern Platonist" (Badiou 2004, 54), and draws upon three crucial aspects of Plato's work to set up this transformation.

First, Badiou maintains that "the independent existence of mathematical structures is entirely relative for Plato" (Badiou 2004, 49). The claim being that Plato's account of anamnesis[13] does not set up the "criterion of the exteriority (or transcendence) of mathematical structures (or objects)" (Badiou 2004, 49). On the contrary, it designates that "thought is never confronted with 'objectivities' from which it is supposedly separated" (Badiou 2004, 49). Badiou considers a mathematical structure to be an "Idea" that is "always already there and would remain unthinkable were one not able to 'activate' it in thought" (Badiou 2004, 49). He maintains that "Plato's fundamental concern is to declare the immanent identity, the co-belonging, of the knowing mind and the known, their essential ontological commensurability" (Badiou 2004, 49). So the problem for Badiou in this respect is to provide an account of how these Ideas are activated in thought, which is facilitated by providing an account of this "essential ontological commensurability."

Second, Badiou reinterprets the famous passage in the *Republic* where Plato opposes mathematics to the dialectic.

The theorizing concerning being and the intelligible which is sustained by the science [*épistémè*] of the dialectic is clearer than that sustained by what are known as the sciences [*techné*] . . . It seems to me you characterize the [latter] procedure of geometers and their ilk as discursive [*dianoia*], while you do not characterize intellection thus, in so far as that discursiveness is established between [*metaxu*] opinion [*doxa*] and intellect [*nous*].[14]

In this passage, Plato singles out the procedures of the geometer, having in mind here the axioms of Euclidian geometry, as operating externally to the norms of thought, i.e. the dialectic. Badiou's modern move here is to embrace the axiomatic approach specifically because of this externality, which addresses that aspect of the problem mentioned above of how these Ideas are activated in thought. Badiou here also reveals his formalist leanings by endorsing the understanding that the theorem follows logically from its axioms, although it is a formalism without the implicit finitism that accompanies its usual presentation in the philosophy of mathematics as the manipulation and interpretation of finite sequences of symbols.

Third, in the *Parmenides* Badiou notes with approval what he considers to be the formulation in the account of a speculative dream of "being" as pure or inconsistent multiplicity [*plethos*] (Badiou 2005, 34). However, he considers Plato to capitulate to the fact that "there is no form of object for thought which is capable of gathering together the pure multiple, the multiple-without-one, and making it consist" (Badiou 2005, 34). The multiple, in this respect, can only be thought in terms of the One, and thus as consistent or structured multiplicity [*polla*]. Plato writes, "It is necessary that the entirety of disseminated being [as inconsistent multiplicity] shatter apart, as soon as it is grasped by discursive thought" (Badiou 2005, 34). Badiou considers this to be where Plato is premodern, by which he specifically means pre-Cantorian, because it is Cantor who was the first to "elucidate the thinking of being as pure multiplicity" (Badiou 2004, 55), an account of which will be given in the next section. In order to maintain the distinction between the two types of multiplicity, *plethos* and *polla*, Badiou suggests transcribing Plato's statement: "If the one is not, nothing is," to "If the one is not, (the) nothing is" (Badiou 2005, 35). This then aligns the Platonic text with the "axiomatic decision" with which Badiou's "entire discourse originates": "that of the non-being of the one" (Badiou 2005, 31). According to Badiou, "under the hypothesis of the non-being of the one, there is a fundamental asymmetry between the analytic of the multiple and the analytic of the one itself" (Badiou 2005, 32). It is only in relation to the "non-being of the one" that multiplicity as pure or inconsistent, the multiple-without-one, is presentable. In axiomatic set theory, which is the first-order formal language that Badiou deploys in his model theoretic approach, the "non-being of the one" is characteristic of the void or empty set, $\emptyset$ (Badiou 2005, 69).

In support of these moves, and of the claim that the status of mathematical objects is a secondary problem, Badiou draws upon comments made by Kurt Gödel about axiomatic set theory and Cantor's continuum hypothesis:

the question of the objective existence of the objects of mathematical intuition (which, incidentally, is an exact replica of the question of the objective existence of the outer world) is not decisive for the problem under discussion here. The mere psychological fact of the existence of an intuition which is sufficiently clear to produce the axioms of set theory and an open series of extensions of them suffices

to give meaning to the question of the truth or falsity of propositions like Cantor's
continuum hypothesis. (Gödel 1983, 485)

With this, Badiou positions Cantor's continuum hypothesis, and the development of
transfinite numbers that underpins it, as of central importance to his approach. Badiou
argues that

> With Cantor we move from a restricted ontology, in which the multiple is still tied
> to the metaphysical theme of the representation of objects, numbers and figures, to
> a general ontology, in which the cornerstone and goal of all mathematics becomes
> thought's free apprehension of multiplicity as such, and the thinkable is definitively
> untethered from the restricted dimension of the object. (Badiou 2004, 46)

Badiou characterizes this "general ontology," which is nothing other than pure
multiplicity, as "being qua being," and, on the basis of Cantor's account of transfinite
numbers, maintains that "it is legitimate to say that ontology, the science of being
qua being, is nothing other than mathematics itself" (Badiou 2005, xiii). Badiou then
presents this "general ontology" as modeled by the Zermelo-Fraenkel axiomatization
of set theory (abbreviated ZF) and the open series of extensions of them, including in
particular those by Gödel and Paul Cohen. In response to Quine's famous formula:
"to be is to be the value of a variable" (Quine 1981, 15), Badiou responds that "the ZF
system postulates that there is only one type of presentation of being: the multiple"
(Badiou 2005, 44). He maintains that "mathematical 'objects' and 'structures,' . . . can
all be designated as pure multiplicities built, in a regulated manner, on the basis of
the void-set alone" (Badiou 2005, 6), and that "[t]he question of the exact nature of
the relation of mathematics to being is therefore entirely concentrated – for the epoch
in which we find ourselves – in the axiomatic decision which authorizes set theory"
(Badiou 2005, 6). In order to characterize this axiomatic decision, an account of the
development of transfinite numbers, which Badiou considers "to prompt us to think
being qua being" (Badiou 2008, 98), is required.

Cantor's account of transfinite numbers or ordinals

To begin with, an ordinal number describes the numerical position or order of an
object, for example, first, second, third, etc., as opposed to a cardinal number which
is used in counting: one, two, three, etc. An ordinal number is defined as "the order
type of a well ordered set" (Dauben 1990, 199). There are finite ordinals, denoted using
Arabic numerals, and transfinite ordinals, denoted using the lower case Greek letter
ω (omega). While the ordinality and cardinality of finite sets are the same, this is not
the case with transfinite ordinals and cardinals, as will be explained in the following
lines. It was Cantor who developed transfinite ordinals as an extension of the whole
numbers, i.e. transfinite ordinals are larger than any whole number. The smallest
transfinite ordinal ω, is the set of all finite ordinals $\{0, 1, 2, \dots \}$, which is the countably
infinite set **N** of natural numbers.[15] The cardinality of this set is denoted $\aleph_0$ (aleph-0)
(Dauben 1990, 179).[16] Note that the cardinality of **Z**, the integers, and **Q**, the rational

numbers, is also $\aleph_0$. Whereas **R**, the set of real numbers, is uncountably infinite, and its cardinality is denoted by *c*, which is called the "continuum" in set theory. Because **R** is the power set of **Z**, where the power set of any set is the set of all of its subsets, and because every set of size or cardinality *n* has a power set of cardinality 2^n, $c = 2^{\aleph_0}$. While there is only one countably infinite cardinal, $\aleph_0$, there are uncountably many countable transfinite ordinals, because like other kinds of numbers, transfinite ordinals can be added, multiplied, and exponentiated:[17]

$$\omega, \omega + 1, \omega + 2, \ldots, \omega \times 2, (\omega \times 2) + 1, \ldots, \omega^2, \omega^2 + 1, \ldots,$$

$$\omega^3, \ldots, \omega^\omega, \ldots, \omega^{\omega^\omega}, \ldots, \varepsilon_0, \ldots$$

The cardinality of the ordinal that succeeds all countable transfinite ordinals, of which there are uncountably many, is denoted $\aleph_1$ (aleph-1) (Dauben 1990, 269). Each ordinal is the well-ordered set of all smaller ordinals, i.e. every element of an ordinal is an ordinal. Any set of ordinals which contains all the predecessors of each of its elements has an ordinal number which is greater than any ordinal in the set, i.e. for any ordinal α, the union $\alpha \cup \{\alpha\}$ is a bigger ordinal $\alpha + 1$. For this reason, there is no largest ordinal. The ordinals therefore "do not constitute a set: no multiple form can totalize them" (Badiou 2008, 98). What this means for Badiou is that the ordinals are the ontological schema of pure or inconsistent multiplicity.

Badiou argues that "[t]he anchoring of the ordinals in being as such is twofold" (Badiou 2008, 98). (1) the "absolutely initial point . . . is the empty set," which is an ordinal, and is "decided axiomatically" as the empty set, $\varnothing$. In ZF, the axiom of the void or empty set states that the empty set exists. As the "non-being of the one," the empty set provides set theory with its only existential link to being and thereby grounds all the forms constructible from it in existence. Badiou defers here to Zermelo's axiom of separation, which states that "if the collection is a sub-collection of a given set, then it exists" (Kunen 1983, 12). Rather than using this axiom to prove the existence of the empty set by specifying a property that all sets do not have, which would be the orthodox Platonist approach since all sets already exist, Badiou argues that in order for the axiom of separation to separate some consistent multiplicity as a sub-collection, some pure multiple, as the multiple of multiples,[18] must already be presented, by which Badiou means the initial multiple, the empty set, which is guaranteed rather by the axiom of the empty set (Badiou 2005, 45). (2) "[t]he limit-point that 'relaunches' the existence of the ordinals beyond . . . the whole natural finite numbers . . . is the first infinite set, ω," which is also "decided axiomatically." The axiom that formalizes the infinite set representing the natural numbers, **N**, is the axiom of infinity, which states that there exists an infinite set. These two axiomatic decisions, which Badiou considers to be crucial for modern thought, represent the ordinals as "the modern scale of measurement" of pure or inconsistent multiplicity. He maintains that these two decisions determine that nothingness, the empty set, "is a form of. . . . numerable being, and that the infinite, far from being found in the One of a God, is omnipresent," as pure or inconsistent multiplicity, "in every existing-situation" (Badiou 2008, 99). Before clarifying what Badiou means here by "every existing-situation," which is dependent upon the model-theoretic implications of his approach, the Platonist implications of axiomatic set theory that Badiou is drawing upon require further explication.

The Platonist implications of axiomatic set theory

ZF and the extensions of it by Gödel and Cohen allow the Cantorian theory to be developed in full while avoiding all known paradoxical constructions, the simplest of which is Russell's paradoxical set of all sets, which Cantor called an inconsistent or absolutely infinite set.[19] The main problem left unanswered by Cantor's theory of transfinite numbers is the hypothesis, which tried to make sense of these inconsistent or absolutely infinite sets, referred to as the continuum hypothesis (abbreviated CH). CH proposes that there is no infinite set with a cardinal number between that of the "small" countably infinite set of integers, denoted $\aleph_0$, and the "large" uncountably infinite set of real numbers, denoted $2^{\aleph_0}$. CH therefore asserts that $\aleph_1 = 2^{\aleph_0}$, where $\aleph_1$ is the cardinality of the ordinal that succeeds all countable transfinite ordinals. Cantor believed CH to be true and spent many fruitless years trying to prove it. If CH is true, then $2^{\aleph_0}$ is the first cardinal larger than $\aleph_0$. However, independently of whether or not CH is true, the question remains as to whether such a cardinal $2^{\aleph_0}$ exists. Cantor argues for the existence of $2^{\aleph_0}$ by invoking the well-ordering principle (abbreviated WO), which simply states that a set is said to be well-ordered by a relation $<$ (less than) of ordering between its elements if every nonempty subset has a first element. This argument implies that every set can be well-ordered and can therefore be associated with an ordinal number. The problem with Cantor's argument is that it assumes there to be a method for making an unlimited number of successive arbitrary choices for each subset to determine this first member. If the set is the set **N**, then there is no problem, since the standard ordering of **N** already provides well-ordering. But if the set is **R**, there is no known method to make the required choice. The assumption of the existence of such an infinite sequence of choices was considered by many to be unjustified.[20] In response to this problem, Zermelo provided a proof of WO on the basis of the axiom of choice (abbreviated AC, and indicated by the "C" in ZFC), which proposes a function that provides for "the *simultaneous choice* from each nonempty subset" of the first element (Feferman 1989, 39). This axiom "reduces the construction of a transfinite sequence of successive choices," which in Cantor's argument appear to proceed through time, "to the assumption of a single simultaneous collection of choices" (Feferman 1989, 39). The main problem with AC for many mathematicians was that it presupposed the independent existence of the function that it proposes, i.e. it asserts existence without explicitly defining the function as a mathematical object and thus lays the axiomatic grounds for orthodox mathematical Platonism in set theory and the problems outlined above associated with it.

While a committed Platonic realist in the philosophy of mathematics who "conceives sets to be arbitrary collections of entities existing independently of human consciousness and definitions" would consider AC to be "immediately intuitively evident" (Feferman 1989, 40), Badiou, on the contrary, considers the acceptance of AC to be solely the result of an axiomatic decision, the reasons for which will become evident once more of the history of dealing with CH is presented. So while both Badiou and the orthodox Platonist accept AC, and therefore that the cardinal $2^{\aleph_0}$ exists, the question that remains to be addressed is whether or not CH is true.

In 1937, Gödel proved that if ZF is consistent then it remains consistent if AC and the Generalized Continuum Hypothesis (abbreviated GCH) are added to it as axioms. The GCH states that if an infinite set's cardinality lies between that of an infinite set and that of its power set, then it either has the same cardinality as the infinite set or the same cardinality as its power set. This is a generalization of CH because the continuum, **R**, has the same cardinality as the power set of integers, **Z**. Gödel also introduced the notion of "constructible set" to show that when the universe of sets, V, is restricted to the class of constructible sets, L, i.e. when V = L, then all the axioms of ZFC and GCH are proved.[21] What this consistency result showed was that any instance of GCH could not be disproved using ZFC.

The notion of constructible sets is problematic for the orthodox Platonist as the restriction to definable objects is contrary to the conception of an independently existing universe of arbitrary sets. Most Platonists would therefore reject V = L, and the proof that relies on it. Badiou, on the contrary, affirms Gödel's notion of constructible sets, i.e. L, as another necessary axiomatic decision, and the result that follows. Badiou argues that by "considering constructible multiples *alone*, one stays within the framework of the Ideas of the multiple" (Badiou 2005, 300) elaborated above.[22]

This result, that GCH could not be disproved using ZFC, did not rule out that some instance of GCH could be proved in ZFC, even CH itself (Feferman 1989, 66–9); however, Gödel projected that CH would be independent or could not be derived from ZFC, and that "new axioms" might be required to decide it (Gödel 1983, 476).

Progress on this problem was not made until 1963 when Paul Cohen (1966) proved that if ZF is consistent then (1) AC is independent or cannot be derived from ZF; (2) CH is independent from ZFC; and (3) V = L is independent of ZFC + GCH.[23] The proof effectively showed that CH does not hold in all models of set theory. The technique he invented and called "the method of forcing" and generic sets involved building models of set theory. This method takes its point of departure in that used by Gödel. Rather than producing only one model by restricting a presumed model of set theory, V, to obtain that of the constructible sets, L, Cohen extended the model of constructible sets, L, by the adjunction of a variety of generic sets without altering the ordinals.[24] In fact, he adjoined sufficiently many generic subsets of $\omega = \{0, 1, 2, \ldots\}$ that the cardinality of this constructed model of ZFC, $\aleph_1$, was greater than $\aleph_0$ but less than c, thus violating CH.

The procedure of forcing starts with a countable transitive model M for any suitable finite list of axioms of ZFC + V = L.[25] The method of forcing is then used to construct a countable transitive model G, called a *generic extension* of M, for a finite list of axioms of ZFC + V = L, such that M contains G, abbreviated as M[G]. M is "the set of all sets which can be constructed from G by applying set-theoretic processes definable in M" (Kunen 1983, 188). As long as M doesn't equal G, G will satisfy V ≠ L. G can also be made to satisfy ¬CH, and "a wide variety of other statements by varying certain details in [the] construction" (Kunen 1983, 185). While Gödel's method of constructability established the consistency of statements true in L, specifically GCH, Cohen's method of forcing "is a general technique for producing a wide variety of models satisfying diverse mathematical properties" (Kunen 1983, 184). It has since become the main method for showing statements to be independent of ZF or ZFC. Cohen's independence results are the basis of Badiou's claim that AC and V = L are "axiomatic decisions," as they are undecidable within the framework of ZF and of ZFC + GCH, respectively. As for CH, it is "demonstrable within the constructible universe, and refutable in certain generic extensions. It is therefore undecidable for set theory without restrictions" (Badiou 2005, 504).

Building on Cohen's work, Easton (1970) shows that for each regular transfinite cardinality of a set, the cardinality of its power set can be any cardinal provided that it is superior to the first and that "it is a successor cardinal" (Badiou 2005, 279), where a successor cardinal is the smallest cardinal which is larger than the given cardinal.[26]

Consonant with Gödel's projection, a number of "new axioms" called strong axioms of infinity, or large cardinal axioms, are candidates or have been newly proposed in the attempt to decide CH. These include the axioms that assert the existence of inaccessible cardinals, or Mahlo cardinals, and stronger axioms for the existence of measurable cardinals, compact cardinals, supercompact cardinals, and huge cardinals.[27] What the large cardinal axioms attempt to do is "to constitute within the infinite an abyss comparable to the one which distinguishes the first infinity, ω_0, from the finite multiples" (Badiou 2005, 311). It is in this way that the large cardinal axioms are considered to be "strong axioms of infinity." However, for each of these axioms, if it has been shown to be consistent with ZFC then it remains consistent regardless of whether CH or $\neg$CH is added. That is, "CH is consistent with and independent from every large cardinal axiom that has been proposed as at all plausible" (Feferman 1989, 72–3). What this means is that "none of them quite succeed" in deciding CH.

On a purely formal level, Kanamori and Magidor argue that interest in large cardinal axioms lies in the "aesthetic intricacy of the net of consequences and interrelationships between them." However, they go further to suggest that the adaptation of large cardinal axioms involves "basic questions of belief concerning what is true about the universe," and can therefore be characterized as a "theological venture" (Kanamori and Magidor 1978, 104). Badiou endorses this suggestion and incorporates large cardinal axioms into his approach as approximations of the "virtual being required by theologies" (Badiou 2005, 284).

The model-theoretic implications of Badiou's "modern Platonism"

The definitive statement of Badiou's model-theoretic orientation in *Being and Event* is in the chapter on the "Theory of the Pure Multiple," where he effectively states that "the object-language (the formal language) . . . which will be that of the theory in which I operate" (Badiou 2005, 39) is axiomatic set theory, specifically ZFC, including, as indicated above, Gödel's axiom of constructability, V = L. What this means is that the object language that Badiou deploys is already itself a model of ZFC insofar as the acceptance of V = L, which in Cohen's terminology is the model M, indicates Badiou's decision to solely accept the existence of constructible sets, or as Badiou refers to them, "constructible multiples" (Badiou 2005, 306). So Badiou's object language already implicates the model M of ZFC that is determined in the first stage of the procedure of Cohen's method of forcing and generic sets.

The metalanguage with which Badiou discusses the object language and that has the resources to make substantial assertions about the ontology attributed to the object language is the "fully developed language" of philosophy itself, specifically Badiou's philosophy, which he refers to as a metaontology. For Badiou, mathematics doesn't recognize that it is ontology; this is left up to philosophy itself whose task is to explain how it is that mathematics is ontology.

The model-theoretic interpretations of the object language are the very generic extensions generated by Cohen's method of forcing, which constructs a *generic extension* G of M, such that M contains G, i.e. M[G]. Cohen's generic extensions themselves are unknowable from the model M of which they are extensions, thus furnishing Badiou with the concept of the indiscernible multiple. This distinction between the indiscernible multiples of the generic extensions and the constructible multiples of M is also characteristic of their evental nature, insofar as "the event does not exist" and is not decided (Badiou 2005, 305) in the latter but is decided and is a condition of the former. Badiou therefore characterizes generic sets, indiscernible multiples, as the "ontological schema of a truth" (Badiou 2005, 510). A procedure of fidelity to the truth of an indiscernible multiple is a *generic procedure* of which Badiou lists four types: artistic, scientific, political, and amorous. He characterizes these generic procedures as "the four sources of truth" (Badiou 2005, 510). In addition to the role as metalanguage to the object language is the role of philosophy "to propose a conceptual framework in which the contemporary compossibility" of these generic procedures "can be grasped" (Badiou 2005, 4). These generic procedures are therefore characterized by Badiou as the conditions of philosophy. This marks an abrupt shift from talking about the sets of the model M as constructible multiples to talking about specific constructible multiples, or as Badiou refers to them, "situations" (Badiou 2005, 178), that are presentable by the model and its generic extensions. This is, however, consonant with Badiou's reorientation of the epistemic problem of the orthodox Platonist in mathematics. By claiming that mathematics is ontology, Badiou reorients the debate from an epistemological question about the nature of the relation between mathematical language and mathematical objects to an ontological question about how being is thought and how mathematics is implicated in this question. Badiou maintains that it "is nothing new to philosophers—that there must be a link between the existence of mathematics and the question of being" (Badiou 2005, 7), and he singles out "the Cantor-Gödel-Cohen-Easton symptom" (Badiou 2005, 280) of mathematics as providing the impetus for rethinking the nature of this link.

In regard to the orthodox epistemic problem, Badiou refuses the reduction of the subject matter of mathematics to the status of objects on the model of empirical objects. In *Being and Event*, he maintains that

> If the argument I present here holds up, the truth is that *there are no* mathematical objects. Strictly speaking, mathematics *presents nothing*, without constituting for all that an empty game, because not having anything to present, besides presentation

itself – which is to say the Multiple –, and thereby never adopting the form of the object, this is certainly a condition of all discourse on being *qua being*. (Badiou 2005, 7)

He rather draws upon Plato's account of anamnesis to reinstate mathematical objects to the status of Ideas. He argues that "A mathematical idea is neither subjective ("the activity of the mathematician"), nor objective ("independently existing structures"). In one and the same gesture, it breaks with the sensible and posits the intelligible. In other words, it is an instance of thinking" (Badiou 2004, 50). Badiou draws upon Cohen's deployment of Gödel's idea of constructible sets to characterize what he refers to as "the being of configurations of knowledge" (Badiou 2005, 284). Badiou argues that the axiom of constructability is "a veritable 'Idea' of the multiple" and that the constructible universe that is a "model" of the ZFC + V = L axioms is "the framework of the Ideas of the multiple" (Badiou 2005, 426). It is the axioms of "the Cantor-Gödel-Cohen-Easton symptom" (Badiou 2005, 280) that present this framework, and it is philosophy as metaontology that articulates how this framework should be thought in relation to the generic procedures. For this reason, Badiou maintains that,

> Mathematical ontology does not constitute, by itself, any orientation in thought, but it must be compatible with all of them: it must discern and propose the multiple-being which they have need of. (Badiou 2005, 284)

The ontology that Badiou proposes is dependent upon his axiomatic decision to present the empty set as the "non-being of the one," which he characterizes as the primitive name of being. This is a metaontological claim that cannot be derived mathematically. The ontology of the hierarchy of constructible sets, which is obtained by iterating the power set operation on the empty set through the transfinite, "is rooted in it" (Badiou 2004, 57). As Cassou-Noguès points out,

> Badiou can not found his axioms and establish that they are true propositions of the ontology of the multiple. But in the perspective that he puts in place, this foundation is not required. It is only necessary to remain faithful to . . . the event of Cantor's work and pursue a process that is thought to be producing truths, without ever being able to establish it. (Cassou-Noguès 2006, par. 33)

This is of course consonant with Badiou's own characterization of philosophy as metaontology, and of ontology as "a rich, complex, unfinishable science, submitted to the difficult constraint of a *fidelity* (deductive fidelity in this case)" (Badiou 2005, 8). The coherence of his approach rests solely upon the fidelity of his philosophy to this event. The consistency with which Badiou can continue to develop his philosophy in response to the ongoing engagement that mathematics has with the presentation of being qua being is the sole testament to this fidelity.

In this respect, Cohen's method of forcing is also behind the shift in focus that occurs in Badiou's second main text, *Logics of Worlds*, which exhibits an attempt to extend this fidelity by experimenting with the category theoretic extension of set theory, Heyting Algebra and Sheaf theory. Kanamori points out that "Forcing has been . . . adapted in a category theory context which is a casting of set theory in intuitionistic logic" (Kanamori 2008, 371). Heyting algebra replaces Boolean algebra in intuitionistic logic, where Boolean algebra is an important instrument in the interpretation of, and is deployed in an alternative approach to, Cohen's original procedures of the method of forcing. Kanamori also indicates that "forcing can be interpreted as the construction of a certain topos of sheaves. The internal logic of the topos of presheaves over a partially ordered set is essentially Cohen's forcing . . . ." (Kanamori 2008, 371). This move on Badiou's part can be seen as an attempt to address the fact of the ongoing engagement that mathematics has with the presentation of being qua being, and the potential limitations of the singular commitment to set theory in *Being and Event* as the definitive statement of this presentation.

It is not at all clear that this requirement of fidelity, which is characteristic of Badiou's metaontology, contributes anything to the debates about the realism of mathematical objects as conducted in the philosophy of mathematics. At best what Badiou is offering is an alternative way of formulating the question of fidelity, which for Badiou is to Cantorian set theory and the nonbeing of the one, rather than to the indispensability argument for Quine and Putnam, or to the existence of mathematical structures for Shapiro. The significant feature of this difference is that it entails accepting a radical alternative formulation of the relation between philosophy and mathematics that purports to render superfluous the empiricist framework within which these debates have to date been conducted. Whether or not Badiou's philosophy is robust enough to displace the indispensability argument or the structuralist program in realism has yet to be demonstrated in any convincing way.

On the difference between set theory and category theory

One of the strengths of Badiou's philosophy is that it does propose a solution to the question of fundamental ontology, the question of being qua being, and this is perhaps its most persuasive feature. It is also what is most dogmatic about Badiou's approach. Even though Badiou claims that philosophy must remain attentive to those truth procedures in mathematics that follow experimental lines of enquiry and that continue to develop new articulations of the presentation of being qua being, just how successful Badiou is in respecting the implications of the experimental lines of enquiry that mathematics opens up for the presentation of being qua being remains an open question.

Category theory is the program in mathematics that has established itself as an alternative power of unification in mathematics that challenges the dominant role set theory has traditionally played in this respect (See Salanskis 2002, 102; Corfield 2003, 198). Although category theory does appear to be the historical continuation of set theory, the concept of "categorization" is not a technical refinement of the concept of set but rather represents a profound conceptual change in mathematics. Category theory, which brackets off fundamental ontological concerns, allows you to work on mathematical structures without the need to first reduce them to sets. It is a general mathematical theory of structures and of the systems of structures. Despite this, Badiou's deployment of category theory in *Logics of Worlds* restricts itself to a particular axiomatic deployment of Grothendieck's topology, namely topos theory, which is the category theoretic presentation of set theory. In his paper "Sets, Categories and Topoi: approaches to ontology in Badiou's later work," Anindya Bhattacharyya notes that "topoi act as the appropriate categorical generalization of sets," which "can bridge the gap between sets and categories" (Bhattacharyya 2012, 92).[28] This narrow deployment of category theory betrays Badiou's work as being both overly bound to its early set theoretical underpinnings, and as being quite limited in its exploration of the full richness of what category theory has to offer for the presentation of being qua being. Bhattacharyya goes as far as to suggest that, in the face of developments in category theory, "the pure ontology of set theory is at the very least dispensable" (Bhattacharyya 2012, 94). This is argued within the context of maintaining "Badiou's subordination of philosophy to its mathematical condition while radically transforming the content of the mathematical ontology that condition prescribes" (Bhattacharyya 2012, 94). While I endorse the value of the project of extending the subordination of philosophy to its mathematical condition by exploring the potential of the mathematical ontology that category theory can provide independently of the pure ontology of set theory, I'd like to suggest that the alternative approach to the relation between mathematics and philosophy that has been canvased in this chapter, and which is represented in the work of Deleuze, is also a strong candidate for thinking through the potential of the mathematical ontology that category theory can provide independently of the pure ontology of set theory.

Category theory "began as a project to study continuous mappings within the program of algebraic topology" (Corfield 2003, 198). Work on the latter was initiated by Henri Poincaré (b.1854–1912) as a project to help develop tools to study differential equations qualitatively.[29] Category theory is much closer to Riemann's mathematical program than to set theory. In fact, the fields of algebraic topology and differential geometry, from which category theory emerged, developed in the wake of Riemann's work and were greatly influenced by it. The difference between algebraic topology and set-theoretic topology is that "the latter is . . . ubiquitous in routine arguments and formulations, but the former is almost unreasonably effective in advancing mathematical understanding" (Macintyre 1989, 366). Deleuze's work should be understood to engage with the kinds of mathematical problematics associated with such transformations in the discipline of mathematics, whether or not they can be given a set theoretical or formal determination. It is these kinds of mathematical problematics that Deleuze traces as an alternative lineage in the history of philosophy. The relevant question to ask as to whether the approach to the relation between mathematics and philosophy that is represented in the work of Deleuze can serve as a candidate for thinking through the potential of the mathematical ontology that category theory can provide independently of the pure ontology of set theory is whether the engagements that Deleuze undertakes with the discipline of mathematics are exhaustive? Or is the logic of Deleuze's engagements able to be repeated in relation to other developments in the discipline of mathematics that are not reducible to set theoretical axiomatics? the purpose of which would be to characterize new mathematical problematics that can be directly redeployed as models for reconfiguring philosophical problematics in relation to the history of philosophy, in order to construct new philosophical concepts.

One way of extending Deleuze's work in relation to category theory would be to think through the relation between the concept of smooth space that Deleuze develops in the chapter of *A Thousand Plateaus* entitled "The Smooth and the Striated," by drawing upon the work of Riemann, more directly in relation to the historical development of smooth infinitesimal analysis in the work of F. William Lawvere (b. 1937–). Lawvere, who is one of the founding figures of category theory, developed smooth infinitesimal analysis in an attempt to provide an axiomatic framework for the use of infinitesimals (Lawvere 1964; 1979), and also its topos theoretic extension, synthetic differential geometry (See Kock 1981).[30]

Mathematics as ontology in Badiou and Deleuze

While Badiou is clear about the relation that he figures philosophy to have to mathematics, i.e. the role of set theory as an ontological foundation for his philosophy (Badiou 2005), the role played by mathematics in the construction of Deleuze's ontology is certainly not stated as clearly from the outset, but is just as surely deployed as such by Deleuze.[31] While the mathematical problem mobilized by Badiou is set theory and its extension by Cohen's account of forcing and generic set, that deployed by Deleuze is primarily algebraic topology, functional analysis, and differential geometry.

By examining each of the different schemas by which Deleuze and Badiou deploy mathematics in their respective philosophies, it is clear that there is a shared focus on extracting mathematical problems from the history of mathematics and deploying them in particular philosophical contexts. However, what sets them apart is that Badiou, in *Being and Event* (2005), isolates and commits to one particular mathematical problematic, namely the axioms of set theory, and therefore to the foundational program in mathematics associated with it, and subsequently, in *Logics of Worlds* (2009), Badiou incorporates within this purview the category theoretic presentation of set theory. Whereas Deleuze, despite engaging with particular mathematical problematics, doesn't attach himself to a particular mathematical program. When he and Guattari comment on "the 'intuitionist' school", they insist that it "is of great importance in mathematics, not because it asserted the irreducible rights of intuition, or even because it elaborated a very novel constructivism, but because it developed a conception of *problems*, and of a *calculus of problems* that intrinsically rivals axiomatics and proceeds by other rules (notably with regard to the excluded middle)" (AT 570 n. 61). Deleuze extracts this concept of the calculus of problems itself as a mathematical problematic from the episode in the history of mathematics when intuitionism opposed axiomatics. It is the logic of this calculus of problems that he then redeploys in relation to a range of episodes in the history of mathematics that in no way binds him to the principles of intuitionism.

Deleuze is very much interested in the particular kinds of mathematical problematics that can be extracted from the history of mathematics that characterize advances in mathematics, and that can be used to characterize developments in the discourse of philosophy. By redeploying these actual mathematical problematics that are extracted from the history of mathematics in relation to the history of philosophy,

Deleuze can therefore also be understood to be redeploying the logic of the generation of mathematical problematics, i.e. the calculus of problems, in relation to the history of philosophy, as a model for the generation of philosophical problematics. It is in relation to the history of philosophy that Deleuze then determines the logic of the generation of philosophical problematics as the logic characteristic of a philosophy of difference.

In order to present an adequate account of the engagements that Deleuze undertakes between developments in the discipline of mathematics and the discourse of philosophy, the mechanism of operation of this logic, as determined in relation to the discipline of mathematics and the mathematical problematics extracted from it, requires explication. This has been the main project of the first four chapters of this book. Far from it being a logic of the relation between Royal science and nomad science, between axiomatics and problematics, or of that between the history of mathematics and the mathematical problematics that are extracted from it; it is rather a logic of the generation of nomad science itself, or of each mathematical problematic itself.

It is a logic that had proved incapable of being formalized by Royal science or axiomatic mathematics, up until the developments in set theory by Paul Cohen (1966). Cohen proved the fundamental theorem of forcing which is essentially the only known way to enlarge a model of set theory. This is of fundamental importance to Badiou's entire project, which can therefore be understood as an attempt to give a formal account of the very logic characteristic of the advances or transformations in mathematics. It is also important for understanding the nature of the difference in approach to this problem by Badiou and Deleuze, which is key to understanding the difference between their respective approaches to philosophy. This logic, the logic of the calculus of problems, is formalized by Badiou in axiomatic set theory and Cohen's extensions of it, and is given an informal characterization by Deleuze who traces its development through an alternative lineage in the history of mathematics from Cauchy through Weierstrassian analytic continuity and Poincaré's qualitative theory of differential equations to Riemann's concept of qualitative multiplicity. It is therefore not simply a logic characteristic of the relative difference between Royal and nomadic science, or between the history of mathematics and its related mathematical problematics. It is rather characteristic of the very logic of the generation of each mathematical problematic itself, whether perceived from the point of view of the foundational approach to the relation between mathematics and philosophy, as presented in the work of Badiou, or from the alternative point of view of the relation between mathematics and philosophy that is interested in exploring the full range of mathematical theories, practices, and developments, as presented in the work of Deleuze. It is this logic that Badiou deploys formally by establishing set theory as the ontological foundation for the system of philosophy that he develops. It is this logic that Deleuze redeploys in relation to the history of philosophy as a logic of difference in order to generate the philosophical problematics that he then uses to construct a philosophy of difference. Developing an understanding of the nature of this logic is the key to understanding the difference between Badiou's formal engagements with set theory and its role throughout his philosophy and Deleuze's informal engagement with the history of mathematics and his use of mathematical problematics throughout his work.

One of the main criticisms that Badiou brings to bear on the mathematical problems with which Deleuze constructs his philosophy is that they fail to characterize the distinction between change understood in terms of a simple consequence or modification, and change understood as innovation or novelty. In effect, Badiou disputes the claim to "newness" in the Deleuzian construction of concepts on the basis of his criticism of the framework of the relation between mathematics and philosophy developed by Deleuze. As a corollary to this criticism, Badiou argues that the mathematical problematic that he presents in his own work does adequately characterize this distinction, and can thereby be used to understand the mechanism that underpins innovative or novel developments, not only in philosophy, but also in other domains (See Gillespie 2008, 19–23). This criticism appears on the surface to be devastating for Deleuze's philosophy. Indeed, this criticism is considered by some to generate a crisis requiring a major re-evaluation of the legitimacy of their work (Alliez 2005, 267; Murphet 2006, 147).

There are two things that need to be kept in mind when considering this criticism, neither of which is clearly laid out by Badiou. First, this criticism is primarily a defense of the foundational approach to the relation between mathematics and philosophy against the alternative nonfoundational approach. Given the emerging role of category theory as an alternative power of unification in mathematics that is in the process of outflanking set theory and the role that it has traditionally played in this respect, and the very real possibility of extending Deleuze's project, and the alternative lineage in the history of mathematics that he traces, directly in relation to category theory, the alternative approach to the relation between mathematics and philosophy that Deleuze deploys is not so easily dismissed. Thus, the actual force of this criticism is severely diminished in the face of current developments in mathematics, namely category theory. Second, the different mathematical problematic that Badiou and Deleuze each extract from the history of mathematics engages with the same problem, the problem of determining the logic characteristic of the very advances and transformations in mathematics, which they each then redeploy in their respective philosophical systems. Badiou provides a formal solution to the problem whereas Deleuze provides an informal solution to the problem. The strength of Badiou's argument rests on the question of whether or not a formal solution renders an informal solution redundant. An example of a development of a formal solution to a mathematical problem in which this was initially thought to be the case, but where subsequent developments in mathematics proved this to be premature, is elaborated in Chapter 1. The formalization of Newton's approach to the infinitesimal calculus by Weierstrass's epsilon-delta method, which deals only with limits, did relegate Leibniz's infinitesimal to the backwaters of mathematical research for half a century until the developments in Non-Standard analysis problematized any assumption that the differential had been irrevocably expunged from the history of mathematics or from current mathematical practice.[32] So just because a formal solution to the problem has been provided, and this formal solution has been extended to its category theoretic presentation, this does not diminish the value and usefulness of the informal approach, particularly since the informal solution is based on quite a different mathematical problematic or set of problems than the formal solution.

There would be grounds to uphold Badiou's criticism of Deleuze if the mathematical problematic that Deleuze deploys did in fact fail to distinguish change in terms of simple consequence or modification from change understood as innovation or novelty; however, this is not the case. The mathematical problem that Deleuze draws upon as a model by tracing an alternative lineage in the history of mathematics accounts for the distinction as follows; change understood as simple consequence or modification is accounted for in the model at the level of Riemann surfaces, which are the product of the power series expansion of a meromorphic function, in terms of a rearrangement of the relations between Riemann surfaces, or because different Riemann surfaces are put in relation with one another. Change understood as innovation or novelty is accounted for in the model as the result of the construction of a new essential singularity or Riemann surface, which is produced by the expansion of the power series of a meromorphic function that results from different analytic functions relating to one another, i.e. as a result of different polynomials of analytic functions forming different meromorphic functions.

The distinction is not a formal distinction; therefore, it is true that the distinction, and therefore the claim to novelty, is not couched in a formal language. However, this is different to the argument that it is incapable of making the distinction in its own terms. Badiou conflates an affirmative determination in the former statement, which is true, with an affirmative determination in the latter argument, which is false. There are two factors that lead to this conflation on Badiou's part. The first of which contributes to the second. The first is the presumption that only the foundational approach to the relation between mathematics and philosophy is able to characterize this distinction. Of course were this in fact the case, then Badiou would be right and the conflation would be a moot point. However, as has been demonstrated in the previous chapters of the present book, this is not the case. The second is that Badiou's account of Deleuze's engagement with the history of mathematics is decidedly partial. In fact, Badiou doesn't provide an account of the mathematics with which Deleuze engages but rather just a summary dismissal of Deleuze's engagement with mathematics based upon it not respecting the question of foundations as Badiou thinks they should be. Contrary to Badiou's stance, it is not the case that in order to respect both the significance and the implications of the Cantorian development of set theory and its subsequent axiomatization, one must adopt a foundational approach to the relation between mathematics and philosophy. The developments in category theory are testament to this. The work of Weyl on Riemann surfaces (Weyl 1913), which is instrumental to the development of Deleuze's approach to mathematics,[33] is also a case in point. Weyl, who makes Riemann's intuitive representations more explicit by using a generalization of Weierstrass's analytic continuation and Hilbert's axiomatic method, is well aware of and working within the framework of Zermelo's axiomatization of set theory (Zermelo 1908), despite not adopting a foundational approach to mathematics. Even Cantor had a concept of a well-ordered set which ensured that his theory of sets was "not vulnerable to the set-theoretic antinomies" (Newstead 2009, 546), in particular that subsequently enshrined in Russell's paradox:[34]

The concept of a *well-ordered* set is thereby shown to be fundamental for the whole of set theory. That it is always possible to bring every *well- defined* set into the form of a *well-ordered* set seems to me to be a law of thought (*Denkgesetz*) rich in consequences and especially remarkable for its general validity. (Cantor 1932, 169)[35]

The problem with Cantor's definition from the foundational point of view is that it relies on intuitive elements and is therefore not adequate to establish mathematical foundations.[36] This is only a problem from the foundationalist point of view, and it is only from this point of view that Cantorian set theory can be considered to be naïve, where by naïve mathematicians mean a set theory that places no restriction on what could count as a set.[37] It is clear from Cantor's definition of well-ordered sets that Cantor does impose restrictions adequate to overcome the antinomy, albeit only intuitive restrictions. It is also clear that these restrictions are inadequate to do the job of providing foundations; however, this is only the case if approaching the problem from the point of view of foundations. Badiou's criticism of Deleuze can therefore be understood to stem from Badiou's refusal to acknowledge not only Deleuze's approach to the relation between mathematics and philosophy, but also any nonfoundational approach to this relation. Badiou's engagement with both the history of mathematics and the history of philosophy is singularly skewed by this presumption. One has to respect the fidelity with which Badiou pursues his own philosophical agenda, but there are more ways of engaging with these issues than he is willing to concede.

While the distinction that Bergson makes between the dogmatic, pure, or radical mechanist and the more epistemologically modest approach to mechanical explanation is not directly transferable from its nineteenth century context in which it was deployed, it is instructive of the distinction that can be understood to be operating between the two different approaches to the relation between mathematics and philosophy that is developed in this chapter. By adopting the foundational approach to the relation between mathematics and philosophy, Badiou also takes on the dogmatism of the pure or radical mechanists, albeit with the formal justification of axiomatic set theory to underwrite his decision. It is dogmatism nevertheless. Deleuze's more epistemologically modest approach doesn't dispute the formal developments upon which Badiou's project stands, but at the same time doesn't accept the dismissal of the nonfoundational approach, neither just for being nonfoundational, nor for actively exploring the value of informal mathematical models to reconfigure philosophical problems and perhaps generate useful solutions. Just as Bergson remains overcommitted to a concept of duration that is distinct from space while the developments in mathematics outpace his arguments, so too does Badiou remain over committed to the pure ontology of set theory while developments in mathematics, namely in category theory, outflank and outpace his attempts to reconcile his work with it.

Conclusion

The "vindication" of Leibniz's account of the differential

A debate about the role of Leibniz's infinitesimal in Deleuze's account of the differential calculus has recently developed, which directly challenges the account of the role of mathematics in Deleuze's philosophy that I have proposed,[1] and which I defend in the this book. In a recent article in *Continental Philosophy Review*, entitled "Hegel and Deleuze on the metaphysical interpretation of the calculus," Henry Somers-Hall claims that "the Leibnizian interpretation of the calculus, which relies on infinitely small quantities is rejected by Deleuze" (Somers-Hall 2010, 567; 2012, 173). While this comment may appear to be claiming that Deleuze rejects Leibniz's interpretation of the calculus, this in fact is not the case. Somers-Hall's claim should rather be understood to be that it is "the Leibnizian interpretation of the calculus" that Deleuze rejects, which Somers-Hall aligns with the subsequent finite interpretation of the calculus that understands the differential quantitatively as "a determinate, if infinitesimal magnitude" (Somers-Hall 2010, 567). This claim does not entail the rejection of Leibniz's infinitesimal, which he considered to be a useful fiction, the conceptual character of which continues to play a part in Deleuze's account of the metaphysics of the calculus. In order to further clarify the terms of this debate, I would like to take up two further issues with Somers-Hall's presentation of Deleuze's account of the calculus in the article, which is largely reproduced in his recent book (Somers-Hall 2012). The first is with the way that my own work on Deleuze's account of the calculus is reduced to what Somers-Hall refers to as "modern interpretations of the calculus," by which he means set-theoretical accounts and which he aligns with the finite interpretation of the calculus. For a start, set theory has not brought all fields of mathematics that develop and deploy the calculus under its wings; examples include algebraic topology, functional analysis, and differential geometry, to name but a few. So it is historically inaccurate to reduce all modern interpretations of the calculus to set theoretical ones. Deleuze is quite aware of this, and the history of the calculus that he charts in a number of places in his work traces the development of the calculus that continues to elude this reduction. So, in addition to the two interpretations of the calculus proposed by Somers-Hall, which include the

> finite interpretations, which understand the differential quantitatively, as a determinate, if infinitesimal magnitude, and the infinite interpretation of Hegel, which only gets as far as the vanishing of the quantum, and therefore leaves its status as vanished (from the realm of quanta at least) untouched. (Somers-Hall 2010, 567)

both of which I agree Deleuze rejects, there is in fact a third interpretation of the calculus, the conceptual character of which is the focus of Deleuze's interest. Historically, the third interpretation was marginalized as a result of efforts to determine the rigorous algebraic foundations of the calculus. It was these efforts that, on Somers-Hall's account, lead to the development of the finite interpretation of the calculus. The alternative that I am referring to is the approach to the calculus that developed the operation of integration as a method of summation in the form of series, rather than the canonical approach that treats integration as the inverse transformation of differentiation.[2] The series dealt with by this alternative version of the calculus are Taylor series or power series expansions, the production of which depends solely on the relations between differentials at a given point, and which converge with differentiable functions, rather than the type of series dealt with by Somers-Hall, which relies on the differential equations of those functions and "the form of series that emerge from the repeated differentiation of the area around a singularity" (Somers-Hall 2010, 568; 2012, 175).[3] The distinction between a series "at a point" and the series of measurements that can be made on either side of a point is not made in Somers-Hall's account. Indeed the former is conflated with and reduced to the latter.

The importance of this distinction is demonstrated in Chapter 2 in relation to the work of Maimon, in Chapter 3 in relation to the work of Bergson, and in Chapter 4 in relation to the work of Lautman. In Chapter 2, it is demonstrated in the discussion of the application of the mathematical rule of the understanding, which is the operation of integration as a method of summation in the form of series, to the elements of sensation, which are modeled on differentials. For Maimon, it is this process that brings the manifolds of sensation to consciousness as sensible objects of intuition. In Chapter 3, this distinction is important for Bergson when discussing the distinction between immediate and useful perceptions (MM 185–6). The "useful" perceptions are characterized as infinitely small elements, and the task of the philosopher, like that of the mathematician, is to reconstitute the real curve from these differential elements by means of the "true work of integration", which, when attempting to determine the function by starting from the differential, is a process of summation in the form of a series. Rather than using simple differentiation as a model, which involves passing from the function to its derivative, this example starts with infinitely small elements and poses the problem of reconstituting from these elements the curve itself. It is also important to Weyl's presentation of Riemann's work in Chapter 3, and in Chapter 4, where Weyl's work on Riemann is used by Lautman to characterize the local-global conceptual couple.

While Somers-Hall does note that Deleuze appeals to another interpretation of the calculus, which Deleuze describes as "barbaric" (Somers-Hall 2010, 556; 2012, 268), Somers-Hall makes no elaboration of this point. He seems to think that to say an interpretation is "barbaric" implies that it is a reference to the distant past, rather than to actual developments on the margins of mathematics that have a robust history of their own and have directly given rise to contemporary practices in mathematics. Deleuze actually says: "barbaric or pre-scientific interpretations of the differential calculus" (DR 171). The reference to the "barbaric or pre-scientific" is not a reference to the temporally pre-scientific, i.e. pre scientific revolution. This is evident from the fact that the thinkers to whom Deleuze refers to in this passage are predominantly eighteenth and nineteenth century mathematicians and post-Kantian philosophers whose responses to Kant draw upon the developments in the differential calculus at the time. What is important to realize is that when Deleuze says that the interpretation is barbaric or pre-scientific this in no way implies that it is a nonmathematical interpretation, indeed the exemplar of this barbarous or prescientific interpretation is the third alternative interpretation of the calculus, which is mathematical and committed to the differential. By calling this interpretation prescientific, I take Deleuze to mean its contested and marginal status with respect to mathematical rigor because of its commitment to the differential. The claim that the barbaric or prescientific interpretation is fundamentally mathematical does not, however, preclude the deployment of its conceptual character in other discourses, such as the philosophical discourses of the post-Kantians, which are crucial to the development of Deleuze's own post-Kantianism.

The second issue that I'd like to take up is that this oversight of Somers-Hall about the alternative interpretation of the integral calculus means that his presentation of Deleuze's account of the calculus is only partial, and the partial character of his presentation leads him to make a number of unnecessary presumptions.[4] I agree with Somers-Hall up to the point in the paper where he correctly identifies the crucial difference between Deleuze's account of the calculus and that of Hegel as being concerned with "the value of the differential equation [which] is to be understood according to its difference from the primitive function" (Somers-Hall 2010, 569). What I disagree with Somers-Hall about is the nature of this difference. Somers-Hall presents only the "first aspect" of this difference. The second aspect involves characterizing the difference between the two different interpretations of integration. The primitive function is calculated by means of the inverse transformation of the integral calculus. The procedure requires the broad derivative function, i.e. the entire function that expresses the relation between the differentials of the differential relation at any point of the curve. If this procedure is supposed to start solely with differentials at a given point, as it is in Deleuze's account, then all that is available are two differentials, dy and dx, in relation to one another in a differential relation, dy/dx, which is the derivative only at one point, but not the broader derivative function itself. So integration to produce the primitive function, which requires the broader derivative function, is unable to be carried out. However, integration can be carried out by means of the method of summation in the form of a series. This method is appropriate in this instance because the coefficients of the function that is produced in this way depend solely on the relation between the differentials at that point. What is produced is a power series expansion, which can be written as a polynomial,[5] the coefficients of each of its terms being the successive differential relations evaluated at that point. Where the differential relation gives the value of the gradient at the given point, the value of the derivative of the differential relation, i.e. the second derivative, indicates the rate at which the gradient is changing at that point, which allows a more accurate approximation of the nature of the differentiable function in the neighborhood of that point. The value of the third derivative indicates the rate at which the second derivative is changing at that point. In fact, the more successive derivatives that can be evaluated at the point, the more accurate will be the approximation of the differentiable function in the immediate neighborhood of that point. As the number of terms approaches infinity, the polynomial of the power series expansion converges with the differentiable function in the neighborhood of the given point.

Deleuze makes the distinction to which Somers-Hall refers in the following passage. In respect of the differential relation, Deleuze argues that

> It is determinable first in qualitative form, and in this connection it expresses a function which differs in kind from the so-called primitive function . . . This is only a first aspect, however, for in so far as it expresses another quality, the differential relation remains tied to the individual values or to the quantitative variations corresponding to that quality (for example, tangent). It is therefore differentiable in turn, and testifies only to the power of Ideas to give rise to Ideas of Ideas. (DR 172)

The qualitative form in which the differential relation is first determinable is considered by Somers-Hall to be the "differential equation," i.e. the equation of the relation between the differentials, which would be the broader derivative function if this were integrable by means of the inverse transformation of differentiation to produce the primitive function. However, as mentioned above, starting solely with differentials at a point does not provide enough information to determine the broader derivative function, just the derivative at that point. What I claim rather is that, while the first aspect in which the differential relation is determinable is the qualitative function, the second aspect in which the differential is determinable is insofar as it is "differentiable in turn", i.e. in the polynomial of the power series expansion, the production of which depends solely on the relations between differentials at that point. This claim is also supported by comments that Deleuze makes about series a few pages later, both in drawing upon Wronski's criticism of Lagrange, when Deleuze argues that "differentials . . . constitute an unconditioned rule . . . for the construction of series or the generation of discontinuities which constitute its material" (DR 175);[6] and in relation to Poincaré, when he refers to the example of the "dips, nodes, focal points, centers" (DR 177).[7] The polynomial of the power series expansion is different in kind from the primitive function insofar as it is generated from differentials rather than produced by the inverse transformation of differentiation to deal "with relations of actual magnitudes" (Somers-Hall 2010, 569).

So while I agree with the specific problematic that Somers-Hall identifies in Deleuze's account of the calculus, I maintain that Somers-Hall provides only a partial account, i.e. only of the "first aspect," and overlooks the second aspect, the alternative version of the integral calculus as integration by means of the method of summation in the form of a series, and the history of its development. This second aspect provides an account of the movement of generation that Somers-Hall calls for, and provides a model of the calculus that Deleuze draws upon in developing his response to Kant, which is elaborated in Chapter 2 in relation to Maimon.

Where I consider Somers-Hall to be misleading in his presentation of my own work is in his stated assumption that my work endorses what he claims to be "relatively standard" in the reading of Deleuze, i.e.

to treat him as using the tools of modern mathematics to cut off the path to Hegelian dialectic by resolving the antinomies at the base of the calculus. This view is clearly implicit in De Landa's interpretation, and is most clearly expressed by Simon Duffy in *The Logic of Expression: Quality, Quantity and Intensity in Spinoza, Hegel and Deleuze*, where he writes that, 'Deleuze . . . establishes a historical continuity between Leibniz's differential point of view of the infinitesimal calculus and the differential calculus of contemporary mathematics thanks to the axioms of non-standard analysis which allow the inclusion of the infinitesimal in its arithmetization; a continuity which effectively bypasses the methods of the differential calculus which Hegel uses in the Science of Logic to support the development of the dialectical logic' (Duffy 2006a, 74–5). I want to argue, contrary to this view, that Deleuze in fact wants to reject both positions in order to develop a theory of the calculus which escapes completely from the dichotomy of the finite and infinite. (Somers-Hall 2010, 566–7; See also 2012, 266–7)

Somers-Hall here identifies my work with the modern finite interpretations of the calculus, which, like Russell's, moves "away from an antinomic interpretation of mathematics" (Somers-Hall 2010, 560) towards a finite interpretation of the calculus which "understands the differential quantitatively, as a determinate, if infinitesimal magnitude" (Somers-Hall 2010, 567). This reduction is unwarranted and betrays the partial grasp that Somers-Hall has demonstrated not only of the history of the calculus, but also of Deleuze's engagement with it. Despite the goal posts having been shifted dramatically by Robinson's nonstandard analysis, the antinomies at the base of the calculus that Deleuze draws upon to develop a metaphysics of the calculus are not resolved by Robinson's proof. It also is important to point out that Robinson's argument, that the nonstandard proof of the infinitesimal "fully vindicated" (Robinson 1996, 2) Leibniz's ideas about using infinitesimals in the calculus, does not actually provide a proof of Leibniz's infinitesimal itself.[8] Robinson's infinitesimals are not, and do not purport to be, Leibniz's infinitesimal. In fact, there have been a number of independent formalizations of the infinitesimal since Robinson (Lawvere 1979, Bell 1998, Connes 2001), none of which are formalizations of Leibniz's infinitesimal, and none of which can be used to resolve the antinomies at the base of the calculus in respect of Leibniz's infinitesimal. In the *Logic of Expression*, I argue that Robinson's axioms allow "Leibniz's ideas to be 'fully vindicated,' as Newton's had been thanks to Weierstrass" (Duffy 2006a, 56).[9] It is quite clear from the context of this argument that Newton's fluxion, while vindicated, is not proved to be correct by Weierstrass. To draw from this paragraph that Leibniz's infinitesimal is somehow differently vindicated, i.e. that it is actually proved to be correct by Robinson, is to misconstrue the argument. It is important to reiterate that Somers-Hall's claim that Deleuze rejects "the Leibnizian interpretation of calculus," which Somers-Hall aligns with the finite interpretation, which understands the differential quantitatively as a determinate if infinitesimal magnitude, does not entail the rejection of Leibniz's infinitesimal, insofar as Leibniz considered it to be a useful fiction, the conceptual character of which continues to play a part in Deleuze's account of the metaphysics of the calculus. What is vindicated by Robinson's proof is Leibniz's introduction of the concept of the infinitesimal to the calculus in the first place, i.e. taking the concept of the infinitesimal seriously despite all of the problems associated with its use. In respect of Leibniz, the proofs are inspirational rather than demonstrative. What Robinson's proof represents is the end of any legitimacy in the impetus to bury the infinitesimal once and for all. Even Badiou is quite clear on this point. In "The Being of Number," he maintains that "non-classical models" of number "open up the fertile path of nonstandard analysis, thereby rendering infinite (or infinitesimal) numbers respectable once again" (Badiou 2004, 59). Deleuze acknowledges that "the interpretation of the differential calculus has indeed taken the form of asking whether infinitesimals are real or fictive" (DR 177), however, for Deleuze, the question is rhetorical, for it is of little importance whether the infinitesimals are real, and if they aren't this doesn't signify the contemptible fictive character of their position. What is important for Deleuze is the very conceptual character of the mathematical problematic that the hypothesis of the infinitesimal introduced to mathematics, and that can be traced through a range of developments in the history of mathematics. The lack of a mention of Robinson by Deleuze in *Difference and Repetition* in no way undermines the significance of his developments to Deleuze's project. Robinson is given a place in this alternative lineage in the history of mathematics in the *Fold*. The upshot of all of this is that Leibniz's infinitesimal, while fictional, no longer warrants contempt, nor do the various guises that the concept of the differential has taken, which have skirted the two interpretations of the calculus put forward by Somers-Hall. As far as Deleuze is concerned, these developments mean that it is no longer a question of reluctantly tolerating their "inexactitude" in one or the other of these interpretations, but rather of embracing them as deployed in this third alternative interpretation of the calculus, as he does. It is the conceptual character of the differential as deployed in this third alternative integral calculus as a method of summation in the form of series, the subsequent developments of which lead to Poincaré's qualitative theory of differential equations,[10] that provides the model for "the extra-propositional or sub-representative element expressed in the Idea of the differential, precisely in the form of a problem" (DR 178). It is in the work of Maimon, specifically Maimon's account of mathematical cognition, that Deleuze finds the criteria to characterize the "Idea of the differential," admittedly only after updating the structure of Maimon's system in response to subsequent developments in the calculus.[11]

On a point of interpretation of *Difference and Repetition*, when Deleuze is distinguishing the zeros of differentials from "quanta as objects of intuition," on the understanding that differentials are not objects of intuition, he argues that "Quanta as objects of intuition always have particular values; and even when they are united in a fractional relation, each maintains a value independently of the relation" (1994, 171). Somers-Hall misreads this statement as being about differentials, rather than as a statement about the distinction between a relation between differentials and a simple relation between "quanta as objects of intuition" (Somers-Hall 2010, 567; 2012, 173). This failure to distinguish between the two further colors Somers-Hall's account, and highlights his enthusiasm to fit the history of the infinitesimal into a schema of finite and infinite interpretations of the calculus, which, I've argued,[12] is a poor fit given the complexity of the developments of the history of mathematics.[13]

As for the claim about modern mathematics "cutting off the path to Hegelian dialectic", what is at stake in the nineteenth century integral calculus, which is completely divorced from the Robinsonian proofs of the infinitesimal, is the difference between integral calculus as the inverse operation of differentiation on the one hand and as a method of summation on the other. Deleuze's championing of the latter doesn't "cut off the path to Hegelian dialectic," but rather provides an alternative path in the history of mathematics to that followed by Hegel, who championed the former. The alternative history of mathematics that Deleuze charts provides the resources to develop an account of the metaphysics of the calculus in which the history of the differential is intimately implicated, rather than sidelined. I therefore maintain that I have not engaged in a project of retrospectively rewriting the history of the calculus in order to make dubious moves against Hegel. What I have tried to do,[14] and which is also the aim of the this book, is to lay bare the history of the concept of the differential in all of its flavors and to give an account of how this history operates in Deleuze's work.

Somers-Hall seems to think that my work in Duffy 2006a makes a "major interpretative error" in overlooking "the propositional/extrapropositional" (Somers-Hall 2012, 6) distinction in Deleuze's work. In response, it is worthwhile mentioning again my comments on the distinction between the static ontological genesis and the static logical genesis made in Chapter 1. It is important to note that the static ontological genesis (LS 109–12) is distinct from the static logical genesis (LS 118–26). While the static logical genesis is correlated with the structure of logical propositions in language, "with its determinate dimensions (denotation, manifestation, signification)" (LS 120), the static ontological genesis, the two levels of which are the focus of the this study, is concerned with "the objective correlates of these propositions which are first produced as ontological propositions (the denoted, the manifested, and the signified)" (LS 120). "The first level of actualization produces . . . individuated worlds and individual selves which populate each of these worlds" (LS 111). This correlates with, or is modeled on, the logic of differen*t*iation. The second level of actualization "opens different worlds and individuals" to the individuated worlds and individual selves of the first level "as so many variables and possibilities" (LS 115). This correlates with, or is modeled on, the logic of differen*c*iation. I maintain that it is in relation to the distinction in the *Logic of Sense* between the static ontological genesis and the static logical genesis that the propositional/extrapropositional distinction should be understood to operate in Deleuze's work.[15] This is also the appropriate context for understanding how my work relates to the propositional/extrapropositional distinction. By sidelining the role of mathematics in the determination of Deleuze's understanding of the static ontological genesis, Somers-Hall leaves out one of the major features of Deleuze's project that establishes the framework for adequately characterizing the nature of the propositional/extrapropositional distinction in his work.

The scienticity debate in Deleuze studies

One obvious antagonistic line of research that Somers-Hall defends his approach against is the materialist tendency in the work of some scholars working in the field of Deleuze studies. From the quotes above, Somers-Hall declares his position in what is referred to by Peter Gaffney as "the scienticity polemic" (Gaffney 2010, 7),[16] according to which there are two divergent approaches to reading of Deleuze's engagement with science evident in Deleuze studies.

> The first compares Deleuze's work to theories and discoveries advanced by contemporary 'radical' science (the notion of complexity in various branches of theoretical science: symbiogenesis in biology; topology in physics and mathematics, etc.). . . . The second approach tries to limit this comparison, using terms that point nonetheless to radical developments in the philosophy of science (intuitionism, constructivism), developments that run parallel to Deleuze's nonepistemic methods and aims. Both approaches render valuable insight into Deleuze's work, but they also represent diverging paths for the future of Deleuzian studies. (Gaffney 2010, 8)

The risk of the first approach is the "general merger of metaphysics and theoretical science" (Gaffney 2010, 9). The second approach counters this risk by drawing a line between physics and metaphysics, in order to highlight "the epistemic truth claims" of the former as they contrast with the "philosophical openness" (Gaffney 2010, 9) of the latter.

The most well known proponent of the first approach is Manuel De Landa. In his various texts, De Landa undertakes to eliminate the concept of metaphysics from science, in favor of an ontology that is appropriate to science. In this way, De Landa advocates the reduction of Deleuze's metaphysics to ontology, and that ontology to a materialist ontology, which is expressed in various complex physical systems. The corollary to this reductive move being that a descriptive account of these complex physical systems is adequate to provide an account of that ontology. De Landa defends this move against what he sees as the "idealist" alternative.[17]

Somers-Hall provides what can be taken as a critical response to De Landa that establishes how he plans to deal with this issue differently (Somers-Hall 2010, 566–7). I happen to agree with Somers-Hall that Deleuze effectively precludes any sense in which his philosophy could be interpreted as either materialist *or* idealist, at least insofar as each of these terms refers only to the exclusion of the categories comprised by the other. Any determination of the metaphysics of the calculus is always the result of an account of how the two are implicated in relation to one another.

Rather than understanding these two approaches in the scienticity debate as competing strategies within Deleuze studies, I see them as two quite distinct approaches to Deleuze's work that have quite different aims. The first is engaged in the project of redeploying, more or less adequately, certain aspects of Deleuze's philosophy specific to a particular task at hand in other domains. Whereas the second approach is engaged in the project of explicating the arguments drawn from the history of philosophy and the history of various disciplines in science that Deleuze draws upon in the construction of his philosophy, which can also be done more or less adequately.

The less adequately that Deleuze's work is redeployed by proponents of the first approach, the more this work can be characterized as operating independently of the framework of Deleuze's philosophy, which is rather being drawn upon solely for inspiration. The cogency of this work should then be judged independently of the adequacy with which it deploys Deleuze's work and rather in terms of its own intrinsic value, or in terms of what it can produce, whether as an extension of Deleuze's philosophy or insofar as it embarks upon lines of enquiry in new and different directions. While De Landa's self described "materialist reconstruction of Deleuzian philosophy" (Gaffney 2010, 330) doesn't follow Deleuze's philosophy to the letter, it does, however, set up the possibility for redeploying this material more adequately in relation to Deleuze's philosophy, which represents its enduring value to Deleuze studies.

This same degree of generosity is operable in relation to the second approach. The problem here is that in attempting to reconstruct the philosophical arguments or scientific heritage that Deleuze draws upon, the proponents of this approach risk offering retrograde appraisals of Deleuze's philosophy by favoring one line of investigation to the detriment of the rich plurality of sources that Deleuze draws upon. In this instance, the best possible outcome would be a range of competing historical accounts of his work, each having its merits and contributing to a broader appreciation of it. The flip side of this would be that a number of speculative dead ends with respect to Deleuze's philosophy itself are explored, but again, the merits of these endeavors should be determined rather in terms of their own intrinsic value or in terms of what they themselves can produce.

There is no reason why there couldn't be a degree of overlap of the two approaches in any particular engagement with Deleuze's work. What is important, however, is maintaining a degree of clarity with respect to the approach that is being deployed at any one time. So it seems to me that the only basis for these different strategies to be perceived as competing with one another is if the proponent of one approach makes false claim to be working under the jurisdiction of the other approach. This is what seems to me to be at stake in "the scienticity polemic", and particularly in the case of De Landa.

Badiou's relation to Lautman and the mathematical real

In *Being and Event*, Badiou openly declares that what he owes to Lautman's writings, "even in the very foundational intuitions for this book, is immeasurable" (Badiou 2005, 482). This aspect of Badiou's work has recently been addressed in an article by Sean Bowden, "Alain Badiou: Problematics and the different senses of Being in *Being and Event*" (Bowden 2008), the main argument of which is largely reproduced in the chapter of the book that I coedited with him, *Badiou and Philosophy* (Bowden and Duffy 2012). Bowden sets up his reading of Badiou's thesis that "ontology = mathematics" by drawing upon what I consider to be quite a problematic understanding of the work of Lautman. This understanding of Lautman was developed by Bowden in relation to the work of Deleuze in *The priority of events* (Bowden 2011a).

Bowden considers Lautman's dialectic of Idea to be "transcendent with respect to mathematics and can be posed outside of mathematics" (Bowden 2008, 36; 2011a, 110–11; Bowden and Duffy 2012, 42), rather than as being the fourth point of view of the mathematical real, which Lautman is quite explicit in claiming (Lautman 2011, 183). Bowden does not distinguish between the mathematical real and mathematical theories, but rather collapses the former into the latter. This effectively allows him to (mis)read Lautman's references to a dialectic of ideas as being references to a general dialectic that exists independently of the mathematics, and to characterize the mathematics as just one of many ways that this general dialectic of ideas is made apparent. His reconstruction of Lautman's thesis is that mathematics provides some kind of evidence of an external and more general dialectic that is equally accessible by means of some kind of analysis performed in regard to or from within other discourses. This is a mischaracterization of what Lautman claims, and indeed of what Lautman can in fact claim given his argument. What seems to be clear in Lautman's work is that he considers himself to be working within the constraints of the discourse of mathematics, and the structure of the dialectic that he presents is determined as operating within the expanded concept of mathematics that he makes claim to: the mathematical real. The dialectic of ideas is independent of the mathematical theories, or the mathematics per se, but not of the expanded understanding of the mathematical real.

Lautman does claim that the structure of the dialectic is not the sole privy of the mathematical real, and that it can therefore also "be found" in other discourses. However, he does not claim that this is the case because the dialectic is able to be generalized, insofar as it is "transcendent" with respect to the mathematical real, as Bowden claims. While Lautman makes strong claim to the unity of mathematics, which was controversial at the time and remains so today, he does not make any claim whatsoever as to the unity of all discourses. What Lautman argues rather is that this is the case because the way that the structure of the dialectic operates in the mathematical real functions as a model for recognizing how it can be understood to operate in other discourses.

One of the problems with Bowden's argument surfaces in the following passage when he argues that "because the 'sufficient reason' for the diversity and development of mathematical theories, along with their progressive integrations and interferences, cannot be found within mathematics itself, one is obliged to affirm the prior existence of something like the dialectic of Ideas" (Bowden 2008, 36; 2011a, 111; Bowden and Duffy 2012, 43). First, Bowden here reduces the mathematical real to "the mathematics", i.e. to mathematical theories. Second, the sufficient reason, to which Bowden refers, is that required to recognize unity in the diversity of mathematical theories and their development. The obligation, as Bowden puts it, therefore refers solely to the impetus of the dialectic to provide an account of this unity, not of the actual development of the mathematical theories themselves, which are meaningful in themselves as theories. Nor does the obligation to affirm the priority of the dialectic extend to affirming its generality with respect to, or its transcendence of, the mathematical real. On the contrary, the dialectic of ideas remains a point of view within the mathematical real.

Lautman maintains that we are able to recognize the logic of relations structured by the dialectic in other discourses solely by virtue of the mathematical theories in which these relations are incarnated, as Lautman argues, "the effectuation of these connections is immediately mathematical theory" (Lautman 2011, 28). That is to say that it is the way in which the mathematical logic is deployed in other discourses that allows such a discourse to be understood to operate according to the dialectic. By dialectic Lautman means here the dialectic of the mathematical real. So mathematics is not privileged over other discourses according to Lautman because, on the one hand, he doesn't consider there to be a definite system of mathematical laws at the base of nature, and, on the other hand, he does consider it to be intimately involved in our understanding of the very dialectical structure of those discourses. What this amounts to is that mathematical theories are not the sole privy of mathematics, or the mathematical real; they also provide the ground for understanding how the dialectic operates in other discourses. So when Lautman argues that "mathematical logic does not enjoy in this respect any special privilege. It is only one theory among others and the problems that it raises or that it solves are found almost identically elsewhere" (Lautman 2011, 28), by privileged, we should also understand exclusive to the mathematical real.

What is important about mathematics, for Lautman, Deleuze and Badiou, is its *a priority*, which allows the dialectic of ideas to be recognized as a component of the mathematical real in a way that is not directly accessible in other discourses. This sets up the mathematical real, and the structure of the dialectic as it operates in the mathematical real, as a model for the structure of other discourses, and for how we can understand these other discourses to operate. It is the conceptual character of mathematical theories or problems that, when deployed in relation to other discourses, allows such a discourse to be understood to operate according to the dialectic, or to be structured by the dialectic. It is by tracing the history of the conceptual character of the differential as deployed in a number of developments in mathematics, and the deployment of the conceptual character of these developments in mathematics in relation to specific problems in the history of philosophy, that the structure of the dialectic of the mathematical real has been developed in this book as an important component of the structure of Deleuze's philosophy.

What is problematic in Bowden's argument, and this is also reflected in his assessment of Badiou and Badiou's interest in Lautman, is that Bowden mischaracterizes Lautman as making some kind of a gesture toward an already existing transcendent dialectical process that subsumes not only mathematics, but also all other discourses. The way that Bowden characterizes this general dialectic is in terms of the question of being, which he presents as "the" general problematic Idea that determines the structure of the dialectic in all discourses, including mathematics (Bowden 2008, 32). It is this problematic reading that allows Bowden to claim that Badiou's thesis that "ontology = mathematics" is simply one possible response to this general problematic Idea, and that Badiou's concept of being is therefore "equivocal", i.e. insofar as it is both the statement "ontology = mathematics" and a response to the problematic Idea (Bowden 2008, 33).

I have two comments to make in defense of Badiou in this respect. First, in relation to Badiou's use of set theory. Badiou includes Cohen's independence results — that CH is independent from ZFC, which effectively showed that CH does not hold in all models of set theory — in his understanding of set theory. Set theory, in this respect, is a formalization of the structure of the dialectic of ideas. It is therefore not a response to the dialectic of ideas, but a formal restatement of its structure, just as Deleuze's provides an informal restatement of its structure. For this reason, Badiou's concept of being is not equivocal as Bowden claims. Second, set theory, as qualified above, operates as the mathematical theory that provides the ground for understanding how the dialectic operates in other discourses, namely the four conditions that Badiou proposes: Science, Politics, Art, Love. So for Badiou, an Event is a dialectical Idea, and felicity to it operates according to the structure of the dialectic of ideas.

Bowden's main problem is what amounts to the dogmatic presumption that there is an overarching dialectic of ideas that subsumes the operations of all discourses.[18] This reduces the work of Lautman, Deleuze, and Badiou to merely providing descriptive accounts of this dialectic of ideas using different terms. Rather than their respective works being arguments for a particular kind of dialectic of ideas that can be understood to operate in relation to other discourses by virtue of the way that it operates in the mathematical real, i.e. the detail of the structure of the dialectic can only be offered in terms of the mathematical real, however, this structure can be used to model the structure and mode of operation of other discourses. So the structure of the dialectic of ideas can indeed be found in other discourses, as Lautman states, however, it is only by virtue of the extent to which the structure of other discourses can be determined to operate according to the model of the mathematical real that this can be achieved.

The research undertaken in this book aims to address the undervalued and neglected question of Deleuze's own mathematical influences, and to highlight the significance of mathematics to an adequate understanding of Deleuze's philosophy. It provides an account of the nature of the relation between developments in mathematics and Deleuze's project of constructing a philosophy of difference. By tracing the conceptual character of the mathematical problems with which Deleuze engages, the alternative lineage in the history of mathematics that Deleuze draws upon has been made apparent as a mathematical problematic, or series of problems. The structure of Deleuze's philosophy, and the role that mathematics plays in determining this structure, has been explicated by providing an account of the philosophical problems that are reconfigured by being modeled on the conceptual character of this mathematical problematic, and by giving an account of the broader framework that Deleuze draws upon in order to adequately deploy these resources within his philosophy. This framework is drawn largely from Lautman's critical program in mathematics, albeit with a Cavaillès inspired qualification about the problem of positing problematic ideas beyond the exigency of the problems themselves. This way of thinking about problems is referred to by Deleuze as the logic of the calculus of problems, which is characteristic of the advances or transformations that occur in the developments in mathematics. While the mathematical resources that Deleuze draws upon to characterize the logic of the calculus of problems, which have been detailed in this book, means that his account of this logic remains informal, whereas because Badiou draws upon axiomatic set theory and Cohen's extensions of it the account of this logic that he provides is formal. This distinction is important for understanding the nature of the difference between the approach of Badiou to mathematics and that of Deleuze, and is key to understand the difference between their respective approaches to philosophy. The argument developed in Chapter 5 in relation to this distinction demonstrates that there is no crisis in legitimacy that results from Badiou's criticism of Deleuze. It therefore puts Deleuze's philosophy and both the philosophical and nonphilosophical deployments of it on a firm footing.

The role of mathematics in determining the structure of Deleuze's philosophy is developed in the late 60s and early 70s in *Difference and Repetition, Expressionism in Philosophy: Spinoza*, and in *The Logic of Sense*, and in the seminars that focus on the topics introduced by each of these books. This structure is then deployed in his subsequent work, including the Capitalism and Schizophrenia books with Guattari, and in Deleuze's later engagements with the works on Bergson, Foucault, Leibniz, and in the *Cinema* books. The research to determine whether or not the detail of this structure is able to be applied to Deleuze's earlier work on Hume and Nietzsche has yet to be done, but could prove useful in settling claims as to the overall structure of Deleuze's philosophy. These two early texts continue to have resonances with developments in Deleuze's later work. This research would give a broader context to the problem of grasping what is at stake in Deleuze's account of the relations between forces in Nietzsche, and of how to figure the transcendental in relation to Hume.

One way of extending Deleuze's work into a fully fledged Deleuzian philosophy would involve an examination of more recent developments in mathematics in response to the mathematical problematics utilized by Deleuze. This could take the form of an examination of their continued status as problematics, or of the altered axiomatics of mathematics post reappropriation of these problematics. It could also take the form of forging new connections between philosophy and more recent developments in mathematics by extending the alternative lineage in the history of mathematics that Deleuze developed throughout his work, one prime example of which would be category theory.[19] The aim of such a philosophy would be to locate and characterize new mathematical problematics which can then be redeployed as models for the reconfiguration of current philosophical problems in relation to the history of philosophy. I have indicated the direct relevance of the work of Lawvere in this respect (Lawvere and Schanuel 1997). This would be achieved by isolating the points of convergence between their conceptual characteristics in order then to redeploy them as philosophical problems in relation to the history of philosophy, thus opening up the potential for the creation of new philosophical concepts, which could offer solutions to those problems.

Not only do the mathematical underpinnings of Deleuze's account of the structure of Leibniz's metaphysics subtend the entire text of *The Fold*,[20] but what has been demonstrated in this book is that the developments in mathematics and the alternative lineage in its history that Deleuze traces subtends the entire body of Deleuze's work from the late 60s onward. I look forward to the research that will clarify whether this framework can be extended retrospectively to include the entire body of Deleuze's work without qualification.

Notes

Introduction

1   Much of the detail of this history is outlined in Chapter 4 of *Difference and Repetition*, "Ideas and the synthesis of difference" (DR 168–184).

Chapter 1

1   Levey 2003, 413. Levey cites Deleuze (FLB 16) as one of the commentators to have picked up on the idea of fractal structure to describe the "folding of matter" in Leibniz's metaphysics.
2   See Hallward 2003, 382; Rajchman 1997, 116; and Simont 2003, 42.
3   For an account of the role of the projective geometry of Dürer and Desargues in Deleuze's account of point of view, see Duffy 2010a, 140–2.
4   Transcendental in this mathematical context refers to those curves that were not able to be studied using the algebraic methods introduced by Descartes.
5   A concept that was already in circulation in the work of Fermat and Descartes.
6   The lettering has been changed to more directly reflect the isomorphism between this algebraic example and Leibniz's notation for the infinitesimal calculus.
7   This example presents a variation of the infinitesimal or "characteristic" triangle that Leibniz was familiar with from the work of Pascal. See Leibniz "Letter to Tschirnhaus (1680)" in Leibniz 1920, and Pascal, "Traité des sinus du quart de cercle (1659)" in Pascal 1904, 61–76.
8   Newton's reasoning about geometrical limits is based more on physical insights rather than mathematical procedures. In *Geometria Curvilinea* (1680), Newton develops the synthetic method of fluxions which involves visualizing the limit to which the ratio between vanishing geometrical quantities tends (Newton 1971, 420–84).
9   Leibniz, *Methodus tangentium inversa, seu de functionibus* (1673), see Katz 2007, 199.
10 While Leibniz had already envisaged the convergence of alternating series, and by the end of the seventeenth century, the convergence of most useful concrete examples of series, which were of limited quantity, if not finite, was able to be shown, it was Cauchy who provided the first extensive and significant treatment of the convergence of series. See Kline 963.
11 For an account of this problem with limits in Cauchy, see Potter 2004, 85–6.
12 While the epsilon-delta method is due to Weierstrass, the definition of limits that it enshrines was actually first proved by Bernard Bolzano (b. 1741–1848) in 1817 using different terminology, however, it remained unknown until 1881 when a number of his articles and manuscripts were rediscovered and published (Ewald 1996, 226).

13   Nonstandard analysis allows "interesting reformulations, more elegant proofs and
     new results in, for instance, differential geometry, topology, calculus of variations,
     in the theories of functions of a complex variable, of normed linear spaces, and of
     topological groups" (Bos 1974, 81).
14   One option is to consider the infinitesimal to be a hyperreal number that exists in
     a cloud of other infinitesimals or hyperreals floating infinitesimally close to each
     real number on the hyperreal number line (Bell 2005, 262). The development of
     nonstandard analysis, however, has not broken the stranglehold of classical analysis
     to any significant extent; however, this seems to be more a matter of taste and
     practical utility rather than of necessity, see Potter 2004, 85. Another option is to
     consider the infinitesimal as a nonzero nilpotent infinitesimal, see Lawvere 1979.
     There is also the distinctive infinitesimal conceptions that arise in Alain Connes
     noncommutative geometry and in p-adic analysis, see Connes 2001.
15   Robinson's Non-Standard Analysis is the most recent development that Deleuze
     refers to in *The Fold* (FLB 129–30), but this is by no means the end, nor indeed the
     beginning, of this story. The history of these developments predates the successful
     formalization of the infinitesimal by Robinson, as does Deleuze's initial engagement
     with this history. There have also been a number of independent formalizations of
     the infinitesimal since Robinson (Lawvere 1979, Bell 1998, Connes 2001), each of
     which allows reformulations, more elegant proofs, and new results in a range of
     areas in mathematics. While there have been a number of different formalizations of
     the infinitesimal, it remains to be seen whether the specific Leibnizian approach can
     be set on a foundation adequate to modern mathematical standards of rigor.
16   For a discussion of recent debates about the importance of this work, see the first
     section of the conclusion entitled "The 'vindication' of Leibniz's account of the
     differential."
17   The concept of neighborhood, in mathematics, which is very different from
     contiguity, is a key concept in the whole domain of topology.
18   It was actually known to the Babylonians 1000 years earlier, although Pythagoras is
     considered to be the first to have proved it.
19   Cache 1995, 34–41, 48–51, 70–1, 84–5.
20   See Lakhtakia et al. 1987, 35–8.
21   For a more extensive account of Deleuze's deployment of the Weierstrassian theory
     of analytic continuity and the role of power series, see Duffy 2006b.
22   See the section of Chapter 4 entitled "The logic of the calculus of problems."
23   See the section of Chapter 3 entitled "The Riemannian concept of multiplicity and
     the Dedekind cut."
24   See Chapter 2 for a discussion of Maimon's role in Deleuze's response to Kantian
     idealism and the development of his distinctive post-Kantian philosophy.
25   The contribution that Wronski makes to the development of Deleuze's philosophy
     is taken up again in the section of Chapter 2 entitled "The rigorous algorithm of
     Wronski's transcendental philosophy."
26   For further discussion of the contribution of Bordas-Demoulin's work to the
     development of Deleuze's argument see the section of Chapter 2 entitled "Bordas-
     Demoulin on the differential relation as 'the universal function'."
27   Note: the primitive function $\int f(x)dx$ expresses the whole curve f(x).
28   It was Charles A. A. Briot (b. 1817–1882) and Jean-Claude Bouquet (b. 1819–1885)
     who introduced the term "meromorphic" for a function which possessed just poles
     in that domain (Kline 1972, 642).

29 Gilbert Simondon (b. 1924–1989) is another important figure for Deleuze whose
    use of the concept of metastable systems to describe the preliminary condition
    of individuation is also informed by these and subsequent developments in
    mathematics related to the modeling of complex systems. Simondon 1964.

30 Mandelbrot qualifies these statements when he says of Poincaré that "nothing I know
    of his work makes him even a distant precursor of the fractal geometry of the visible
    facets of Nature" (1982, 414).

31 Leibniz's distinction between the three kinds of points: physical, mathematical, and
    metaphysical, will be returned to in the following section.

32 This would also hold for propositions of the form "A is A," which is the propositional
    form of the expression of the Principle of the identity of indiscernibles A = A, and
    for those such as "Matter is extended," where it is a logical necessity to introduce the
    concept of extension when thinking the concept of matter. Another example of this
    latter case would be "A triangle has three angles," as distinct from the proposition "A
    triangle has three sides," which is analytic by inclusion, but not identical. See Sem. 15
    Apr 1980.

33 In *Difference and Repetition*, Deleuze argues that "for each world, a series which
    converges around a distinctive point," or singularity "is capable of being continued
    in all directions in other series converging around other points, while the
    incompossibility of worlds, by contrast, is defined by the juxtaposition of points
    which would make the resultant series diverge" (DR 48).

34 "Principles of Nature and Grace" (1714), §13, Leibniz 1969, 636–42.

35 In the preface to *New Essays on Human Understanding*, Leibniz says that
    "noticeable perceptions arise by degrees from ones which are too minute to be
    noticed" (1996, 56).

36 Letter to Simon Foucher (1693), Leibniz 1965, 415–16.

37 A summary of which appears in Leibniz's *Monadology*, 1714 (Leibniz 1991, 68–81).

38 Huygens in his 1656 study *De Motu corporum ex percussione* ("On the Motion
    of Bodies by Percussion"), parts of which were published in 1669 (Huygens
    1888–1950). Newton also handles accelerated motion in essentially this way in the
    Principia (1687).

39 "The whole thing therefore reduces to this: at any moment which is actually
    assigned we will say that the moving thing is at a new point" (Leibniz
    2001, 208).

40 See the earlier explanation of the third set of transformations in the section
    "The character of a *point-fold* as reflected in the point of reflection."

41 Leibniz 1989, 120; 1996, 165, 216.

42 See Leibniz 1965, IV, 468–70; 1969, 432–3.

43 Panofsky 1959, 259. This method was systematized by Gaspard Monge
    (b. 1746–1818) in what he called "descriptive geometry" (Monge 1799).

44 Leibniz 1989, 146. See Garber 2004, 34–40.

45 See Grene and Ravetz 1962, 141. Deleuze also poses the question of whether this
    topological account can be extended to Leibniz's concept of the vinculuum (FLB
    111). If so, the topology of the vinculuum would have to be isomorphic to that of
    matter; however, it would be so within each monad, and would be complicated by
    itself being a phenomenal projection. For further discussion of the vinculuum in
    Leibniz, see Look "Leibniz and the substance of the *vinculum substantial.*"

46 See DR 49, where Deleuze characterizes the limitations of the concept of
    convergence in Leibniz's philosophy.

47   The "jump" of the variable across the domain of discontinuity also corresponds to the "leap" that Deleuze refers to in *Expressionism in Philosophy* when an adequate idea of the joyful passive affection is formed (Deleuze 1990, 283). It characterizes the "leap" from inadequate to adequate ideas, from joyful passive affections to active joys, from passions to actions. For a further explication of the correspondence between the "jump" and the "leap" in Deleuze's engagement with Spinoza, see Duffy 2006a, 158–63, 185–7.

48   The concept of individuation that is being used here is that developed by Deleuze in relation to Spinoza. This concept, and its relevance to Deleuze's reading of Leibniz, is addressed in Duffy 2006a. The work of Gilbert Simondon (b. 1924–1989) is also important for the development of Deleuze's concept of individuation. For an account of the relation between the work of Simondon, Spinoza, and Deleuze, see Del Lucchese 2009.

49   This aspect of Deleuze's Neo-Leibnizianism is also clearly expressed in *The Logic of Sense*, in particular in the "Sixteenth series of the static ontological genesis," where Deleuze writes that "Instead of each world being the analytic predicate of individuals described in series, it is rather the incompossible worlds which are the synthetic predicates of persons defined in relation to disjunctive syntheses" (LS 115).

50   See in particular Chapters 1 and 4.

51   The correlate distinction in the *Logic of Sense* is between the first two levels of the static ontological genesis. "The first level of actualization produces . . . individuated worlds and individual selves which populate each of these worlds" (LS 111). This correlates with the logic of differentiation. The second level of actualization "opens different worlds and individuals" to the individuated worlds and individual selves of the first level "as so many variables and possibilities" (LS 115). This correlates with the logic of differenciation. It is important to note that these two levels of the static ontological genesis (LS 109–12) are distinct from the static logical genesis (LS 118–26). While the static logical genesis is correlated with the structure of logical propositions in language, "with its determinate dimensions (denotation, manifestation, signification)" (LS 120), the static ontological genesis, the two levels of which are the focus of the present study, is concerned with "the objective correlates of these propositions which are first produced as ontological propositions (the denoted, the manifested, and the signified)" (LS 120). For a useful account of the structure of the static logical genesis in the *Logic of Sense*, see Bowden 2012. For an extended analysis of Bowden's understanding of the role of mathematics in Deleuze see my comments in the conclusion.

Chapter 2

1   Recall that there is an analytic relationship between two concepts when one of these concepts is contained in the other.

2   Kant's constructability thesis . . .: in order to grasp the relation between the subject and predicate concepts of an arithmetic proposition, one must "go beyond" the subject concept to the intuition that corresponds to it and identify properties that are not analytically contained in the concept yet still belong to it (Kant 1998, B15; A718/ B746; Shabel 2006, 13).

3   Contrary to the standard interpretation of what is referred to as the "argument from geometry," which is advanced by Guyer (1987, 367); Allison (1983, 99); and

Friedman (2000, 193), and which maintains that Kant, in the "Transcendental Exposition of the Concept of Space" (Kant 1998, B40–1), provides an analysis of geometric cognition in order to establish that we have a pure intuition of space, I maintain that the "argument from geometry" establishes that geometric cognition itself develops out of a pure intuition of space. This contrary interpretation has been proposed by Carson (1997) and Warren (1998), and eloquently defended by Shabel (2004). The counter claim is that the section of the "Transcendental Exposition of the Concept of Space" that contains the "argument from geometry" actually contains Kant's argument to connect his metaphysical theory of space as pure intuition, already established in the "Metaphysical Exposition" (Kant 1998, A22–5/ B37–40), with his mathematical theory of pure geometry. Shabel maintains that the argument from geometry "shows that this pure intuition of space explains and at least partially accounts for the synthetic a priority of our geometric cognition" (2004, 206). To account for the applicability of this geometric cognition, according to Shabel, Kant goes on to argue that "our pure intuition of space is that 'immediate representation' that allows us to form our intuitions of outer objects. Thus, the 'argument from geometry' is meant to show that a pure intuition of space provides an epistemic foundation for geometry as a synthetic a priori science" (2004, 207).

4 It is important to note that while this principle is common to geometric textbooks at the time, it does not appear in Euclid's *Elements*, and is therefore not a Euclidean principle.

5 These rules are consonant with the description of the difference between mathematical and philosophical cognition that Kant provides in "The discipline of pure reason in dogmatic use," where Kant writes that "Philosophical cognition thus considers the particular only in the universal, but mathematical cognition considers the universal in the particular, indeed even in the individual, yet nonetheless *a priori* and by means of reason, so that just as this individual is determined under certain general conditions of construction, the object of the concept, to which this individual corresponds only as its schema, must likewise be thought as universally determined" (Kant 1998, A715/B742).

6 When Kant says that algebra "achieves by a symbolic construction equally well what geometry does by an ostensive or geometrical construction (of the objects themselves)" (Kant 1998, A717/B745), what he means is that the algebraic expression symbolizes the construction of arithmetic and geometric concepts in the form of figures. Kant therefore seems to have taken algebraic expressions to be symbolic of the proportions between magnitudes represented in the geometrical or arithmetic intuitions of mathematical concepts. Accordingly, the individual magnitudes of geometrical or arithmetic problems are each assigned a symbol, and the relations between these magnitudes are represented as proportions in the algebraic symbolism. Thus algebraic expressions function for Kant as reductions of the geometric or arithmetic constructions themselves. See Shabel 2003, 129.

7 According to Maimon, "what is justified is what is legitimate, and with respect to thought, something is justified if it conforms to the laws of thought or reason" (Maimon 2010, 363).

8 However, unlike Kant, Maimon deduces the formal forms from the categories, rather than the inverse, and Maimon does not recognize the category of quantity. See Bergman 1967, 117–20. The latter point will be returned to later in the chapter.

9 For a discussion of the implications of these developments for the concept of space deployed by Deleuze, see the section of Chapter 3 entitled "The Riemannian concept of multiplicity and the Dedekind cut."

10   Maimon's theory of the differential has proved to be a rather enigmatic aspect of his
     system. Commentators have argued either that it plays a central role in determining
     the structure of this system (Atlas 1964, Bergman 1967), or on the contrary that
     it as too incoherent to do so (Buzaglo 2002). Alternatively they have focused on
     the importance of other aspects of Maimon's work because it is too ambiguous to
     play such a central role (Beiser 1987, Bransen 1991, Franks 2005). Peter Thielke
     provides a more balanced approach to the concept of the differential as it operates in
     Maimon, without however taking his analysis as far as it could, and arguably should,
     be taken (Thielke 2003, 115–9). In a recent article, Florian Ehrensperger remarks
     on this enigmatic status by noting that "Despite its prominence, an in-depth study
     of the differential in Maimon is still a desideratum" (Ehrensperger 2010, 2). What I
     propose to offer in this chapter is a study of the differential and the role that it plays
     in the *Essay on Transcendental Philosophy* (1790) by drawing upon mathematical
     developments that had occurred earlier in the century and that, by virtue of the
     arguments presented in the *Essay*, Maimon was aware of.

11   The Leibnizian syncategorematic definition of the infinitesimal and the example of
     the calculus of infinite series is discussed in the section of Chapter 1 entitled "The
     mathematical representation of matter, motion and the continuum" in relation to
     the infinitangular triangle and the differential calculus. For further discussion of the
     Leibnizian syncategorematic or fictional definition of the infinitesimal, see Jesseph
     2008, 215–34.

12   See the section of Chapter 1 entitled "Leibniz's law of continuity and the
     infinitesimal calculus," and Duffy 2006a, 53–4.

13   Taylor 1715. See the section of Chapter 1 entitled "Subsequent developments in
     mathematics: Weierstrass and Poincaré," and Duffy 2006a, 70–1. Taylor actually
     adopts the Newtonian methodology of "fluxions" in his account of power series
     expansions, the importance of which to Maimon will be returned to in the final
     section of this chapter. While Lagrange, a contemporary of Maimon's, did attempt to
     provide an algebraic proof of Taylor's theorem as early as 1772, the work in which it
     was published did not appear until 1797, after Maimon had written the *Essay* (2010).
     For a detailed introduction to the techniques of Taylor series approximation, see
     Arfken 1985.

14   Note that the greater the number of terms, the greater the degree of approximation.

15   If the differential of a third quantity has a relation with either of the other two,
     then it in turn can also be determined as a sensible object by means of the same
     procedure.

16   Maimon to Kant, 20 September 1791.

17   Maimon is drawing here upon Leibniz's account of the differential and the
     differential relation. For an account by Leibniz of the method by means of which
     the differential relation is determined independently of its terms, see Leibniz 1969,
     542–6. See also the section of Chapter 1 entitled "Leibniz's law of continuity and the
     infinitesimal calculus," and Duffy 2006a, 50–1.

18   See Newton 1981, 123–9. See also the section of Chapter 1 entitled "Newton's
     method of fluxions and infinite series."

19   For an analysis of how the a priori/pure a priori distinction is implicated in
     Maimon's account of the infinite intellect, see Lachterman 1992 and Buzaglo 2002.

20   For a useful discussion of the role of the differential in Deleuze's reading of Maimon,
     see Lord 2011 and Voss 2012. For more general approaches to this material, see
     Bryant 2008, Jones 2009, and Kerslake 2009.

21 It is in relation to the work of Carnot that Deleuze defines a "problematic" as "the ensemble of the problem and its conditions" (DR 177).

22 It wasn't until 1882 that the squaring of the circle was proved to be impossible when Ferdinand von Lindemann proved that π, the mathematical constant whose value is the ratio of any circle's circumference to its diameter and which is implicated in the determination of the area of the circle (πr^2), was a transcendental number, i.e. nonalgebraic and therefore nonconstructible.

23 See the section of Chapter 1 entitled "The development of a differential philosophy."

24 As an example of the permutations of roots, consider the quadratic equation $x^2 - 2 = 0$, which can also be expressed by $(x - \sqrt{2})(x + \sqrt{2}) = 0$, the roots of which are $\sqrt{2}$ and $- \sqrt{2}$. Either of these roots will satisfy this equation, and there is a symmetry of the roots insofar as one can be swapped with the other. To swap one for the other is called a permutation of the roots. Importantly, any polynomial equation with $\sqrt{2}$ as a root also has $- \sqrt{2}$ as a root. Now consider the quartic equation $x^4 - 5x^2 + 6 = (x^2 - 2)(x^2 - 3) = 0$, the roots of which are $\sqrt{2}, -\sqrt{2}, \sqrt{3}, -\sqrt{3}$. The roots $\sqrt{2}$ and $- \sqrt{2}$ are symmetrical and can be permuted, as can the roots $\sqrt{3}$ and $-\sqrt{3}$. However, $\sqrt{2}$ and $\sqrt{3}$ are not symmetrical and therefore cannot be permuted.

25 According to this procedure, in order to determine the roots of a cubic, all that is required is that the elementary symmetric polynomial be solved, where the elementary symmetric polynomial is the expression of the symmetric roots of the cubic as a function, which happens to be a polynomial equation of lesser degree and therefore a quadratic equation. This is also the case for quartics, i.e. the elementary symmetric polynomial, which is a cubic, needs to be solved. When it comes to the quintic however, this procedure generates a polynomial equation of greater degree, degree six, which doesn't facilitate solving the original quintic, but rather complicates the matter.

Chapter 3

1 See the section of Chapter 2 entitled "The laws of sensibility."

2 There is an important resonance here with the work of Maimon, according to which sensible objects of the intuitions are represented to the understanding as being extra-cognitive. Maimon explains that this is an illusion, and that sensible objects appear as external objects to us when in fact they are the product of our understanding. See the section of Chapter 2 entitled "The laws of sensibility."

3 See B 75–6; Deleuze 1999, 45–6; Boundas 1996, 104.

4 See the section of Chapter 1 entitled "Subsequent developments in mathematics: Weierstrass and Poincaré."

5 See Plotnitsky 2009, 198. I am indebted to Arkady Plotnitsky's careful consideration of this material in Plotnitsky 2006; 2009.

6 Gilles Châtelet (b. 1944–1999) also singles out this passage for comment in his paper "sur une petite phrase de Riemann. . ." (Châtelet 1979), which provides an account of the advances in group theory that led up to Einstein's development of general relativity (Châtelet 1979, 72–3). For further discussion of the role of mathematics in the determination of the concept of space, see Châtelet 2000.

7 Bergson considers space itself to be a composite of matter and duration. He even speaks of them as inverse tendencies. Duration is a tendency whose principle is

contraction, as illustrated in the contraction and condensation associated with isolated or dominant memories, and matter is a tendency whose principle is expansion. See CE 55.

8 Deleuze is aware of Weyl's work on Riemann via Lautman's commentary on Weyl, which Deleuze cites in *A Thousand Plateaus*, 485. The importance of Lautman's work to Deleuze's engagement with mathematics in *Difference and Repetition* is explored in Chapter 4.

9 Remmert points out that "Contrary to what has often been said, the book does not give a complete symbiosis of the concepts of Riemann and Weierstrass: The question whether every connected non-compact Riemann surface is isomorphic to a Weierstrassian analytic configuration, is not dealt with" (Remmert 1998, 218). In fact no convincing proof was known at the time. The problem had been stated by Koebe in 1909 (Koebe 1909), dealt with again by Stoilow in 1938 (Stoilow 1938), and again by Behnke and Stein in 1947 (1949); however, a theorem to this effect that completed the symbiosis of Riemannian and Weierstrassian function theory was not proved until 1948, by Herta Florack (Florack 1948). See Remmert pp. 218–22. For the purposes of this book, I am assuming the proof of this theorem and that Deleuze, who is engaging with this material two decades after the Florack proof, is operating on the same assumption, i.e. that there is a complete symbiosis of the ideas of Weierstrass and Riemann.

10 It is generally acknowledged that Weyl's book placed Riemann surfaces on a firm footing and thereby had a marked impact on the development of mathematics. Jean Dieudonné refers to the book as "a classic that inspired all later developments of the theory of differentiable and complex manifolds" (Dieudonné 1976, 283).

11 See Chapter 1.

12 Weyl discusses essential singularities at Weyl 1913, 38.

13 See Duffy 2006a, 131–3, 220–25.

14 These developments also apply to Deleuze's conception of the second level of the static ontological genesis (LS 109–12).

15 See the section of Chapter 1 entitled "Overcoming the limits of Leibniz's metaphysics."

16 See Duffy 2006a, 220–25.

17 It is this distinction between the virtual and the actual, as modeled on Riemann space, that finds its way into all of Deleuze's subsequent work, including that with Guattari.

18 While my concern here is with providing a structural account of this distinction, rather than an account of how these different conceptions of change are actually registered, Deleuze's work on Spinoza does provide one account of how this distinction is registered. Deleuze notes Spinoza's distinction between joyful actions and sad passions, and then tries to draw out the implications of a finer distinction between joyful passions and active joys, which correlates with the distinction between change understood as consequence or modification, which is registered as either joyful or sad passions, and change understood as novelty or innovation, which is registered as an active joy. See Duffy 2007; 2010c.

19 See in particular the comments about Maimon's account of space and time as being derived from conceptual relations in the section of Chapter 2 entitled "Maimonic reduction."

20 The following passage from *A Thousand Plateaus* clearly articulates Deleuze's understanding of how the first stage of these developments relate to the second stage.

"All of these points already relate to Riemannian space, with its essential relation to 'monads' (as opposed to the unitary Subject of Euclidean space) . . . . Although the 'monads' are no longer thought to be closed upon themselves, and are postulated to entertain direct step-by-step local [Riemannian-space-type] relations, the purely monadological point of view proves inadequate and should be superseded by a 'nomadology' (the identity of striated spaces versus the realism of smooth space)" (TP 573–74).

Chapter 4

1   The axiomatic method is a way of developing mathematical theories by postulating certain primitive assumptions, or axioms, as the basis of the theory, while the remaining propositions of the theory are obtained as logical consequences of these axioms.

2   The Bourbaki project explicitly espoused a set-theoretic version of mathematical structuralism.

3   According to mathematical structuralism, mathematical objects are defined by their positions in mathematical structures, and the subject matter that mathematics concerns itself with is structural relationships in abstraction from the intrinsic nature of the related objects. See Hellman 2005, 256.

4   The main aim of Hilbert's program, which was first clearly formulated in 1922, was to establish the logical acceptability of the principles and modes of inference of modern mathematics by formalizing each mathematical theory into a finite, complete set of axioms, and to provide a proof that these axioms were consistent. The point of Hilbert's approach was to make mathematical theories fully precise, so that it is possible to obtain precise results about properties of the theory. In 1931, Gödel showed that the program as it stood was not possible. Revised efforts have since emerged as continuations of the program that concentrate on relative results in relation to specific mathematical theories, rather than all mathematics. See Ferreirós 2008, ch. 2.6.3.2.

5   See Largeault 1972, 215, 264.

6   The term "metamathematics" is introduced by Hilbert in Hilbert 1926.

7   See Brunschvicg 1993.

8   It is important to keep in mind that for Lautman, following Hilbert, every branch of mathematics goes through naive, formal, and critical periods. See Hilbert 1896, 124. My thanks to Colin McLarty for pointing this out.

9   A mathematical definition is impredicative if it depends on a certain set, $\mathbf{N}$, being defined and introduced by appeal to a totality of sets which includes $\mathbf{N}$ itself. That is, the definition is self-referencing.

10   The law of the excluded middle states that every proposition is either true or false. In propositional logic, the law is written "P $\neg$P" ("P or not-P").

11   See Petitot 1987, 81.

12   See Chevalley 1987, 61.

13   Dumoncel 2008, 199. Translation modified.

14   See also Lautman 2011, 189–90, 40–2; Barot 2003, 7n2.

15   See Chevalley 1987, 60.

16   Which are also referred to and operate as "dualities." See Alunni 2006, 78.

17   Which he therefore also refers to as "logical schemas." See Lautman 2011, 83.

18 From Lautman's correspondence with Fréchet dated 1 February 1939.

19 See Chevalley 1987, 50.

20 See Lautman 2011, 211.

21 A cautionary word along the lines of Cavaillès's warning of "possible
    misunderstandings" of Lautman's references to Heidegger (From correspondence
    dated 7 November 1938, cited in Granger 2002, 299): if Lautman were to be
    considered Heideggerian, or to be embarking on a project of fundamental ontology,
    because of the few places in his work where he makes brief allusion to specific
    conceptual distinctions in Heidegger's work that serve as analogies for his own
    undertakings in relation to mathematics, a more detailed reading of Lautman, which
    I hope to have provided here, should lead to revising such an understanding. It is in
    this vein that I briefly clarify Lautman's relation to Heidegger.

22 This is Lautman's gloss of Heidegger.

23 See Heidegger 1969, 160–1.

24 This is one of the key aspects of Lautman's work that Deleuze takes up in his own
    project of constructing a philosophy of difference.

25 See Barot 2003, 10; Chevalley 1987, 63–4.

26 For an account of the role that this example of the local–global conceptual pair
    plays in Deleuze, see the section of Chapter 4 entitled "Deleuze's rehabilitation and
    extension of Bergson's project."

27 See Petitot 1987, 113.

28 See also Barot 2003, 6, 16n1. For a Deleuzian account of an alternative logic to the
    Hegelian dialectical logic, one that implicates the work of Lautman, see Duffy 2009b.

29 Salanskis 1996; 1998; Smith 2003; Duffy 2006b.

30 See Salanskis 1998, "Contre-temoinage."

31 When Deleuze and Guattari comment on "the 'intuitionist' school (Brouwer,
    Heyting, Griss, Bouligand, etc)," they insist that it "is of great importance in
    mathematics, not because it asserted the irreducible rights of intuition, or even
    because it elaborated a very novel constructivism, but because it developed a
    conception of problems, and of a calculus of problems that intrinsically rivals
    axiomatics and proceeds by other rules (notably with regard to the excluded
    middle)" (TP 570 n. 61). Deleuze extracts this concept of the calculus of problems
    itself as a mathematical problematic from the episode in the history of mathematics
    when intuitionism opposed axiomatics. It is the logic of this calculus of problems
    that he then redeploys in relation to a range of episodes in the history of
    mathematics that in no way binds him to the principles of intuitionism. See Duffy
    2006a, 2–6.

32 For an account of Deleuze's engagement with Galois, see the section of Chapter 3
    entitled "Abel and Galois on the question of the solvability of polynomial equations."
    See also Châtelet 2006, 41; Salanskis 2006, 52–3; 1998; Smith 2006, 159–63.

33 See Chapter 2, where the complex concept of the logic of differen*t/c*iation is
    demonstrated to be characteristic of Deleuze's "philosophy of difference." See also
    Duffy 2006c.

34 See Widder 2001 for an account of Deleuze's reversal of Platonism and its implied
    idealism. See also Livingston 2011, who argues that "Deleuze develops a theory
    of the Platonic Idea which, though it owes nothing to 'Platonism' traditionally
    conceived, nevertheless plausibly captures the very formal relationship which Plato
    calls 'participation'" (Livingston 2011, 95).

35 See Smith 2006 for an account of the operation of the relation between Royal and
    nomad science and between axiomatics and problematics in Deleuze's work.

36 Deleuze argues that "Ideas always have an element of quantitability, qualitability and potentiality; there are always processes of determinability, of reciprocal determination and complete determination; always distributions of distinctive and ordinary points; always adjunct fields which form the synthetic progression of a sufficient reason" (DR 181).

37 See Duffy 2004; 2006c.

38 See Chapter 3.

Chapter 5

1 Recent work on this topic has pointed out the decidedly partial nature of Badiou's engagement with Deleuze. See Jon Roffe's critical assessment of Badiou's claim that Deleuze "obstinately reaffirms that the thought of the multiple demands that being be rigorously determined as One" in *Deleuze: The Clamor of Being* (Badiou 2000, 44) (Roffe 2012, 246). Mogens Laerke provides one of the most succinct critiques of Badiou's engagement with Deleuze on this point by examining their respective deployments of the work of Spinoza (Laerke 1999). Badiou's "interpretation" of Deleuze unapologetically moves within the theoretical constraints of Badiou's own mathematical and philosophical commitments. What remains problematic in Badiou's approach is that he maintains that the account of Deleuze that is thereby generated is a faithful rendition of Deleuze's philosophy, rather than a caricature of Deleuze that is used as a polemical foil in the construction and defense of his own theoretical position. See also Gil 1998 and Toscano 2000.

2 It is important to note that Deleuze also eschews characterizing his relation to mathematics as simply analogical or metaphorical. See the Introduction.

3 See Hallward 2003, 55.

4 See Benacerraf 1973, 661–79.

5 See Quine 1964; 1981, and Putnam 1979.

6 See Shapiro 2000, 46.

7 For an account of a model-theoretic framework, see Marker 1996, 754–5; Shapiro 2000, 46–8.

8 Putnam 1981, 72–4; Shapiro 2000, 67.

9 Plato 1997, *Gorgias* 451A–C.

10 Plato 1997, *Theatetus* 198A–B; see also *Republic* VII 522C.

11 Plato 1997, *Gorgias* 451A–C; see also *Charmides* 165E–166B.

12 See Shapiro 2000, 76–7.

13 The Platonic doctrine of anamnesis holds that all learning is recollection, and that perception and inquiry remind us of what is innate in us (Plato 1997, *Meno* 80A–86C; *Phaedo* 73C–78B).

14 Plato 1997, *Republic* VI 511C–D. Badiou's translation. See Badiou 2004, 44.

15 A countable set is any set that is either finite or the same size as $\mathbf{N}$. An uncountable set is any set bigger than $\mathbf{N}$.

16 Note that $\mathbf{N}$, ω, and $\aleph_0$ all name the same set, i.e. the set of natural numbers.

17 See Dauben 1990, 103–111.

18 i.e. the multiple from which all other multiples are constructed.

19 Russell's paradox raises the question of whether the set of all sets which are not members of themselves is a set. If the set exists, then it is included as one of its own sets, i.e. it is both a member and not a member of itself, which is a contradiction.

20 See Feferman 1989, 37.

21 Gödel's "constructible sets" are sets defined solely in terms of the subsets of the previous stage of construction that have already been constructed, rather than the set of all subsets, as it is in V.

22 He maintains that "the constructible universe is a *model* of these axioms [i.e., ZFC + V = L] in that if one applies the constructions and the guarantees of existence supported by the Ideas of the multiple, and if their domain of application is restricted to the constructible universe, then the constructible [universe] is generated in turn" (Badiou 2005, 300).

23 The method of showing that a certain statement is not derivable from or is not a logical consequence of given axioms is to exhibit a model in which the axioms are true but the statement is false. This is indicted by the following notation:
    1) ZF + ¬AC; 2) ZFC + ¬CH; 3) ZFC + GCH + V ≠ L. See Kanamori 2008, 361.

24 See Kanamori 2008, 360.

25 According to Kunen, "Cohen's original treatment made forcing seem very much related to the constructible hierarchy. His M was always a model for V = L" (Kunen 1983, 235).

26 See Roitman 1990, 91–2.

27 See Kanamori 1994, 472.

28 See Bhattacharyya 2012 for a detailed description of how Badiou's phenomenology of topoi aims to extend his pure ontology of sets.

29 The importance of this aspect of Poincaré's work for Deleuze is addressed in Chapters 1, 3, and 4.

30 For an account of the ongoing attempt to defend this program, see Hellman 2006.

31 Salanskis notes that Deleuze's engagement with mathematics provides Deleuze with "a decisive resource for the edification of his . . . original ontological contribution" (Salanskis 2008, 28).

32 See the section of Chapter 1 entitled "Subsequent developments in mathematics: the problem of rigor."

33 See the section of Chapter 3 entitled "Deleuze's rehabilitation and extension of Bergson's project."

34 Newstead notes that both Hallett 1984 and Lavine 1994 "support the contention that Cantorian set theory was always free from paradox" (Newstead 2009, 545).

35 See Newstead 546. See also Hallett 1984, 155; Lavine 1994, 53.

36 For Russell's account of the development of the set theoretic paradox from the foundational point of view, which refers to Cantor's antinomy as "Cantor's paradox," see Russell 1992, 362.

37 It is Zermelo's commitment to the problem of foundations that played a role "in creating the impression that Cantorian set theory was naïve" (Newstead 2009, 544). See also Hallett 1984, 238–9.

Conclusion

1 See Duffy 2004; 2006a; 2006b; 2009b.
2 See Chapter 1.
3 For an account of the history of the development of this method of integration see Duffy 2004, 203–11; 2006a, 70–93; 2009b, 466, 479, and Chapter 1.

4 Some of which are shared by other idealist readings of Deleuze. See in particular my comments in the following two sections.

5 See Duffy 2006a, 271, and Chapter 1.

6 For an account of the relation between power series expansions and discontinuities, see Duffy 2006a, 82.

7 For an account of the role of Poincaré's qualitative theory of differential equations in Deleuze's account of the calculus, see Duffy 2006a, 81.

8 See Duffy 2006a, 56; 2009b, 465, and Chapter 1.

9 See also the section of Chapter 1 entitled 'Subsequent developments in mathematics: the problem of rigor.'

10 See Duffy 2006a, 81, and the section of Chapter 1 entitled 'Subsequent developments in mathematics: Weierstrass and Poincaré.'

11 See DR 173–4, and the section of Chapter 2 entitled 'Maimon's infinite intellect is displaced by a theory of problems.'

12 Contrary to Somers-Hall's claim that I endorse the schema, see Somers-Hall 2012, 6.

13 See Duffy 2009b, and Chapter 2.

14 See Duffy 2006a, 44–68; 2009b.

15 For an account of how this distinction operates in *Difference and Repetition*, see Hughes 2008, 105–26.

16 See also May 2005, 251.

17 See Gaffney 2010, 329.

18 Bowden shares implicitly Somers-Hall's explicit predilection for Hegelianizing Deleuze, which is quite unnecessary. Bowden outlines his idealist reading of Deleuze in Bowden 2011b.

19 De Landa's work also remains a useful resource in this respect.

20 This is the claim made in the introduction to Chapter 1 of this book, and in Duffy 2010a.

Bibliography

Alliez, Eric. 2005. 'Badiou. The Grace of the Universal.' *Polygraph* 17: 267–73.

Allison, Henry. 1983. *Kant's Transcendental Idealism: An Interpretation and Defense*. New Haven: Yale UP.

Alunni, Charles. 2006. 'Continental Genealogies. Mathematical confrontations in Albert Lautman and Gaston Bachelard' in Duffy 2006d.

Arfken, George. 1985. 'Taylor's expansion.' *Mathematical Methods for Physicists*. Orlando: Academic.

Atlas, Samuel. 1964. *From Critical to Speculative Idealism: The Philosophy of Solomon Maimon*. The Hague: Nijhoff.

Badiou, Alain. 2000. *Deleuze: The Clamor of Being*. Trans. L. Burchill. Minneapolis: Minnesota UP. Original edition, *Deleuze: La clameur de l'Etre*. Paris: Hachette, 1997.

—. 2001. *Ethics: An Essay on the Understanding of Evil*. Trans. P. Hallward. London: Continuum. Original edition, *L'éthique: essai sur la conscience du mal*. Paris: Hatier, 1998.

—. 2004. *Theoretical Writings*. Ed. and trans. R. Brassier and A. Toscano. London: Continuum.

—. 2005. *Being and Event*. Trans. O. Feltham. London: Continuum. Original edition, *L'Etre et l'Evénement*. Paris: Seuil, 1988.

—. 2006. 'Mathematics and Philosophy,' in Duffy 2006d.

—. 2008. *Number and Numbers*. Trans. R. Mackay. Cambridge: Polity. Original edition, *Le nombre et les nombres*. Paris: Seuil, 1990.

—. 2009. *Logics of Worlds*. Trans. A. Toscano. London: Continuum. Original edition, *Logiques des mondes*. Paris: Seuil, 2006.

Barot, Emmanuel. 2003. 'L'objectivité mathématique selon Albert Lautman: entre Idées dialectiques et réalité physique.' *Cahiers François Viète* 6: 3–27.

—. 2009. *Lautman*. Paris: Belles Lettres.

Barrow-Green, June. 1997. *Poincaré and the Three Body Problem*. Providence: American Mathematical Society.

Bassler, O. Bradley. 1998. 'Leibniz on the indefinite as infinite.' *Review of Metaphysics* 51(4): 849–75.

Behnke, Heinrich and Karl Stein. 1949. 'Entwicklung analytischer Funktionen auf Riemannschen Flächen.' *Mathematische Annalen* 120: 430–61.

Beiser, Frederick C. 1987. *The Fate of Reason: German Philosophy from Kant to Fichte*. Cambridge: Harvard UP.

Bell, John L. 1998. *A Primer of Infinitesimal Analysis*. Cambridge: Cambridge UP.

—. 2005. *The Continuous and the Infinitesimal in Mathematics and Philosophy*. Milano: Polimetrica.

Benacerraf, Paul. 1983. 'Mathematical Truth.' *Philosophy of Mathematics: Selected Readings*, Eds P. Benacerraf and H. Putnam. Cambridge: Cambridge UP.

Bergman, Samuel H. 1967. *The Philosophy of Solomon Maimon*. Trans. Noah J. Jacobs. Jerusalem: Magnes.

Bergson, Henri. 1910. *Time and Free Will: An Essay on the Immediate Data of Consciousness*. Trans. F. Pogson. London: Allen & Unwin. Original edition, *Essai sur les donnés immédiates de la conscience*. Paris: Alcan, 1889.

—. 1911a. *Matter and Memory*. Trans. N. Paul and W. Palmer. New York: Macmillan. Original edition, *Matière et memoire*. Paris: Alcan, 1896.

—. 1911b. *Creative Evolution*. Trans. A. Mitchell. New York: Holt. Original edition, *L'Evolution créatrice*. Paris: Alcan, 1907.

—. 1972. *Mélanges*. Eds A. Robinet, M.-R. Mossé-Bastide, M. Robinet and M. Gauthier. Foreword H. Gouhier. Paris: Presses Universitaires de France.

—. 1992. *The Creative Mind*. Trans. M. Andison. New York: Citadel. Original edition, *La Pensé et le mouvant: essais et conferences*. Paris: Presses Universitaires de France, 1938.

—. 1999a. *An Introduction to Metaphysics*. Trans. T. Hulme. Indianapolis: Hackett. Original edition, 'Introduction à la métaphysique,' *Revue de métaphysique et de morale* 11.1 (1903): 1–36.

—. 1999b. *Duration and Simultaneity*. Ed. R. Durie. Manchester: Clinamen. Original edition, *Durée et simultaniété*. Paris: Alcan, 1921.

Bhattacharyya, Anindya. 2012. 'Sets, Categories and Topoi: Approaches to Ontology in Badiou's Later Work,' in Bowden and Duffy 2012.

Birkhoff, Garrett. 1937. 'Galois and group theory.' *Osiris* 3: 260–8.

Bordas-Demoulin, Jean. 1843. *Le Cartésianisme, ou la Véritable Rénovation des Sciences*. Intro. F. Huet. Paris: Hetzel.

Bos, Henk J. M. 1974. 'Differentials, higher-order differentials and the derivative in the Leibnizian calculus.' *Archive for History of Exact Sciences* 14(1): 1–90.

Boundas, Constantin V. 1996. 'Deleuze-Bergson: an ontology of the virtual.' *Deleuze: A Critical Reader*, Ed. Paul Patton. London: Blackwell.

Bowden, Sean. 2008. 'Alain Badiou: Problematics and the different senses of Being in Being and Event.' *Parrhesia* 5: 32–47.

—. 2011a. *The Priority of Events: Deleuze's Logic of Sense*. Edinburgh: Edinburgh UP.

—. 2011b. 'Paul Redding's Continental Idealism (and Deleuze's continuation of the idealist tradition).' *Parrhesia* 11: 75–9.

—. 2012. 'The Set-Theoretical Nature of Badiou's Ontology and Lautman's Dialectic of Problematic Ideas,' in Bowden and Duffy 2012.

Bowden, Sean and Simon B. Duffy (eds). 2012. *Badiou and Philosophy*. Edinburgh: Edinburgh UP.

Boyer, Carl B. 1959. *The History of the Calculus and its Conceptual Development*. New York: Dover.

Bransen, Jan. 1991. *The Antinomy of Thought: Maimonian Skepticism and the Relation between Thoughts and Objects*. Dordrecht: Kluwer.

Brassier, Ray. 2005. 'Badiou's materialist epistemology of mathematics.' *Angelaki* 10(2): 135–50.

Brunschvicg, Léon. 1993. *Les Etapes de la philosophie mathématique*. Paris: Blanchard. Original edition, 1912.

Bryant, Levi R. 2008. *Difference and Givenness: Deleuze's Transcendental Empiricism and the Ontology of Immanence*. Evanston: Northwestern UP.

Buzaglo, Meir. 2002. *Solomon Maimon: Monism, Skepticism, and Mathematics*. Pittsburgh: Pittsburgh UP.

Cache, Bernard. 1995. *Earth Moves: The Furnishing of Territories*. Trans. Anne Boyman. Ed. Michael Speaks. Cambridge: MIT Press.

Cantor, Georg. 1932. 'Grundlagen einer allgemeine Mannigfaltigkeitslehre (1883).' *Georg Cantor Gesammelte Abhandlungen*, Ed. E. Zermelo. Berlin: Springer. Reprinted 1962 by Hildesheim: Olms. Trans. W. Ewald as 'Foundations of a General Theory of Manifolds: A Mathematico- Philosophical Investigation into the Theory of the Infinite,' in Ewald 1996.

Carson, Emily. 1997. 'Kant on intuition in geometry.' *Canadian Journal of Philosophy* 27(2): 489–512.

Cassou-Noguès, Pierre. 2006. 'L'excès de l'état par rapport à la situation dans L'être et l'événement de A. Badiou.' *Methodos* 6. http://methodos.revues.org/471, accessed 28 Aug 2012.

Cavaillès, Jean. 1994. *Oeuvres complètes de philosophie des science*. Ed. B. Huisman. Paris: Hermann.

Cavaillès, Jean and Albert Lautman. 1946. 'La pensée mathématique. Séance du 4 février 1939.' *Bulletin de la Société Française de Philosophie* 40(1): 1–39. Reprinted in Cavaillès 1994.

Châtelet, Gilles. 1979. 'sur une petite phrase de Riemann. . . ' *Analytiques (Psychanalyse-Écritures-Politiques)* 3: 67–75.

—. 2000. *Figuring Space: Philosophy, Mathematics, and Physics*. Trans. R. Shore and M. Zagha. Dordrecht: Kluwer.

—. 2006. 'Interlacing the singularity, the diagram and the metaphor,' in Duffy 2006d.

Chevalley, Catherine. 1987. 'Albert Lautman et le souci logique.' *Revue d'Histoire des Sciences* 40 (1): 49–77.

Cohen, Paul. J. 1966. *Set Theory and the Continuum Hypothesis*. New York: Benjamin.

Cohn, Harvey. 1967. *Conformal Mapping on Riemann Surfaces*. New York: McGraw-Hill.

Connes, Alain. 2001. 'Noncommutative geometry, Year 2000.' *Visions in mathematics: Geometric and functional analysis (GAFA) Special Volume, Part II*. Edited by N. Alon, J. Bourgain, A. Connes. Basel: Birkhäuser, 481–559.

Corfield, David. 2003. *Towards a Philosophy of Real Mathematics*. Cambridge: Cambridge UP.

Dauben, Joseph W. 1990. *Georg Cantor: His Mathematics and Philosophy of the Infinite*. Princeton: Princeton UP.

De Landa, Manuel. 2002. *Intensive Science and Virtual Philosophy*. New York: Continuum.

Dedekind, Richard. 1963. 'Continuity and Irrational Numbers.' *Essays on the Theory of Numbers*, ed. and trans. W. Beman. New York: Dover. Original edition, *Stetigkeit und irrationale Zahlen*. Vieweg: Braunschweig, 1872.

Dedron, Pierre and Jean Itard. 1974. *Mathematics and Mathematicians*. Trans. J. Field. Vol. 2. London: Transworld.

Del Lucchese, Filippo. 2009. 'Monstrous individuations: Deleuze, Simondon, and relational ontology.' *Differences: A Journal of Feminist Cultural Studies* 20(2–3): 179–93.

Deleuze, Gilles. 1971–87. *Seminars*. 22, 29 Apr 1980, *sur Leibniz*, trans. C. Stivale; 12 Apr 1983, *sur Bergson*. Université Paris VIII Vincennes and Vincennes St-Denis, http://www.webdeleuze.com, accessed 28 Aug 2012.

—. 1986. *Cinema 1: The Movement-Image*. Trans. Hugh Tomlinson and Barbara Habberjam. London: Athlone. Original edition, *Cinéma 1: L'image-mouvement*. Paris: Minuit, 1983.

—. 1989. *Cinema 2: The Time-Image*. Trans. Hugh Tomlinson and Robert Galeta. London, Minneapolis, Athlone: University of Minneapolis Press. Original edition, *Cinéma 2: L'image-temps*. Paris: Minuit, 1985.

—. 1990a. *The Logic of Sense*. Trans. M. Lester with C. Stivale. Ed. C. Boundas. New York: Columbia UP. Original edition, *Logique du sens*. Paris: Minuit, 1969.

—. 1990b. *Expressionism in Philosophy: Spinoza*. Trans. M. Joughin. New York: Zone. Original edition, *Spinoza et le problème de l'Expression*. Paris: Minuit, 1968.

—. 1991. *Bergsonism*. Trans. H. Tomlinson and B. Habberjam. New York: Zone. Original edition, *Le Bergsonisme*. Paris: Presses Universitaires de France, 1966.

—. 1993. *The Fold: Leibniz and the Baroque*. Trans. T. Conley. Minneapolis: Minnesota UP. Original edition, *Le pli: Leibniz et le Baroque*. Paris: Minuit, 1988.

—. 1994. *Difference and Repetition*. Trans. P. Patton. London: Athlone. Original edition, *Différence et répétition*. Paris: Presses Universitaires de France, 1968.

—. 1995. *Negotiations, 1972–1990*. Trans. M. Joughin. New York: Columbia UP. Original edition, *Pourparlers, 1972–1990*. Paris: Minuit, 1990.

—. 1999. 'Bergson's concept of difference.' *The New Bergson*, Ed. John Mullarky. Manchester: Manchester UP. Original edition, 'La conception de la différence chez Bergson,' *Les Etudes bergsoniennes* 4 (1956): 77–112.

Deleuze, Gilles and Félix Guattari. 1987. *A Thousand Plateaus: Capitalism and Schizophrenia*. Trans. B. Massumi. Minneapolis: Minnesota UP. Original edition, *Mille plateaux, Capitalisme et schizophrénie*. Paris: Minuit, 1980.

—. 1994. *What is Philosophy?* Trans. H. Tomlinson and G. Burchill. London: Verso. Original edition, *Qu'est-ce que la philosophie?*. Paris: Minuit, 1991.

Dennis, David and Jere Confrey. 1995. 'Functions of a curve: Leibniz's original notion of functions and its meaning for the parabola.' *College Mathematics Journal* 26(2): 124–30.

Dieudonné, Jean. 1976. 'Weyl, Hermann.' *Dictionary of Scientific Biography*. 14: 281–5.

—. 1977. 'Foreword.' Lautman 1977.

Duffy, Simon B. 2004. 'Schizo-Math. The logic of different/ciation and the philosophy of difference.' *Angelaki* 9(3):199–215.

—. 2006a. *The Logic of Expression: Quality, Quantity, and Intensity in Spinoza, Hegel and Deleuze*. Aldershot: Ashgate.

—. 2006b. 'The differential point of view of the infinitesimal calculus in Spinoza, Leibniz and Deleuze.' *Journal of the British Society for Phenomenology* 37(3): 286–307.

—. 2006c. 'The Mathematics of Deleuze's differential logic and metaphysics,' in Duffy 2006d.

—. 2006d. *Virtual Mathematics: The Logic of Difference*, Ed. S. Duffy, Manchester: Clinamen.

—. 2007. 'The ethical view of Spinoza's theory of relations.' *Sensorium: Aesthetics, Art, Life*, Eds F. Colman, B. Bolt, G. Jones, A. Woodward. Newcastle upon-Tyne: Cambridge Scholars Press.

—. 2009a. 'Deleuze and the mathematical philosophy of Albert Lautman.' *Deleuze's Philosophical Lineage*, Eds G. Jones and J. Roffe. Edinburgh: Edinburgh UP.

—. 2009b. 'The role of mathematics in Deleuze's critical engagement with Hegel.' *International Journal of Philosophical Studies* 17(4): 463–82.

—. 2010a. 'Deleuze, Leibniz and projective geometry in *The Fold*.' *Angelaki* 15(2): 129–47.

—. 2010b. 'Leibniz, mathematics and the monad.' *Deleuze and The Fold. A Critical Reader*, Eds N. McDonnell and S. van Tuinen. Hampshire: Palgrave Macmillan.

—. 2010c. 'The role of "joyful passions" in Spinoza's theory of relations.' *Spinoza Now*, Ed. Dimitris Vardoulakis. Minneapolis: Minnesota UP.

—. 2012. 'Badiou's Platonism: the mathematical Ideas of post-Cantorian set theory,' in Bowden and Duffy 2012.

Dumoncel, Jean-Claude. 2008. 'Review of Lautman, Albert. 2006. *Les mathématiques, les idées et le réel physique*. Paris: Vrin.' *History and Philosophy of Logic* 29(2): 199–205.

Easton, William B. 1970. 'Powers of regular cardinals.' *Annals of Mathematical Logic* 1: 139–78.

Ehrensperger, Florian. 2010. 'The philosophical significance of Maimon's *Essay on Transcendental Philosophy*.' *Journal for Jewish Thought* 1, Univ. Toronto. http://cjs. utoronto.ca/tjjt/node/11, accessed 28 Aug 2012.

Euclid. 1956. *The Thirteen Books of Euclid's Elements*. 2d ed. Trans. T. Heath. New York: Dover Publications.

Euler, Leonhard. 1988. *Introduction to Analysis of the Infinite*. Trans. J. Blanton. New York: Springer.

Ewald, William Bragg. 1996. *From Kant to Hilbert: A Source Book in the Foundations of Mathematics*. Oxford: Oxford UP.

Feferman, Solomon. 1989. *In the Light of Logic*. Oxford: Oxford UP.

Ferreirós, José. 2007. 'The crisis in the foundations of mathematics.' *The Princeton Companion to Mathematics*, Eds T. Gowers, J. Barrow-Green and I. Leader. Princeton: Princeton UP.

Florack, Herta. 1948. 'Reguläre und meromorphe Funktionen auf nicht geschlossenen Riemannschen Flächen.' *Schriftenreihe des Mathematischen Instituts der Universität Münster*, 1. Münster: Kramer.

Franks, Paul W. 2005. *All or Nothing: Systematicity, Transcendental Arguments, and Skepticism in German Idealism*. Cambridge: Harvard UP.

Friedman, Michael. 2000. 'Geometry, construction and intuition in Kant and his successors.' *Between Logic and Intuition: Essays in Honor of Charles Parsons*, Eds G. Sher and R. Tieszen. Cambridge: Cambridge UP.

Gaffney, Peter (ed.). 2010. *The Force of the Virtual: Deleuze, Science, and Philosophy*. Minneapolis: Minnesota UP.

Garber, Daniel. 2004. 'Leibniz on body, matter and extension.' *Supplement to the Proceedings of The Aristotelian Society* 78(1): 23–40.

—. 2009. *Leibniz: Body, Substance, Monad*. Oxford: Oxford UP.

Gil, José. 1998. 'Quatre méchantes notes sur un livre méchant.' *Futur Antérieur* 43.

Gillespie, Sam. 2008. *The Mathematics of Novelty: Badiou's Minimalist Metaphysics*. Melbourne: re.press.

Gödel, Kurt. 1931. 'Uber formal unentscheidbare Sätze der *Principia mathematica* und verwandter Systeme I.' *Monatshefte für Mathematik und Physik* 37: 173–98. Trans. J. van Heijenoort in van Heijenoort 1967.

—. 1983. 'What is Cantor's Continuum problem? [1947, revised 1964].' *Philosophy of Mathematics: Selected Readings*, Eds P. Benacerraf and H. Putnam. Cambridge: Cambridge UP.

Granger, Gilles-Gaston. 2002. 'Cavaillès et Lautman: deux pionniers.' *Revue philosophique de la France: Philosopher en France, 1940–1944* 3: 293–301.

Gray, Jeremy. 2002. 'Poincare, topological dynamics.' *The Investigation of Difficult Things: Essays on Newton and the History of the Exact Sciences*, Eds P. Harman and A. Shapiro. Cambridge: Cambridge UP.

Grene, Marjorie and Jerome Ravetz. 1962. 'Leibniz's cosmic equation: a reconstruction.' *The Journal of Philosophy* 59(6): 141–6.

Gueroult, Martial. 1929. *La philosophie transcendantale de Salomon Maimon*. Paris: Alcan.

Guyer, Paul. 1987. *Kant and the Claims of Knowledge*. Cambridge: Cambridge UP.

Hallett, Michael. 1984. *Cantorian Set Theory and Limitation of Size*. Oxford: Clarendon Press.

Hallward, Peter. 2003. *Badiou: A Subject to Truth*. Minneapolis: Minnesota UP.

Heidegger, Martin. 1962. *Being and Time*. Trans. J. Macquarie and E. Robinson. London: Blackwell.

—. 1967. 'The question concerning technology.' *The Question Concerning Technology and Other Essays*. Trans. W. Lovitt. New York: Harper & Row.

—. 1969. *The Essence of Reason*. Trans. T. Malick. Evanston: Northwestern UP.

Hellman, Geoffrey. 2005. 'Structuralism.' *The Oxford Handbook of Philosophy of Mathematics and Logic*, Ed. S. Shapiro. Oxford: Oxford UP.

—. 2006. 'Mathematical pluralism: the case of smooth infinitesimal analysis.' *Journal of Philosophical Logic* 35: 621–51.

Hilbert, David. 1923. 'Die logischen Grundlagen der Mathematik.' *Mathematische Annalen* 88(1): 151–65. Trans. W. Ewald as 'The logical foundations of mathematics' in Ewald 1996.

—. 1926. 'Uber das Unendliche.' *Mathematische Annalen* 95: 161–90. Trans. S. Bauer-Mengelberg as 'On the Infinite,' in Van Heijenoort 1967.

Houël, Jules. 1867. *Essai critique sur les principes fondamentaux de la géométrie élémentaire*. Paris: Guathiers-Villars.

Hughes, Joe. 2008. *Deleuze and the Genesis of Representation*. London: Continuum.

Huygens, Christiaan. 1888–1950. *Oeuvres Complète de Christiaan Huygens*. 22 vols. The Hague: Société Hollandaise des Sciences.

Jesseph, Douglas. 2008. 'Truth in fiction: origins and consequences of Leibniz's doctrine of infinitesimal magnitudes.' *Infinitesimal Differences: Controversies between Leibniz and his Contemporaries*, Eds U. Goldenbaum and D. Jesseph. Berlin: Gruyter.

Jones, Graham. 2009. 'Salomon Maimon.' *Deleuze's Philosophical Lineage*, Eds Graham Jones and Jon Roffe. Edinburgh: Edinburgh UP.

Kanamori, Akihiro. 1994. *The Higher Infinite. Large Cardinals in Set Theory from their Beginnings*. New York: Springer.

—. 2008. 'Cohen and set theory.' *Bulletin of Symbolic Logic* 14(3): 351–78.

Kanamori, Akihiro and Menachem Magidor. 1978. 'The evolution of large cardinal axioms in set theory.' *Higher set theory: Lecture Notes in Mathematics*. Vol. 669, New York: Springer.

Kant, Immanuel. 1967. *Philosophical Correspondence, 1759–1799*. Ed. and trans. A. Zweig. Chicago: Chicago UP.

—. 1998. *Critique of Pure Reason*. Ed. and trans. P. Guyer, A. Wood. Cambridge: Cambridge UP.

Katz, Victor J. 2007. 'Stages in the history of algebra with implications for teaching.' *Educational Studies in Mathematics* 66: 185–201.

Kerslake, Christian. 2009. *Immanence and the Vertigo of Philosophy: From Kant to Deleuze*. Edinburgh: Edinburgh UP.

Klein, Felix. 1882. *Ueber Riemann's Theorie der algebraischen Functionen und ihrer Integrale*. Leipzig: Teubner.

Klein, Jacob. 1968. *Greek Mathematical Thought and the Origin of Algebra*. Trans. E. Brann. Cambridge: MIT Press.

Kline, Morris. 1972. *Mathematical Thought from Ancient to Modern Times*. London: Oxford UP.

Knopp, Konrad. 1996. *Theory of Functions, Parts 1 & 2*. Trans. F. Bagemihl. New York: Dover.

Kock, Anders. 1981. *Synthetic Differential Geometry*. Cambridge: Cambridge UP.

Koebe, Paul. 1909. 'Fonction potentielle et fonction analytique ayant un domaine d'existence donné à un nombre quelconque (fini ou infini) de feuillets.' *Comptes Rendus de l'Académie des Sciences* 148: 1446–8.

Kolmogorov, Andrej N. and Adolph P. Yushkevich (eds). 1998. *Mathematics of the 19th Century*. Trans. R. Cooke. Berlin: Birkhäuser.

Kunen, Kenneth. 1983. *Set Theory: An Introduction to Independence Proofs*. Amsterdam: North Holland.

Lachterman, David. 1992. 'Mathematical construction, symbolic cognition and the infinite intellect: reflections on Maimon and Maimonides.' *Journal of the History of Philosophy* 30(4): 497–522.

Laerke, Mogans. 1999. 'The voice and the name: Spinoza in the Badiouian critique of Deleuze.' *Pli* 8: 86–99.

Lagrange, Joseph Louis. 1770. 'Réflexions sur la résolution algébrique des équations.' In Lagrange 1869.

—. 1797. *Théorie des fonctions analytiques*. L'Imprimerie de la République.

—. 1869. *Œuvres de Lagrange,*. Ed J.-A. Serret. Vol. 3. Paris: Gauthier-Villars.

Lakhtakia, A., V. K. Varadan, R. Messier, and V. V. Varadan. 1987. 'Generalisations and randomisation of the plane Koch curve.' *Journal of Physics A: Mathematical and General* 20: 3537–41.

Lakoff, George and Rafael E. Núñez. 2000. *Where Mathematics Comes From: How the Embodied Mmind Brings Mathematics into Being*. New York: Basic Books.

Largeault, Jean. 1972. *Logique mathématique. Textes*. Paris: Armand Colin.

Laubenbacher, Reinhard and David Pengelley. 1998. *Mathematical Expeditions: Chronicles by the Explorers*. New York: Springer.

Lautman, Albert. 1938a. *Essai sur l'unité des sciences mathématiques dans leur développement actuel*. Hermann. Trans. S. Duffy as 'Essay on the Unity of the Mathematical Sciences in their Current Development,' in Lautman 2011, 45–86.

—. 1938b. *Essai sur les notions de structure et d'existence en mathématiques. I. Les Schémas de structure. II. Les Schémas de genèse*. Paris: Hermann. Trans. S. Duffy as 'Essay on the Notions of Structure and Existence in Mathematics. I. The Schemas of Structure. II. The Schemas of Genesis,' in Lautman 2011, 87–196.

—. 1977. *Essai sur l'unité des mathématiques et divers écrits*. Foreword by Jean Dieudonné, Olivier Costa de Beauregard and Maurice Loi. Paris: Union générale d'éditions. New edition, Lautman 2006.

—. 2006. *Les mathématiques, les idées et le réel physique*. Intro. F. Zalamea. Paris: Vrin. Original edition, Lautman 1977.

—. 2011. *Mathematics, Ideas and the Physical Real*. Trans. S. Duffy. London: Continuum. Trans. of Lautman 2006.

Lavine, Shaughan. 1994. *Understanding the Infinite*. Cambridge: Harvard UP.

Lawvere, F. William. 1964. 'An elementary theory of the category of sets.' *Proceedings of the National Academy of Science of the USA* 52: 1506–11.

—. 1979. 'Categorical dynamics.' *Topos Theoretic Methods in Geometry*. Aarhus University Institute of Mathematics, Various Publications Series 30: 1–28.

Lawvere, F. William and Stephen H. Schanuel. 1997. *Conceptual Mathematics: A First Introduction to Categories*. Cambridge: Cambridge UP.

Leibniz, Gottfried Wilhelm. 1673. *Methodus tangentium inversa, seu de functionibus*. In Leibniz 1962, vol. 3 (See note p. 251).

—. 1676. *Pacidius Philalethi*. In Leibniz 2001.

—. 1714. *Monadology*. In Leibniz 1991.

—. 1920. *The Early Mathematical Manuscripts of Leibniz*. Trans. J. Child. London: Open Court.

—. 1962. *Mathematische Schriften*. 7 vols. 1849–63. Ed. C. Gerhard. Hildesheim: Olms.

—. 1965. *Die philosophischen Schriften*. 7 vols. 1875–90. Ed. C. Gerhard. Berlin: Weidman.

—. 1969. *Philosophical Papers and Letters*. 2d ed. Ed. and trans. L. Loemker. Dordrecht: Reidel.

—. 1989. *Philosophical Essays*. Ed. and trans. R. Ariew and D. Garber. Indianapolis: Hackett.

—. 1991. *Discourse on Metaphysics and other essays*. Ed. and trans. D. Garber and R. Ariew. Indianapolis: Hackett.

—. 1996. *New Essays on Human Understanding*. Ed. and trans. P. Remnant and J. Bennett. Cambridge: Cambridge UP.

—. 2001. *The Labyrinth of the Continuum: Writings on the Continuum Problem, 1672–1686*. Ed. and trans. R. Arthur. New Haven: Yale UP.

Levey, Samuel. 2003. 'The interval of motion in Leibniz's Pacidius Philalethi.' *Nous* 37(3): 371–416.

Livingston, Paul. 2011. *The Politics of Logic: Badiou, Wittgenstein, and the Consequences of Formalism*. London: Routledge.

Livio, Mario. 2006. *The Equation That Couldn't Be Solved: How Mathematical Genius Discovered the Language of Symmetry*. London: Simon & Schuster.

Loi, Maurice. 1977. 'Foreword.' Lautman 1977.

Look, Brandon. 2000. 'Leibniz and the substance of the vinculum substantial.' *Journal of the History of Philosophy* 38(2): 203–20.

Lord, Beth. 2011. *Kant and Spinozism: Transcendental Idealism and Immanence from Jacobi to Deleuze*. London: Palgrave.

Macintyre, Angus. 1989. 'Trends in logic.' *Logic Colloquium '88*, Eds C. Bonotto R. Ferro, S. Valentini, and A. Zanardo. Amsterdam: Elsevier.

Mahoney, Michael. 1990. 'Infinitesimals and transcendent relations: the mathematics of motion in the late seventeenth century.' *Reappraisals of the Scientific Revolution*, Eds D. Lindberg and R. Westman. Cambridge: Cambridge UP.

Maimon, Salomon. 2004. *Versuch über die Transzendentalphilosophie*. Ed. F. Ehrensperger. Hamburg: Meiner.

—. 2010. *Essay on Transcendental Philosophy*. Trans. N. Midgley, H. Somers-Hall, A. Welchman and M. Reglitz. London: Continuum. Note: page numbers in the text are to Maimon 2004.

Mandelbrot, Benoit. 1982. *The Fractal Geometry of Nature*. San Francisco: Freeman.

Marker, David. 1996. 'Model theory and exponentiation.' *Notices of the American Mathematical Society* 43: 753–9.

May, Tod. 2005. 'Deleuze, difference, and science.' *Continental Philosophy of Science*, Ed. G. Gutting. Oxford: Blackwell.

Monge, Gaspard. 1789. *Géométrie descriptive*. Paris: Baudouin.

Murphet, Julian. 2006. 'Cultural Studies and Alain Badiou.' *New Cultural Studies: Adventures in Theory*, Eds G. Hall and C. Birchall. Athens: Georgia UP.

Newstead, Anne. 2009. 'Cantor on infinity in nature, number, and the divine mind.' *American Catholic Philosophical Quarterly* 83(4): 533–53.

Newton, Isaac. 1729. *The Mathematical Principles of Natural Philosophy*. 2 vols. Trans. A. Motte, pref. R. Cotes. London: Motte. Original edition, *Philosophiae Naturalis Principia Mathematica*. London: Royal Society, 1687.

—. 1736. *The Method of Fluxions and Infinite Series, 1671*. Trans. J. Colson. *The Mathematical Papers of Isaac Newton*. Ed. D. Whiteside. Vol. 3: 1670–1673. Cambridge: Cambridge UP.

—. 1971. *The Mathematical Papers of Isaac Newton*. Ed. D. Whiteside. Vol. 4: 1674–1684. Cambridge: Cambridge UP.

—. 1981. 'On the quadrature of curves, 1704.' *The Mathematical Papers of Isaac Newton*. Ed. D. Whiteside. Vol. 8: 1697–1722. Cambridge: Cambridge UP.

Panofsky, Erwin. 1955. *The Life and Art of Albrecht Dürer*. Princeton: Princeton UP.

Pascal, Blaise. 1914. *Oeuvres de Blaise Pascal*. Eds L. Brunschvicg, P. Boutroux and F. Gazier. Vol. 9, Paris: Hachette.

Petitot, Jean. 1987. 'Refaire le Timée. Introduction à la philosophie mathématique d'Albert Lautman.' *Revue d'Histoire des Sciences* 40(1): 79–115.

—. 2001. 'La dialectique de la vérité objective et de la valeur historique dans le rationalisme mathématique d'Albert Lautman.' *Sciences et Philosophie en France et en Italie entre les deux guerres*, Eds J. Petitot and L. Scarantino. Napoli: Vivarium.

Plato. 1997. *Plato: Complete Works*. Ed. J. Cooper. Indianapolis: Hackett.

Plotnitsky, Arkady. 2006. 'Manifolds: on the concept of space in Riemann and Deleuze,' in Duffy 2006d.

—. 2009. 'Bernhard Riemann's Conceptual Mathematics and the Idea of Space,' *Configurations* 17(1): 105–30.

Potter, Michael. 2004. *Set Theory and its Philosophy: A Critical Introduction*. Oxford: Oxford UP.

Putnam, Hilary. 1979. 'What is Mathematical Truth.' *Mathematics Matter and Method: Philosophical Papers*. Cambridge: Cambridge UP.

—. 1981. *Reason, Truth and History*. Cambridge: Cambridge UP.

Quine, Willard V. 1964. *From a Logical Point of View*. Cambridge: Harvard UP.

—. 1981. *Theories and Things*. Cambridge: Harvard UP.

Rajchman, John. 1997. *Constructions*. Cambridge: MIT Press.

Remmert, Reinhold. 1998. 'From Riemann surfaces to complex spaces.' *Seminaires et congrès* 3, *Société mathématique de France*. Paris: SMF, 203–241.

Riemann, Bernhard. 1963. 'On the hypotheses which lie at the bases of geometry, 1868.' *Nature* 8 (183–4): 14–17, 36–7. Trans. W. Clifford.

Robinson, Abraham. 1996. *Non-Standard Analysis*. Princeton: Princeton UP. Original edition, Amsterdam: North-Holland, 1966.

Roffe, Jon. 2012. 'One Divides into Two: Badiou's Critique of Deleuze. '*Badiou and Philosophy*. Edited by Sean Bowden and Simon B. Duffy. Edinburgh: Edinburgh University Press.

Roitman, Judith. 1990. *Introduction to Modern Set Theory*. New York: Wiley.

Russell, Bertrand. 1992. *The Principles of Mathematics*. London: Routledge. Original edition, 1903.

Salanskis, Jean-Michel. 1996. 'Idea and Destination.' *Deleuze: A Critical Reader*, Ed. Paul Patton. Oxford: Blackwell.

—. 1998. 'Pour une épistémologie de la lecture.' *Alliage* 35–6. http://www.tribunes.com/ tribune/alliage/accueil.htm, accessed 28 Aug 2012.

—. 2002. 'Les mathématiques chez x avec x = Alain Badiou.' *Penser le multiple*, Ed. C. Ramond. Paris: Harmattan.

—. 2006. 'Mathematics, metaphysics, philosophy,' in Duffy 2006d.

—. 2008. *Philosophie des mathématiques*. Paris: Vrin.

Shabel, Lisa. 2003. *Mathematics in Kant's Critical Philosophy: Reflections on Mathematical Practice*. New York: Routledge.

—. 2004. 'Kant's "Argument from Geometry".' *Journal of the History of Philosophy* 42(2): 195–215.

—. 2006. 'Kant's Philosophy of Mathematics.' *The Cambridge Companion to Kant*, Ed. Paul Guyer. 2nd ed. Cambridge: Cambridge UP.

Shapiro, Stewart. 2000. *Philosophy of Mathematics, Structure and Ontology*. Oxford: Oxford UP.

Simondon, Gilbert. 1964. *L'individu et sa genèse physico-biologique*. Paris: Presses Universitaires de France.

Simont, Juliette. 2003. 'Intensity, or: the "Encounter".' *An Introduction to the Philosophy of Gilles Deleuze*, Ed. J. Khalfa. London: Continuum.

Smith, Daniel W. 2003. 'Mathematics and the theory of multiplicities: Deleuze and Badiou revisited.' *Southern Journal of Philosophy* 41(3): 411–49.

—. 2006. 'Axiomatics and Problematics as two modes of formalization: Deleuze's Epistemology of Mathematics,' in Duffy 2006d.

Somers-Hall, Henry. 2010. 'Hegel and Deleuze on the metaphysical interpretation of the calculus.' *Continental Philosophy Review* 42(4): 555–72.

—. 2012. *Hegel, Deleuze, and the Critique of Representation: Dialectics of Negation and Difference*. Albany: SUNY Press.

Stoilow, Simion. 1938. *Leçons sur les principes topologiques de la théorie des fonctions analytiques*. Paris: Gauthier-Villars.

Taylor, Brook. 1715. *Methodus Incrementorum Directa et Inversa*. London: Innys.

Thielke, Peter. 2003. 'Intuition and diversity: Kant and Maimon on space and time.' *Salomon Maimon: rational dogmatist, empirical skeptic. Critical assessments*, Ed. G. Freudenthal. Dordrecht: Kluwer.

Tignol, Jean-Pierre. 2001. *Galois' Theory of Algebraic Equations*. London: World Scientific.

Toscano, Alberto. 2000. 'To have done with the end of philosophy.' *Pli* 9: 220–38.

van Heijenoort, Jean (ed.). 1967. *From Frege to Gödel: A Source Book in Mathematical Logic, 1879–1931*. 3rd ed. Cambridge: Harvard UP.

Voss, Daniela. 2012. *Deleuze and the Transcendental Conditions of Thought*. Edinburgh: Edinburgh UP.

Vuillemin, Jules. 1962. *La philosophie de l'algébre*. Paris: Presses Universitaires de France.

Warren, Daniel. 1998. 'Kant and the apriority of space.' *Philosophical Review* 107(2): 179–224.

Weyl, Hermann. 1913. *Ider der Riemannschen Fläche*. Leipzig: Teubner. Third edition 1955. Trans. G. MacLane as *The Concept of a Riemann Surface*, Reading: Addison–Wesley, 1964.

—. 1918. *Das Kontinuum: kritische Untersuchungen über die Grundlagen der Analysis*. Leipzig: Viet. Reprinted 1932, Berlin: Gruyter. Trans. S. Pollard and T. Bole as *The Continuum: A Critical Examination of the Foundation of Analysis*. New York: Dover, 1987.

—. 1921. *Raum Zeit Materie*. Berlin: Springer. Trans. H. Brose as *Space-Time-Matter*, London: Methuen, 1922.

Whittaker, E. and G. Watson. 1990. 'Forms of the remainder in Taylor's series.' *A Course in Modern Analysis*. 4th ed. Cambridge: Cambridge UP.

Widder, Nathan. 2001. 'The rights of simulacra: Deleuze and the univocity of being.' *Continental Philosophy Review* 34: 437–53.

Woodard, Jared. 2006. 'Recovering mathematics after Heidegger.' *Ereignis* 4. http://www.beyng.com/ereignis4.html, accessed 28 Aug 2012.

Wronski, Hoëné. 1814. *Philosophie de l'infini.* Paris: Didot.

—. 1817. *Philosophie de la technie algorithmique.* Paris: Didot.

Zermelo, Ernst. 1908. 'Neuer Beweis für die Möglichkeit einer Wohlordnung.' *Mathematische Annalen* 65: 107–28. Trans. S. Bauer-Mengelberg as 'A new proof of the possibility of a well-ordering,' in van Heijenoort 1967.

Index

Printed in Germany
by Amazon Distribution
GmbH, Leipzig

19819360R00130